Comparing Postcolonial Literatures

Comparing Postcolonial Literatures

Dislocations

Edited by

Ashok Bery

and

Patricia Murray

Published by PALGRAVE
Houndmills, Basingstoke, Hampshire RG21 6XS and
175 Fifth Avenue, New York, N.Y. 10010
Companies and representatives throughout the world

PALGRAVE is the new global academic imprint of St. Martin's Press LLC Scholarly
and Reference Division and Palgrave Publishers Ltd (formerly Macmillan Press Ltd).

ISBN 978-0-333-72339-5

This book is printed on paper suitable for recycling and made from fully managed
and sustained forest sources.

A catalogue record for this book is available from the British Library.

Library of Congress Cataloging-in-Publication Data
Comparing postcolonial literatures : dislocations : edited by Ashok Bery
and Patricia Murray.
p. cm
Chiefly papers presented at a conference.
Includes bibliographical references and index.
Contents: Postcolonial studies and Ireland / C.L. Innes — Crossing the hyphen of history : the
Scottish borders of Anglo-Irishness / Willy Maley — The politics of hybridity / Gerry Smith —
Inside-out : literature, cultural identity and Irish migration to England / Aidan Arrowsmith — States
of dislocation : William Trevor's Felicia's journey and Maurice Leitch's Gilchrist / Liam Harte and
Lance Petitt — It's a free country / Geraldine Stoneham — I came all the way from Cuba so I
could speak like this? / Nara Araújo — Border anxieties : race and psychoanalysis / David Marriott
— Nationalism's brandings : women's bodies and narratives of the partition / Sujala Singh —
Internalized exiles ; three Bolivian writers / Keith Richards — Writing other lives : Native American
(post)coloniality and collaborative (auto)biography / Susan Forsyth — "The Limits of goodwill" : the
values and dangers of revisionism in Keneally's "aboriginal" novels / Denise Vernon — The trickster
at the border : cross-cultural dialogues in the Caribbean / Patricia Murray — Between speech and
writing : "la nouvelle littérature antillaise" / Sam Haig — Hybrid texts : family, state and empire in
a poem by black Cuban poet Excilia Saldaña / Catherine Davies — Beyond Manicheism : Derek
Walcott's Henri Christophe and Dream on Monkey Mountain / John Thieme — "Canvas of Blood"
Okigbo's African modernism / David Richards — Closing statement : apprenticeship to the furies /
Wilson Harris.
ISBN 978-0-312-22781-4
1. Literature, Comparative — Themes, motives Congresses
2. Decolonization in literature Congresses. 3. Postcolonialism
Congresses. I. Bery, Ashok, 1951– . II. Murray, Patricia, 1965–.
PN56.C63C66   1999
809—dc21   99–43179
                                                CIP

Transferred to digital printing 2005

Contents

Acknowledgements

We would like to thank the British Academy for a conference travel grant which enabled Professor Nara Araújo to come to Britain in order to deliver the paper which forms the basis for her essay in this book. We would also like to thank our students and colleagues at the University of North London for their support during the 'Border Crossings' conference, at which many of the papers in this volume were first delivered.

We are grateful to *Casa de las Américas* for permission to reproduce Excilia Saldaña's poem 'Monólogo de la esposa', which is discussed by Professor Catherine Davies in her essay.

Notes on the Contributors

Nara Araújo is Professor of Comparative Literature at the University of Havana, but is currently a Visiting Professor at the Universidad Autónoma Metropolitana in Mexico City. She has published particularly on issues of race, ethnicity, gender and nation as factors in shaping cultural identity. Her work incorporates a strong comparative focus between the Hispanic and francophone areas of the Caribbean.

Aidan Arrowsmith is a Lecturer in Literary Studies at Staffordshire University. His previous publications include articles on postcolonialism, diaspora and Irish culture and his current research develops these interests into a study of second-generation 'Irish-English' writing.

Ashok Bery is a Senior Lecturer in English at the University of North London. His research interests include modern poetry and postcolonial literature and theory. He has published on the novels of R. K. Narayan and is currently working on a comparative study of modern poetry.

Catherine Davies is Professor of Spanish at the University of Manchester. Her publications include *A Place in the Sun? Women Writers in Twentieth-Century Cuba, Spanish Women's Writing 1849–1996*, and (as co-editor) *Latin American Women's Writing: Feminist Readings in Theory and Crisis*.

Susan Forsyth is currently completing her PhD at Christ Church College, Canterbury. Her subject is Native American literature, culture and politics, with particular emphasis on the Lakota. Her interests include postcolonial literature and theory.

Sam Haigh is a Lecturer in French Studies at the University of Warwick, where she teaches courses on francophone Caribbean writing and francophone Literatures. She has recently edited a volume of essays entitled *An Introduction to Caribbean francophone Writing: Guadeloupe and Martinique* and has just completed a book, *Mapping a Tradition: francophone Women's Writing from Guadeloupe*.

Wilson Harris is a distinguished writer and essayist. His many novels include *The Guyana Quartet*, *The Carnival Trilogy* and, most recently,

Jonestown. He was awarded the Premio Mondelo dei Cinque Continenti in 1992. A collection of his essays entitled *The Unfinished Genesis of the Imagination* has recently been published.

Liam Harte is a Senior Lecturer in Irish Studies at St Mary's University College in London. He is the co-author of *Drawing Conclusions: a Cartoon History of Anglo-Irish Relations, 1798–1998* (1998) and a contributing co-editor of *Contemporary Irish Fictions: a Collection of Critical Essays* (1999). He has published essays on contemporary Irish fiction and poetry, and is currently working on an anthology of autobiographical prose by the Irish in Britain.

C. L. Innes is Professor of Postcolonial Literatures at the University of Kent. She is also a member of the Centre for Colonial and Postcolonial Research at the University. Her books include *The Devil's Own Mirror*, a comparative study of Irish and Black literature and cultural nationalism, *Woman and Nation in Irish Literature and Society*, and a study of Chinua Achebe. She is currently working on a history of Black and South Asian writing in Britain.

Willy Maley is a Reader in English Literature at the University of Glasgow, author of *A Spenser Chronology* (1994) and *Salvaging Spenser: Colonialism, Culture and Identity* (1997), and co-editor (with Brendan Bradshaw and Andrew Hadfield) of *Representing Ireland: Literature and the Origins of Conflict, 1534–1660* (1993), (with Bart Moore-Gilbert and Gareth Stanton) of *Postcolonial Criticism* (1997) and (with Andrew Hadfield) of *A View of the Present State of Ireland: from the First Published Edition* (1997).

David Marriott lectures at Queen Mary and Westfield College, University of London. His book, *Black Male Fantasies*, is forthcoming from Edinburgh University Press and he is currently writing a book on Frantz Fanon, race and psychoanalysis.

Patricia Murray is a Senior Lecturer in English at the University of North London. She has published articles on Latin American, Caribbean and contemporary British writing. She has a book forthcoming, *Shared Solitude: the Fiction of Wilson Harris and Gabriel García Márquez*.

Lance Pettitt lectures at St Mary's University College in London and is the author of *Ireland on Screen* (1999) and essays on gay representation in

Irish film in *Sex, Nation and Dissent* (1997), Irish migrant writing in *Under the Belly of the Tiger* (1997) and 'Troubles' TV drama in *The Mechanics of Authenticity* (1998). He has also published articles on contemporary gay culture in *South Atlantic Quarterly* (1996) and the alternative press in Ireland in *Irish Communications Review* (1998).

David Richards is a Senior Lecturer in English and Deputy Director of the African Studies Unit at the University of Leeds. His publications include *Masks of Difference: Cultural Representations in Literature, Anthropology and Art*, and many articles on Caribbean, African and Canadian literature. He is currently working on a book about spatial representations, ethnography and postcolonial writing.

Keith Richards is Assistant Professor at the University of Richmond, Virginia. His doctoral thesis was on contemporary Bolivian literature, and he has published articles on that subject. His interests include Latin American cultural studies, especially literature and cinema, on which he has also published.

Sujala Singh is a Lecturer in English at the University of Southampton. She has published on popular culture in South Asia and is currently working on a book project, *Faithful Representations? Religion, Nation and Identity in South Asian Narratives*.

Gerry Smyth is a Lecturer in Cultural History at Liverpool John Moores University. He has written two books, *The Novel and the Nation: Studies in the New Irish Fiction* (1997) and *Decolonisation and Criticism: the Construction of Irish Literature* (1998). His current research interests are in the areas of spatial theory and ecocriticism, and he is working on a new project entitled *Paddy's Green Shamrock Shore: Space and the Irish Cultural Imagination*.

Geraldine Stoneham is a Senior Lecturer at South Bank University. She works in the fields of Australian literature, postcolonial studies and women's writing. Her publications include chapters on postmodernism and postcolonialism in *Postmodern Subjects/Postmodern Texts*, edited by Jane Dowson and Steven Earnshaw, and *Just Postmodernism*, edited by Steven Earnshaw. She has also published in the journal *Wasafiri*. She is currently working on a book on the Australian author Miles Franklin.

John Thieme is a Professor and the Head of English Studies at South Bank University. He previously taught at the Universities of Guyana, North London and Hull. His publications include books on V. S. Naipaul (1985 and 1987) and Derek Walcott (1998) and *The Arnold Anthology of Post-Colonial Literatures in English* (1996). He edits the *Journal of Commonwealth Literature* and is the General Editor of the Manchester University Press Contemporary World Writers Series.

Denise Vernon teaches drama and cultural studies at the University of Salford. Her research interests include postcolonial studies, Australian literature and theatre. She is currently the Treasurer of the British Australian Studies Association.

Introduction

Ashok Bery and Patricia Murray

I

This collection of essays has its origins in a conference on postcolonial literatures entitled 'Border Crossings' which was held at the University of North London. The borders which we hoped the conference would traverse and transgress were disciplinary, linguistic and cultural ones. These borders – and the geographical ones which underpin some of them – exist for a variety of reasons; most obviously, of course, the historical, cultural and political legacies of colonialism, such as the identity and language of the colonizing power in a particular part of the world, or the political entities left behind as the empires receded into history. But they are reinforced by other pressures, including pedagogic and institutional demarcations, some of them related to the historical development of academic disciplines, which, as Edward Said and others have shown, are themselves in many cases shaped by the experience and ideologies of empire.[1]

Such contingencies have produced anomalies which postcolonial studies have only begun to address relatively recently. In organizing the conference, we were particularly conscious of two such anomalies, one concerning linguistic boundaries, the other relating to the problematic situation of the British Isles in postcolonial studies.

Postcolonial literatures in the various European languages – English, French, Spanish and others – are usually read, studied and discussed in isolation from each other. Yet the increasing pace of the internationalization of literatures as we approach the end of the millennium makes such isolation seem increasingly incongruous. Cross-currents between literatures are not exclusively twentieth-century phenomena; but, for obvious material and technological reasons, among others, the process

1

has been accelerating over the years. As Vinay Dharwadker points out in a helpful summary, internationalization is a product of a variety of intellectual, cultural and material forces, including the production, distribution and reception of books, migrations of readers and writers, and the flow of ideas and literary influences – all of which speed up with the advance of technology.[2]

Of course, internationalization is not confined to postcolonial literatures. One thinks, for instance, of the impact that Chinese and Japanese poetry have had in this century on the poetry of the USA, from Ezra Pound to Gary Snyder and beyond. More recently, British and US poets have learnt much from the example of East European and Latin American writers. But for nineteenth- and twentieth-century writers in colonized (or formerly colonized) countries, the process of international influence was and is more complicated. For such writers, one of the most powerful engines of internationalization has been the culture of the colonizing power. And although, as we suggest later, this particular influence can be overemphasized, it nevertheless enmeshes writers in difficult but also creative dilemmas of cultural identity. Much has been written on the difficulty and ambivalence of those dilemmas; it is only fairly recently that their potential for creativity has been debated more widely, as writers, critics and cultural theorists have become increasingly conscious of, and articulate about, issues of hybridity and transculturation. These perspectives help us move away from hegemonic, top-down models in which cultural influence flows from colonizer to colonized; they enable us to place more emphasis on the selective agency, the *bricolage*, the creative distortions carried out by colonized peoples as they negotiate the meetings of cultures.

Yet even the recent emphasis on such phenomena does not, we feel, always do justice to the complexity and multiplicity of the processes of internationalization. Cross-cultural influence precedes the advent of modern colonialism; cultural interaction is not just built into modern colonialism and neo-colonialism, it is also part of the development of cultures more generally – examples as diverse as Renaissance Europe and Islamic-Hindu India attest to this fact. Contemporary India, for instance, is not simply a product of the confluence of *two* cultures – British and Indian cultures since the European Renaissance. That apparently monolithic term 'Indian' opens up to reveal considerable diversity, some aspects of which are summed up in the hyphenated adjective 'Islamic-Hindu' used above. (The term 'British' also contains its own diversity, as we suggest below.) In other words, cross-cultural influence is a multiple rather than binary process. Discussions of hybridity and transculturation need to recognize this, and avoid being trapped by a binary framework involving the colonizer and the colonized.

Another source of multiplicity is that postcolonial writers have often made attempts to circumvent the direct influence of the colonial culture by seeking out alternatives. Thus anglophone postcolonial poets searching for models different from those offered by the English poetic tradition have been known to look to US poetry and, more recently, to Latin American and non-anglophone European poetry.[3] In postcolonial fiction, 'lo real maravilloso' (somewhat inadequately translated into English as 'magical realism'), interacting in complex and varied ways with different native narrative traditions, has constituted one of the most prominent of these cross-cultural currents, linking writers from diverse parts of the world.[4] Linguistic isolationism tends to encourage the reading of postcolonial literatures in relation to the language and culture of the former colonial power and, in so doing, to undervalue multiple processes of influence, thus subtly reasserting the binary models of colonial thinking. A consciously comparative approach is one way of circumventing these dilemmas.

We recognize that there are difficulties in attempting to read postcolonial literatures along the lines being sketched out here. As we have suggested, internationalization is not a purely literary phenomenon, since the development of cross-cultural interaction is affected by economic and political elements, which in part determine, for instance, the availability of translations. Thus, who gets translated from what languages and into what languages is decided not only by questions of quality or representativeness but also by considerations which include the economics of publishing and the relative material and cultural power of readers in different parts of the world. This means that elements of neo-colonial relationships must inevitably enter into the process of translation, since the balance of material and cultural power tends to lie with the former colonizers. The selective availability of translations in turn produces selective notions of regional literatures; the title of Montserrat Ordoñes's 'One Hundred Years of Unread Writing', for instance, points to the narrow focus of publishing houses that continually try to reinvent the Colombia of García Márquez at the expense of female, local, regional and specialist perspectives.[5] The picture is further complicated by more random and contingent factors, such as the availability of translators, since literary translation, unlike commercial translation, is often a self-selecting activity. Such features of translation and the economics of translation clearly affect and even distort our perspectives on literatures in languages other than our own. Nonetheless, despite these obstacles, we feel that an increasingly important aspect of postcolonial literary study in the future will be an emphasis on cross-cultural, transnational and comparative elements.

Located as the editors are in the United Kingdom, the second anomaly we were particularly conscious of was the awkward and ambivalent position which three constituent parts of the British Isles – Scotland, Ireland and Wales – occupy in the field of postcolonial studies. This ambivalence is partly a matter of historical record. Colonized nations themselves, they were also often intricately and ambiguously implicated in the colonial enterprise, many of their inhabitants going on to take part in the establishment and maintenance of the British Empire. But the ambiguous position of these nations is also related to disciplinary demarcations. Although the situation has been changing recently, Scottish, Welsh or Irish literatures, whether in English or indigenous languages, tend not to be considered within postcolonial frameworks; and, when written in the English language, they have often been subsumed in university syllabuses and texts under the category 'British'. Such occlusions and confusions were nicely illustrated in the early 1980s by the publication of Blake Morrison and Andrew Motion's *Penguin Book of Contemporary British Poetry*, which included a number of Northern Irish poets and brought forth a well-known riposte from Seamus Heaney, in his poem, *An Open Letter*:

> This "British" word
> Sticks deep in native and *colon*
> Like Arthur's sword.
>
> . . . .
> British, no, the name's not right[6]

It is also true to say that it was previously in the interests of postcolonial writers and critics, at least in the anglophone field, to assume a homogeneous notion of Britishness to write back to, though such a monolith began to disintegrate in a developing stage of postcolonial studies, and the construction of 'Britishness' is itself now a part of the field of study. This includes a related issue, but one which we did not have space to address in any detail at the conference, concerning the pressure on definitions of Britishness created by the now-established presence in the British Isles of the communities who trace their origins to countries which were once part of the British Empire. And, as with the Irish case just mentioned, here, too, many writers – Salman Rushdie and

Timothy Mo, among others – have been engaged in the process of exploring their complicated relationship to the notion of Britishness. These pressures of cultural and national definition, sharpened by the phenomena of migration and diaspora, are, of course, replicated in other literatures and cultures as well, and, particularly in the USA, the setting of more than one of our contributors' investigations of hybridity in the metropolis.[7]

Our aims in organizing the conference included the highlighting of such anomalies, and an attempt to move towards a dislocation of the largely anglophone perspective on postcolonial literatures which tends to predominate in the British, if less so in the US, academy. Consequently, our initial call for papers emphasized the project of bringing together work on a variety of literatures in different languages; in particular, we wanted to encourage material on Ireland and on the francophone and hispanic literatures of Latin America and the Caribbean. Such aims perhaps explain the prominence of these areas in this volume. Although few of the individual essays themselves make cross-cultural comparisons in any detail, we hope to have assembled in this volume some materials which may be used for comparative purposes. Our comments in the second part of this introduction provisionally trace some interconnections between the essays and between the cultures, languages and literatures which they discuss.

Our intended title for this volume was *Border Crossings*. The change to the present title was partly brought about by our publisher's advice that a number of books with our preferred original title already existed; but, as we pondered a variety of alternatives, other, more significant considerations began to impose themselves on us. It became increasingly apparent to us that what was at issue was not just the crossing of already existing borders whose existence could unproblematically be taken for granted; rather, as much recent work in the postcolonial field has been emphasizing, the borders themselves mask problems; and the spaces which are supposed to be delineated by those borders are not as clear-cut or unambiguous as they were thought to be. The word *Dislocations* in our title, we feel, points more clearly towards some of the current boundary disputes and debates within the field: the preoccupations with inbetweenness, hybridity, migrancy, fragments, internal colonialisms and so forth which occupy prominent positions in postcolonial studies today. In the next section of the introduction, we suggest, in a preliminary way, how some of these debates might connect up with a comparative approach to postcolonial literatures.

II

One of the important figures in the debates mentioned at the end of the preceding section has been Homi Bhabha, and, although we did not deliberately intend to evoke the echo, *Dislocations* may remind readers of his title *The Location of Culture*.[8] This introduction is not the place for a detailed assessment of Bhabha's work; yet his essays are, of course, prominent among those writings which have helped to question the boundaries and borders which are part of the stock-in-trade of colonialism and colonialist discourses – in particular, the hierarchical binary division between self and other, colonizer and colonized. Part of the concern of Bhabha's work has been to indicate ways in which such terms are dislocated by the supposed *objects* of colonialist discourses – the colonized peoples themselves. Thus Bhabha takes issue with those elements in Edward Said's work on Orientalism which seem to accord total and totalizing power to the authority of colonial discourses. By opening up the spaces and contradictions within these discourses, Bhabha, to some degree, uncovers the powers of resistance possessed by the colonized. However, while we recognize the significance of Bhabha's work for postcolonial studies, we are also aware that it is not unproblematic, and the contributors to this collection who draw on his work often do so with reservations.[9] In particular, we did not want simply to reinforce what has been described as the 'Holy Trinity' of Said, Bhabha and Spivak as postcolonial critics,[10] but were also concerned to draw attention to important earlier, as well as contemporary, critical work that covers vital, and sometimes similar, ground, if not always in the academic language of post-structuralist theory.

This probing of borders has occurred not just in relation to complicating and blurring the binary divide *between* colonized and colonizer, but also *within* the spaces demarcated by these terms and a number of others. For instance, concepts such as national and cultural identity, which played an important role in the formation of anti-colonial discourses have also been subjected to a process of unravelling. In his well-known essay, 'Cultural Identity and Diaspora', Stuart Hall acknowledges that one version of cultural identity – identity defined as an essential 'oneness', as 'a sort of collective "one true self", hiding inside the many other, more superficial or artificially imposed "selves", which people with a shared history and ancestry hold in common' – has played 'a critical role in all post-colonial struggles'. But he then goes on to stress the significance of a very different conception of identity which stresses 'critical points of deep and significant *difference*':

In this perspective, cultural identity is not a fixed essence at all, lying unchanged outside history and culture. . . . Cultural identities are the points of identification, the unstable points of identification or suture, which are made, within the discourses of history and culture. Not an essence but a *positioning*. Hence, there is always a politics of identity, a politics of position, which has no absolute guarantee in an unproblematic, transcendental 'law of origin'.[11]

In that essay, Hall's focus is on exploring the implications of this view for notions of Caribbean identity. But parallel debates have taken place in other contexts. Another example of this fissuring of notions of cultural identity can be found in the field of Indian historiography, where a number of scholars – mostly associated with the *Subaltern Studies* project – have been emphasizing the degree to which even nationalists and nationalist historians continued to operate within colonial paradigms – paradigms to do with the nation state in its relationship with modernity. Anti-colonial nationalist history, like imperialist history, Dipesh Chakrabarty suggests, was 'written within problematics posed by. . . [a] transition narrative, of which the overriding (if often implicit) themes are those of development, modernization, capitalism'.[12] Such nationalisms, and the histories they produce, are, in Partha Chatterjee's well-known formulation, 'derivative discourses'.[13] These narratives are, as *Subaltern Studies* essays repeatedly point out, homogenizing ones. Indeed, Dipesh Chakrabarty argues that colonialism, third-world nationalism and the whole 'academic discourse of history' between them have made 'Europe' universal, and that:

'Europe' remains the sovereign, theoretical subject of all histories, including the ones we call 'Indian', 'Chinese', 'Kenyan', and so on. There is a peculiar way in which all these other histories tend to become variations on a master narrative that could be called 'the history of Europe'.

To counter such homogenizing tendencies, Chakrabarty calls for a project of 'provincializing "Europe"', of displacing a 'hyperreal Europe from the center toward which all historical imagination currently gravitates'. In historiography, he argues, this provincializing can be done through writing 'into the history of modernity the ambivalences, contradictions, the use of force, and the tragedies and the ironies that attend it'.[14] In questioning the homogenizing paradigms, these scholars have investigated internal fissures and borderlines within the nation.

Chatterjee and Gyanendra Pandey have both emphasized the significance of the 'fragment' and of fragmentary discourses in unravelling hegemonic definitions of the anti- and postcolonial nation as a unified entity. Pandey, for instance, writes of the need in the Indian context to:

> foreground [the] state-centered drive to homogenize and 'normalize', and to foreground also the deeply contested nature of the territory of nationalism. Part of the importance of the 'fragmentary' point of view lies in that it resists the drive for a shallow homogenization and struggles for other, potentially richer definitions of the 'nation' and the future political community.[15]

In their different ways and different contexts, then, the two examples just discussed – the Caribbean and South Asia – have contributed to the debate on what Hall terms 'unstable points of identification or suture' (a phrase which points clearly to the problematic nature of the border).

What relevance, however, do such formulations have in the present context? We would argue that they resonate with debates in postcolonial literary study, and indicate strategies of reading which can be brought to bear on the literatures with which we are concerned. One example of such resonance is with the famous argument for the 'abolition of the English Department' propounded by Ngugi Wa Thiong'o and some of his colleagues at the University of Nairobi. This department, they suggested, should be replaced by a comparative studies model in which the aim should be:

> to orientate ourselves towards placing Kenya, East Africa, and then Africa in the centre. All other things are to be considered in their relevance to our situation, and their contribution towards understanding ourselves.[16]

Ngugi's arguments in favour of reading African literatures beside American and Caribbean literatures indicate that Chakrabarty's phrase 'provincializing "Europe"' has suggestive possibilities in the field of literary study as well: it outlines an aim that can be applied to the task of promoting a comparative study of postcolonial literatures. For there is a sense in which Europe continues to remain the subject of these literatures, the centre towards which literary imagination and critical thought gravitate. The way that the study of postcolonial literatures is predominantly constituted today – that is to say, demarcated by reference to the (European metropolitan) languages in which they are written – tends to isolate one literature from another and makes the metropolitan cultures the absent centres round which these literatures revolve, thus perpetuating hierarchical relationships. A good example of this is a feature that has been commented on by a number of critics: the fact that the category 'postcolonial literature' is never thought to include also the literature of the former imperial powers, although they too are postcolonial states, which have not only helped to shape their former colonies, but have themselves been irrevocably shaped by the experience and loss of empire. As Salman Rushdie sardonically put it in his comments criticizing the term 'Commonwealth literature': 'It would never do to include English literature, the great sacred thing itself, with this bunch of upstarts, huddling together under this new and badly made umbrella.'[17] The consideration of European literatures in the same frameworks as the literatures of the former colonies is a major task, and not one which we can even begin to approach in this volume. But we do wish to stress the significance of a horizontal, comparative framework which will, we hope, help in the project mentioned above – the project of dislocating and provincializing Europe.

This project also touches on a number of related debates concerning postcolonial identities; some of these have already been mentioned, but it will be useful to conclude this section of the introduction by returning briefly to the topic. The study of postcolonial literatures in isolation from each other, we have been suggesting, encourages the process of making Europe the absent centre. This, in turn, reinforces the idea that the colonial experience was pervasive in the fashioning of the modern identities of the former colonies. It would be foolish to dispute the obvious fact that colonialism was a very significant influence; yet, in many cases, it was only one factor among others, as the Indian novelist Nayantara Sahgal has forcefully pointed out in her essay 'The Schizophrenic Imagination':

> So is 'colonial' the new Anno Domini by which events are to be everlastingly measured? My own awareness as a writer reaches back to x-thousand B.C., at the very end of which measureless timeless time the British came, and stayed, and left. And now they're gone, and their residue is simply one more layer added to the layer upon layer of Indian consciousness. Just one more.[18]

Similarly, in *The Discovery of India*, Nayantara Sahgal's kinsman Jawaharlal Nehru described his country as 'an ancient palimpsest on which layer upon layer of thought and reverie had been inscribed, and yet no succeeding layer had completely hidden or erased what had been written previously'.[19]

These metaphors – the fragment, the layer, the palimpsest – all point towards a blurring of borders and of ideas of unitary identity; they are equally relevant to Africa (see, for instance, Chantal Zabus's *The African Palimpsest*[20]), to the Caribbean and Latin America (as the work of Wilson Harris has long been urging us to recognize), or to Australia, with its complicated patterns of relationship between indigenous populations, descendants of earlier waves of colonists, and more recent migrants from Europe and Asia. Australia, as Peter Childs and Patrick Williams suggest, can be considered 'coloniser, colonised and post-colonial . . . all at once'.[21] Central to this notion of complex, multi-layered cultures, as Zabus's perspective indicates, is the question of the relationship of the postcolonial to language. We have touched earlier on the tendencies towards isolating postcolonial literatures written in English, say, from those in French or Spanish. There is a further dimension, however, to the issue of language. Why, some scholars have asked, is the postcolonial implicitly held to exist only in the language of the colonizer? Why – as in the case of India – should it not include the writer in Marathi or Bengali or Tamil? Do bilingual writers become 'postcolonial' when they write their books in English, but not when they do so in Marathi? Is the Ngugi of *Matagari* less 'postcolonial' than the writer of *A Grain of Wheat*? Perhaps a more productive way in which to see such writers as these is the way in which Arvind Krishna Mehrotra does – as possessing a '"continuous" language or idiolect', through which they can move,[22] and through which, as Zabus argues, the Europhone language also becomes indigenized. The horizontal and comparative perspective we have been outlining briefly provides a better framework in which to consider the complex relationship between writing in the metropolitan languages and – where they exist – writings in indigenous languages.

Failure to take this dimension into account leads to an overvaluation of work written in the metropolitan languages and of work dealing with themes (such as cultural conflict) which preoccupy those writers who are the products of a certain kind of education and class. Aijaz Ahmad cites as an example of such tendencies the *New York Times*'s description of *Midnight's Children* as 'a continent finding its voice'. The implication, as Ahmad comments, is that 'one has no voice if one does not speak in English'.[23] In an issue of the *New Yorker* commemorating the fiftieth anniversary of Indian independence, Bill Buford – inadvertently, no doubt, but symptomatically – manages to make Indian literature coextensive with Indian literature *written in English* when he refers to a picture of 11 English-language writers printed in that issue as a picture of 'India's leading novelists'.[24] At best, one can take such statements as examples of pardonable ignorance; at worst, as a version of cultural neo-colonialism.

What is at issue in a number of the examples we have been looking at is the question of homogeneity in discussions of the colonial and the postcolonial. This is a topic which has been well-aired by now, and it would be superfluous to go over it at any length here.[25] While we welcome the increasing emphasis on plurality, and hope that the work gathered here will aid the project of plurality, we are also conscious that a comparative enterprise of the kind that this book proposes runs a risk of getting lost in some blurred realm of the 'postcolonial'. There is a need, therefore, to negotiate a difficult path between competing pressures and dangers: on the one hand, there is the task of attempting to question the idea of the boundary, and, on the other, there is the problem of trying to retain some sense of historical and cultural specificity.

We have tried to respond to this dilemma by including both a number of general and theoretical essays, and essays focusing on specific texts. This division also reflects two important aspects of the questioning of existing boundaries and definitions. One is that this questioning is taking place on a theoretical and discursive level in academic institu-tions, journals and books; the other – perhaps more important – is that, in a number of different locations across the world, such questioning is taking place, as it were, concretely and 'on the ground', in the work of recognizable authors such as Wilson Harris and Salman Rushdie as well as collaborating writers such as Rigobeta Menchú, and in the realm of politics and society, where competing definitions of national and cul-tural identities contest these issues.

III

In the essays collected together here, the 'border crossings' theme takes a variety of forms, ranging from narratives of partition in Bolivian and South Asian writing to ambivalent migrant journeyings through Cuban and Irish diasporas, and the creative collapsing of borders in hybrid fictions that emerge out of multiple cultural inheritances. The essays are also written in a variety of styles, reflecting the different locations of the individual authors and sometimes the different critical moments with which they are engaged. Those contributors who are attempting to bring attention to less visible themes and issues (such as indigenous subalternity) are necessarily engaged in the sorts of historical contextualizing that may not be so pertinent to specifically theorized readings. While some of the contributors are bilingual, and some only recently arrived in the British academic metropolis, all are native English speakers apart from Nara Araújo, a Cuban scholar who highlights the neocolonialism which operates through language and which forces her to speak in English if she is to cross-culturalize her own field of study.

While each of the contributors is involved in his or her own cross-cultural project, further areas of comparative overlap emerge when the essays are read as a whole. We have attempted to suggest some of these directions through the sections we provisionally map, as well as through the order of the individual essays, although we recognize, of course, that alternative groupings might be made, and other directions highlighted. The essays in the opening section, 'On the Border', all use the example of Ireland to explore some borders which are discursive and political as much as they are geographical. Lyn Innes notes the tendency – now on the decline – to exclude Ireland from the study of the postcolonial, and suggests that the example of Ireland might fruitfully 'complicate the usual postcolonial paradigms', paradigms which she traces partly to the academic origins of postcolonial studies in Commonwealth Literature, Third World/Black Studies and post-structuralism. Willy Maley's essay, too, is engaged in the questioning of paradigms, in his case the exclusion of Scotland from the postcolonial. Noting that 'thinking in threes has never been popular', he proceeds to explore the implications of inserting Scotland as a third term into the binary relationship between England and Ireland, concluding that this third term is a 'borderline case whose implications are crucial for postcolonial criticism'. In the final essay of this section, Gerry Smyth argues that the currently most fashionable example of border crossing, hybridity, ought perhaps to be viewed more sceptically. He suggests that, although hybridity is touted as a method of 'breaking out of the prisonhouse of oppositionalist logic', it might in fact be 'hegemonically recuperable, easily absorbed by those with an interest in denying the validity of a coherent discourse of resistance'.

Where Part I deals with such general issues, the other essays in the book, by and large, are based on analyses of individual texts. Part II, 'Diasporas', continues the preceding section's emphasis on Ireland, while also introducing one of the other themes signalled earlier in this introduction – the juxtaposition of the Americas with the more usual (at least for British audiences) anglophone studies. Aidan Arrowsmith's paper, and the following paper co-written by Liam Harte and Lance

Pettitt, continue to engage with the issues introduced by Gerry Smyth and, like him, strike a note of caution about the concept of hybridity. For Arrowsmith, inbetweenness is 'not always experienced as a liberated and productive space', since migration disturbs some of the parameters of our identities. His essay acknowledges the longing for return characteristic of so many migrants, and, through a discussion of works by Yeats, Beckett and Anne Devlin, among others, considers the possibility of fruitfully negotiating identities amongst the pulls and tensions of essentialism and anti-essentialism. Liam Harte and Lance Pettitt examine two novels by writers who have spent most of their careers in England – William Trevor's *Felicia's Journey* and Maurice Leitch's *Gilchrist*. These texts, they observe, 'exemplify... the disruptive and transformative energies of migrancy'. Yet they too are wary about uncritical celebrations of hybridity and migrancy. The central characters of the two novels discussed occupy a more ambiguous, troubled and troubling state, 'a state of dislocation, marginalized but surviving, negotiating their hybrid difference'; and Harte and Pettitt point to crucial elements of patriarchy, sexuality, Protestantism and Catholicism which radically disrupt any straightforward sense of Irish migration to England. Geraldine Stoneham's essay shifts our attention to the US metropolis, drawing on Homi Bhabha's distinction between the performative and the pedagogic in the narration of the nation to look at novels by Bharati Mukherjee and T. Coraghessan Boyle. Mukherjee's vision, she concludes, is 'based on a metaphor of genetic mutation rather than hybridity', and consequently 'reinscribes the old immutable myths of the nation with new and mutable ones'; for Boyle the contradictions in the narrative of the nation are 'papered over by a moribund but powerful national identity', and his Mexican border crossers are shown to be as bereft and vulnerable as their Irish counterparts in England. Nara Araújo's essay follows on from Stoneham's analysis of hybridity in the US metropolis and looks at a body of work that is little known in Britain – the literature of the Cuban diaspora in the United States. She notes the heterogeneity of this literature, fissured as it is by issues of cultural location, generational difference, political stances and language, and, following Stuart Hall, argues that, rather than trying to 'find an essence to Cubanamerican literature, one should try to think in terms of a positioning'. These considerations are focused through a discussion of two works, Cristina García's *Dreaming in Cuban* and Achy Obejas's *We Came All the Way from Cuba so You Could Dress Like This?*

Two themes run through a number of essays in Part III: one is the condition of internal exile experienced by marginalized groups; the other is the tension between self-representation and representation by others. In the most theoretical of these pieces, David Marriott uses Fanon's 'cultural politics of the unconscious' to examine the fantasies underlying negrophobia and to show how the 'mirage of white narcissism ... comes to occupy the black psyche through cultural imposition'. Narratives about the partition of India constitute the subject of Sujala Singh's essay, which examines how contending Hindu, Muslim and Sikh nationalisms inscribed themselves on women's bodies, while at the same time attempting to silence the retrieval and representation of the violence done to women. Through an analysis of Amrita Pritam's novella *Pinjar*, she investigates the 'investitures and exclusions that are crucial to the nationalistic discourses of subject-formation'. Keith Richards's paper, which lends its title to this section of the book, usefully contextualizes the place of Latin America in postcolonial studies before looking at the relatively neglected literature of Bolivia, a country which has also been produced out of partition and which, for political, geographical and historical reasons, he argues, suffers from a feeling of marginality and low self-esteem. The three writers he discusses – Jesús Urzagasti, Néstor Taboada Terán and René Poppe – depict this estrangement through the metaphor of exile. 'Bolivia', he argues, 'inexorably imposes the terms of its own marginality upon its writers', though Richards does also indicate some of the strategies for self-identification (such as contemporary reworkings of indigenous myths) that begin to emerge in the literature. Issues of silence, representation, authorship and agency – how subaltern classes might speak out of discourses and publications that are imposed on them, or shape them – also form some of the recurrent threads of Susan Forsyth's analysis of native North American autobiographies. Forsyth examines how these works are constituted in the midst of a variety of contending forces: collaborative authorship, the interaction of native oral traditions with autobiographical and ethnographical forms of writing, pressure from publishers' sense of the market, and so on. Part III concludes with Denise Vernon's account of the 'aboriginal' novels of Thomas Keneally. Like Singh and Forsyth earlier, Vernon engages with important debates concerning self-representation and the legitimacy of representations of the other. The shifts in Keneally's representations of Aboriginal peoples, she suggests, have reflected the changing patterns of race relations in Australia. Although Keneally's writing has been marked by an increasing sense of humility and self-doubt concerning the representation of the other, inevitably it runs up against the 'limits of goodwill', the limits of the 'well-meaning, but ethnocentric authorial voice', the voice of the 'guilt-ridden liberal'.

A number of papers in this collection, we have noted, exhibit a salutary caution about some of the claims made for the idea of hybridity. The essays in Part IV, while aware of these doubts, highlight more positive aspects through a discussion of a variety of texts in a number of different forms and from a variety of locations. Patricia Murray's essay places the Caribbean in terms of the wider cross-culturality of the Americas and analyzes a short story by Wilson Harris as an example of the 'multiple border crossings and trickster-like shape-shifting' that permeate the Caribbean imagination. Fragmentary and hybridized even before contact with Europe, the indigenous culture has a creative potential which energizes much of Harris's work, and which suggests the possibility of dialogue even amidst the brutality of conquest. Sam Haigh's essay continues the investigation of Caribbean narrative, this time from a francophone perspective, by looking at a recent collection of Antillean short stories which, she argues, reflects a change in attitude by Antillean writers. Instead of trying to assimilate themselves to European culture, these writers are now asserting their difference, 'proclaiming their position on the borders of dominant culture' by returning to the Antillean form of the folktale. In Sylviane Telchid's 'Mondésir', the mythical river woman, Manman Dlo, is a 'creole figure *par excellence* – at once precolonial and colonial, oral and written: created out of, renewed and adapted, and now indistinguishable from all of these traditions and more'. Telchid, like other Antillean writers, is 'actively deploying the "creoleness" – the contradictions and ambivalences – at the heart of the Antillean literary tradition', and, like Wilson Harris, is shown to be utilizing the resources of the past, whilst refusing its temptation to nostalgia. Catherine Davies's piece continues the theme of creolization, analyzing a poem by the Cuban poet Excilia Saldaña in order to show how it uses intertextuality to inscribe 'a plurality of discourses across cultural and gender boundaries', and to 'reinvent a cultural space from a dissonant, feminist point of view'. Like Telchid, Saldaña is attempting to write her way out of the straitjackets of characterization and expectation that continue to limit the woman writer in the Caribbean, and, Davies argues, as a black Cuban poet she forces critics to rethink some of the parameters of their theoretical frameworks. John Thieme returns us to the anglophone Caribbean, but to a writer who, in his exploration of creole hybridity, is acutely aware of the lessons of comparative study. Thieme examines the 'literary staging of creolization' in two of Derek Walcott's earlier plays, *Henri Christophe* and *Dream on Monkey Mountain*. Although the character Henri Christophe, Thieme argues, is enmeshed in, and perpetuates, Manichean racial divisions, the play in a sense 'erode[s] the borders drawn by colonial discourse, since it dramatizes the tragic consequences facing the protagonist who succumbs to a view that casts him as the inferior partner in the hierarchized Manichean equation'. In *Dream on Monkey Mountain*, on the other hand, the characters 'exorcize the stultifying legacy of... cultural essentialism and the play promotes a positive view of creolization'. The final essay in Part IV, David Richards's discussion of Christopher Okigbo, focuses on a complex series of cultural exchanges between European modernism and African writing. Noting that Picasso's painting *Les Demoiselles d'Avignon* was influenced by the discovery of a set of African masks in the Trocadero, Richards shows how Picasso's appropriation of African art emptied that art of 'autonomous content', reducing Africans to 'anonymous, "primal", primary and unknowing contributors of source materials'. More than half a century on, however, Okigbo found in Picasso's work – particularly *Guernica* – a source for his own poetics, a 'poetics of collaged fragments' which enabled him to 'recover from modernist primitivism a version of African modernity', disavowing 'the modernist version of African primitivism' and countering 'notions of African historylessness'.

Wilson Harris, as we mentioned earlier, has, in his own inimitable way, long been engaged in exploring cross-cultural encounters. It is appropriate, therefore, that this volume should finish with 'Apprenticeship to the Furies', his closing address to the 'Border Crossings' conference. Here, he confronts head-on the potency for terror unleashed by the revenge-syndrome in the late twentieth century and tries to suggest an alternative reading of the Furies, one which may inspire, instead, 'regeneration of oneself, of one's age, one's community'. Steeped in his own postcolonial history and his experience of writing anti-colonialist dramas, Harris argues that the 'theatre of culture' in which we are engaged has trapped us in 'a dead-end in which to shore up the ruins of a loss of resurrectionary soul, a death of god, a death of cosmic love', and suggests that a departure from such 'one-track mind-set or psychology of brute realism' may be the most challenging of all border crossings. This can be achieved through 'a different kind of fiction from conventional realism', a fiction which makes use of the 'sweep of imageries sprung from different times and ages':

> All this is pertinent to the vessel of the person steeped in spectralities and concretions through which to transcend individual one-track destiny which may ally itself with freedom but, in fact, is intent on cementing a fortressed ego or super-ego for itself. Freedom should

mean, I think, the action of memory to acquaint us deeply, profoundly, with the perilous voyages of humanity out of its cradles of dream in space and time so that the grain of cosmic love may come home to us in all its astonishing reality and fragility and originality.

We hope that the attempts in this book to dislocate some of the disciplinary, linguistic and cultural borders that continue to divide postcolonial studies may suggest more dynamic ways in which to read such 'fictions' in the future.

Part I

On the Border

1
Postcolonial Studies and Ireland

C. L. Innes

Recently I was asked to contribute an essay on cultural nationalism to a book on postcolonial literatures. I accepted the invitation and submitted a comparative discussion which drew on nationalist writing from Africa, Australia and Ireland. The editor returned the essay with the request that I remove the sections on Ireland, since he did not feel that they belonged to the category of 'postcolonial literature'. There was a long exchange of letters, resulting finally in the acceptance and publication of the essay with the Irish sections included.

This exchange led me to reflect further not only about whether it is fruitful to think of Ireland in the context of the postcolonial, but also about the ways in which the category of the postcolonial has been addressed and theorized, and who does the theorizing. Does the inclusion of Ireland lead one to modify our thinking about the nature of colonial and postcolonial relationships, histories and cultures? And why have discussions of the 'postcolonial' made relatively little reference to Ireland? Although Irish literary critics have begun to invoke Said, Fanon and others, and to see them as providing a useful perspective from which to view the relationships between Irish and British cultural history,[1] the major theorists in the postcolonial arena have generally ignored Ireland.[2] I want to suggest that the example of Ireland may lead us to question certain kinds of oppositions and divisions common to a number of discussions of the postcolonial, which in my view do not adequately distance themselves from constructions of race and culture deriving from the colonial period. Moreover, the areas addressed by postcolonial studies, and, in many cases, the assumptions which continue to inform them, are still circumscribed by their origins in three main areas of academic scholarship: Commonwealth Literature, Third-World or Black Studies and post-structuralist theory.

Each of these bases for the development of postcolonial studies has had specific consequences, which I will discuss in greater detail later in this essay. The development of Commonwealth literary studies into the 'postcolonial', marked most notably by the publication of *The Empire Writes Back* in 1989,[3] renamed 'Commonwealth literature' as 'postcolonial literature', thus endorsing an emphasis on literature written in English within the Commonwealth. This excluded literature in indigenous languages or European languages other than English, and also endorsed the assumption of a common metropolitan centre, specifically England. Outside the Commonwealth framework, however, postcolonial studies grew from the North American institutionalization of Black Studies and Third-World Studies. Such groupings often had a more interdisciplinary orientation than the Commonwealth literary one, and endorsed the categorization of cultures and societies in terms of race, colour and racial/cultural divisions or oppositions. Frederic Jameson's 1986 essay on 'Third-World Literature in the Era of Multinational Capitalism'[4] has been one of the more influential and controversial examples of such oppositions between 'First' and 'Third' worlds in which the latter includes all non-white peoples, whether African or Asian. The third base for the development of postcolonial studies has been post-structuralist theory, especially developing from aspects of Foucault and Derrida, with an emphasis on the links between discourse and institutional power, difference and othering. Such theories have strongly influenced, and overlapped with, the first two areas of scholarship briefly outlined above, but Edward Said's *Orientalism* set the agenda for another focus of study, the discourse of the centre rather than the texts which 'wrote back'.[5]

Because of its emphasis on the imperialist programme informing or endorsed by literary and academic texts, Said's book marked a turning point in some areas of literary study, although his general point had been made earlier by African writers like Chinua Achebe (for example in his 1974 lectures, 'Colonialist Criticism', and 'An Image of Africa'[6]), or even forty years earlier by African-American critics such as Sterling Brown. But much less discussion had taken place with regard to the relationship with 'the East', and few had demonstrated so forcefully and with such a wide range of reference the dubiousness and slipperiness of the whole category of 'the Orient'. Nor had many critics drawn on the work of Foucault so extensively with regard to imperialism (an area Foucault himself ignored), and the uses of academic and literary discourse in the underpinning of imperial command over colonized countries. Not only did he define Orientalism as an 'enormously systematic discipline by which European culture was able to manage – *and even produce* – the Orient politically, sociologically, militarily, ideologically, scientifically and imaginatively during the post-Enlightenment period', he also sought to show that 'European culture gained in strength and identity by setting itself off against the Orient as a sort of surrogate and even underground self' (my italics).[7]

Said demonstrated persuasively that the culture of imperialism must be brought home to the imperialists, that the study of the postcolonial cannot be separated from the study of the colonizing power; and he argued for the contextualizing of European literature as one of a number of discourses – anthropological, historical, religious and travel writings. Following Said's example, such work has now been done extensively with regard to India, Africa and the Caribbean, but very little attention has been paid to the study of all kinds of written texts produced in England in the context of England's construction of Irishness or Celticism.

But that 'or Celticism' touches on one of the important issues which has been raised in relation to Said's work. *Would* a narrative of the discourse of Celticism, embracing Julius Caesar, Giraldus Cambrensis, Edmund Spenser, Shakespeare, Ernest Renan, Gauguin, Matthew Arnold and Sir Walter Scott, be a coherent narrative? Does the Celticism which includes Brittany, Wales, Ireland and Scotland stem from the same kind of project to control peoples and territories? Would one not wish to make some quite significant distinctions in terms of the kinds of Celticism directed towards each area, from where, and the uses to which it was put at very specific historical moments? And where would one place Sir Walter Scott or Sir Samuel Ferguson in this project or narrative? As a number of critics have asserted, Said's narrative of Orientalism raises comparable questions. Is it possible to conflate French and English and Greek and German Orientalism into the same category? But more relevant to the focus of this essay is the issue of different kinds of 'othering' within imperial discourses. Said discusses at some length Ernest Renan's categorizing of the Oriental; he does not refer to Renan's views of the Celtic races and their culture, views which strongly influenced Matthew Arnold. Said argues persuasively that Orientalism involves the Westerner's construction of himself and of the Oriental as other, but it is interesting to ask how such constructions of the self in relation to the Oriental compare with constructions of the Anglo-Saxon or Germanic in relation to the Celt. Such comparisons could allow us to discriminate more precisely between different varieties of 'othering', and to ask what circumstances influence those differences. Further, we might ask where Irish men and women placed themselves with regard to such dichotomies between the West and the Orient. Where and in what ways does the Orientalism of Thomas Moore or William Butler Yeats intersect with Celticism, and does it align with or subvert English and French versions of Orientalism?

A recent study by Javed Majeed of the context of James Mill's *History of British India* has a very interesting chapter on the ways in which Thomas Moore used the Orient to give voice to his anti-imperialist views in *Lalla Rookh*, his epic poem set in the context of Hindu and Parsee resistance to Islamic imperialism in the fifteenth century. Majeed points out that many Catholic authors writing about the same time likened Protestant-ism to Islam, and depicted Muhammed as a prototype of the evangelical Protestant.[8] In a note to one section of the epic, in which a young Hindu prince gives his life fighting for the liberty of his nation, Moore makes quite clear his sympathetic identification with his Hindu hero:

> It is no disparagement of the word 'liberty' to apply it to that national independence, that freedom from the interference of foreigners, without which, indeed, no liberty of any kind can exist, and for which both Hindoos and Persians fought against their Mussulman invaders with, in many cases, a bravery that deserved much better success.[9]

Here Moore's distinction between different oriental groups, and his identification with one rather than another, places Orientalism, and even the historical prejudice against Islam, in a different frame. So do Lady Gregory's passionate defence of the Egyptian nationalist leader Arabi in 1882 and Maud Gonne's articles on Indian women nationalists in her newsletter, *Irlande Libre*, in the late 1880s.[10] Yeats's first poems, such as 'The Indian to His Love', drew on Oriental subjects until he was persuaded that Celtic subjects would serve as well.

Although Said turned his attention to anti-colonial writers in his later book, *Culture and Imperialism*, published in 1993, it is the work on imperialist and Orientalist discourse which has been most influential. Frederic Jameson, on the other hand, has had a particular impact on discussions of nationalist and postcolonial writing. His assertion in the 1986 essay referred to above that all 'Third-World' literature could (indeed must) be read as 'national allegory' has been taken up by many postcolonialist critics, including Stephen Slemon and Timothy Brennan. Jameson's argument is based on several questionable premises: that there is a clear distinction between 'First' and 'Third' worlds, not merely in terms of economic and political structures, but also with regard to cultural production; that the Third World is at an earlier stage of literary production, still likely to be caught up in the age of realist fiction and so cannot 'offer the satisfactions of Proust or Joyce';[11] that Third-World literature is instructive and remedial because it is still concerned with community as a whole; that all Third-World countries share a common history of imperial domination and colonialism; that this is the most important factor in their history, and so all 'Third-World texts...necessarily project a political dimension in the form of national allegory'.[12] Jameson takes two texts to illustrate his thesis, one by the Chinese writer Lu Xun, and the other by the Senegalese writer, Ousmane Sembène.

As much in anger as in sorrow, the Indian scholar Aijaz Ahmad has forcefully attacked Jameson's premises and the argument as a whole, particularly with regard to the essentialist and problematic division of the globe into First and Third Worlds.[13] Certainly the term 'Third World' is used by Jameson and others with considerable lack of coherence and precision. What it mainly seems to incorporate in this common usage is a division between European and non-European, or white and non-white, a division which is then conflated with oppositions between modernity and tradition, wealth and poverty, capitalist and feudal, colonizers and colonized. But if it is a history of colonization and decolonization which is the common factor distinguishing the Third World from the First, where does Ireland fit? And where does one place writers of the Indian, African or Irish diaspora resident in the 'First World'? And how does one situate Japan or Hong Kong? Jameson's binary division between the two worlds avoids such complications, and reinforces the categorization of all non-European peoples as other – in terms of race, colour and culture.

In his critique of Jameson, Aijaz Ahmad rejects not only the binary opposition between First and Third World (and then seeks to reinstate the 'Second World') but also Jameson's assumption that he can categorize Third-World literature on the basis of a very few texts written in, or translated into, European languages. Taking India as his example, Ahmad argues that the greater part of the literature written in that country during the late nineteenth and early twentieth centuries was in indigenous languages, and that the preoccupation of these texts, especially the fictional ones, was not with 'the national narrative' but with the *mores* and manners of the emerging middle classes. Neither Ahmad nor Jameson discusses oral forms such as the tale or ballad, despite the importance of both to much nationalist literature.

Turning to the Irish example, one finds that the question of the status and relevance of Gaelic as opposed to English-language literature has been one of the most heated issues for cultural nationalists. On the other hand, if one considers Irish literature that might be read as national allegory along the lines discerned by Jameson, one might think first of works by English and Anglo-Irish men and women who have a very ambivalent relationship to Ireland – Swift's *Story of an Injured Lady*, Maria Edgeworth's *Castle Rackrent*, Lady Morgan's *Wild Irish Girl*, Yeats's *Cathleen ni Houlihan*, Shaw's *Pygmalion*. Joyce indicated that *Dubliners* should be read as an account of the moral history of his nation. (Of course many Gaelic texts, including the *aisling* poems, can also be read as national allegories.)

Commonwealth literary studies stem from an earlier era than the work of Said and Jameson, and until recently had been largely ignored in American academic institutions. A major turn in this field is marked by the publication of *The Empire Writes Back*, in which Ashcroft, Griffiths and Tiffin sought to graft discourse theory and Black Studies insights onto Commonwealth literary studies. The result is reviewed in an essay by Vijay Mishra and Bob Hodge, 'What is Post(-)colonialism?', which criticizes the book on two counts: 1) its conflation of the experience of white settler colonies and black nations; and 2) its preoccupation with the novel and exclusion of poetry, drama and other genres.[14] Mishra and Hodge go on to argue that race and language mark the crucial difference between white settler colonies and black nations. In my view, however, Mishra and Hodge share with the authors they castigate a failure to escape the confines of the Commonwealth Studies arena, which, with added impetus from Black and Third World Studies, excludes other models, and reinscribes the colonial assumption that there is always an absolute division between colonizer and colonized, or settler and native.

The Irish experience might lead one to question such divisions, not only with regard to Ireland itself, but also with regard to the Irish diaspora. The Mishra/Hodge/Jamesonian emphasis on black/white divisions conceals the extent to which race is not a given, but something that is *constructed*. Ireland's history prior to the twentieth century, and even into the twentieth, is a history of apartheid, in which those who spoke Irish, adhered to Irish culture or dress, or married an Irish person were driven 'beyond the Pale', or, at a later date, disenfranchised. Catholic Irish tenants were driven from their land, treated as serfs, and had no recourse to the law. Here one can see clearly the construction of racial difference to justify economic interests, British rule and the creation of rigid class divisions. Anthropologists argued that the Irish were descended from Africans and closest to them in the evolutionary scale.

This construction of racial difference between white settlers and white natives in the context of British rule, as well as the unease arising from the fact that the Irish were not quite not-white, is illustrated in a letter that the liberal reformer, Charles Kingsley, wrote to his wife when he was travelling in Ireland in 1861 (just over a decade after the devastation of the Great Famine):

> But I am haunted by the human chimpanzees I saw along that 100 miles of horrible country. I don't believe they are our fault. I believe there are not only more of them than of old, but that they are happier, better, more comfortably fed and lodged under our rule than they ever were. But to see white chimpanzees is dreadful; if they were black, one would not feel it so much, but their skins, except where tanned by exposure, are as white as ours.[15]

The political and social history of Ireland suggests the degree to which the opposition between settler and native contributes to, rather than derives from, constructions of racial difference, which frequently concealed the fact that in reality the barriers had to do with divisions of class rather than race. The distance between settler and native in Ireland varied from decade to decade according to particular political demands, both internal and external, as Yeats's career vividly illustrates. What chiefly distinguished the Anglo-Irish plantocracy and the working-class Protestant and Presbyterian settlers from those of Celtic descent was not race or colour – or even religion – but the degree of choice available to them when it came to declaring an Irish or non-Irish identity, and the possibility of laying claim to some of the privileges that the latter entailed. Mishra and Hodge emphasize the differences between settler colonies and black nations. Ireland was, and some would assert in part still is, a settler colony, and yet the example of Irish nationalism has been cited as a model by African-American, African and Caribbean cultural nationalists and activists.

The histories of Irish emigration might also encourage us to modify received orthodoxies about the absolute divide between settlers and natives. After the 1798 rebellion led by Wolfe Tone in Ireland, nine convict shiploads of Irish rebels were sent to Australia, arriving in 1800. In these and other voyages carrying Irish convicts, the death rate was around 37 per cent.[16] The British military governors, and the Anglican clergymen who went out with them, spoke of the Irish in very similar terms to those they used to describe the Aboriginal inhabitants. Samuel Marsden, the chief Anglican clergyman of the time, whose name lives on in Australian school histories as one of the founders of the Australian sheep industry, wrote of these convicts as belonging to 'the most wild, ignorant and savage race – their minds devoid of every principle of Religion and Morality – always alive to Rebellion and Mischief... extremely superstitious, artful and treacherous'.[17] There were a number of rebellions by Irish convicts in the new colony, and there exist from the early nineteenth century ballads in which evicted and transported Irishmen compare themselves with the Aborigines dispossessed from their lands in Australia. Later, more famously, we find folk heroes such as Ned Kelly, the son of Irish immigrants, writing in an open letter to the people of Australia in 1879: 'Port McQuarrie Toweringabbie Norfolk island and Emu plains and in those places of tyranny and condemnation many a blooming Irish man rather than subdue to the Saxon yoke were flogged to death and bravely died in servile chains.'[18]

There are analogies here with the brutal transportation of Africans to North and South America and the Caribbean, and their unwilling involvement in the dispossession of native American peoples. The history of Australia, with the gradual emergence of an Irish-Australian and anti-monarchic leadership also makes it comparable to the Caribbean, with the emergence of an Afro-Caribbean or Indo-Caribbean leadership rejecting Anglo-Saxon rule and influence, but still leaving its native population marginalized and impoverished. Such parallels should at the very least modify the settler colony/black nation distinctions asserted by Mishra and Hodge and others. The Caribbean analogy perhaps could also encourage a reading of Shakespeare's *The Tempest* in terms of an Irish as well as a Caribbean context. Might not Prospero be read as Spenser or Walter Raleigh, both of whom were involved in the conquest of Ireland, and, if Caliban evokes the Caribbean, might not Ariel evoke Eire?

There are other ways in which the Irish example complicates the usual postcolonial paradigms and encourages us to think in terms of divisions which derive from class rather than race, and which are more fluid than much postcolonial theory allows. Oscar Wilde, on his tour of America in the 1880s, at one and the same time declared his fervent desire for Irish independence and his sympathy with Jefferson Davis and the defeated American South, whose plight he saw as analogous to that of Ireland. Maud Gonne shared with many Irish nationalists profound identification with the Boers, whom they saw as a peasant nation like Ireland, oppressed and colonized by the hated British imperialists. Her husband, John McBride, was one of a group of Irishmen who fought on the side of the Boers in the Boer War, and later was executed as one of the leaders of the Easter Rising in 1916.

The plays of Oscar Wilde and George Bernard Shaw take on another perspective if read in the light of Homi Bhabha's discussions of mimicry as a strategy for subversion within the colonial context. *The Importance of Being Earnest* and *Pygmalion* become not merely quintessentially English comedies, but quintessentially anti-English farces, which expose and ridicule class structures, the masculinist ethos which underpins imperialism and the discourses which sustain them.[19] But whereas Bhabha's reflections on mimicry and hybridity assume a duality rather than a spectrum of cultures and identities, and often ignore issues of gender and class, Wilde and Shaw evoke and constantly subvert gender, class and cultural boundaries. Shaw's 'Irish play' – perhaps too Irish for the Abbey Theatre – *John Bull's Other Island*, takes on a full spectrum of 'othered' and 'othering' subjects, and reveals the multiple facets of power politics and power play among English capitalists, Irish exiles and land-owners, Catholic, Protestant and in-between, each adapting to the images which best allow them economic and psychic survival. Shaw's *Pygmalion* and *John Bull's Other Island* are both remarkable for their awareness of the interplay between cultural and economic power, and for their dramatization of the economic, psychic and symbolic significance of cultural adaptation or adoption or imposition. Such awareness emerges throughout twentieth-century Irish writing – in the fiction of Joyce, the drama of O'Casey and Friel, and the poetry of Paul Muldoon, among many others.

The study of Irish literature has suffered from its co-option into English literary studies which erase an Irish historical and political context. Conversely, it has within Ireland itself too frequently been confined to a nationalist narrative, which emphasizes the distinctive qualities of Irish literature. A postcolonial perspective can enlarge our understanding not only of texts written by Irish authors and the ways in which they can and cannot be compared with the literatures, cultures and narratives of other peoples who experienced colonization, but also of texts and narratives originating from England and marked by England's encounter with Ireland. But I would also claim that the inclusion of Ireland within postcolonial studies would encourage us to question some of the assumptions that have become too quickly embedded in postcolonial theories and critiques. One of these assumptions is that racial categories are given, and that there are clear divisions between 'white' imperialists and 'coloured' natives. The case of Ireland indicates how readily racial categories are 'constructed' and how fluid these may be, depending on the economic and political demands of those who seize the power to define. Issues of class rather than colour division are also brought to the fore when one studies Ireland in this context. And the interrelationship between imperialists and their victims, through which those who have been dispossessed and victimized may themselves become tools and ultimately beneficiaries of empire, is also clearly illustrated through the stories of those millions of Irish men and women who were transported or forced to emigrate during the nineteenth century to North America and Australia. Such histories also question the assumption that we can make an easy distinction between 'settler' and indigenous 'Black' colonies.

2
Crossing the Hyphen of History: the Scottish Borders of Anglo-Irishness

Willy Maley

The *Concise Oxford Dictionary of Current English* defines the 'Border', with a capital letter, as the 'boundary and adjoining districts between England and Scotland, N. Ireland and the Irish Republic, US and Mexico, etc.'. This is an interesting choice of examples. A 'borderer', on the other hand is a 'dweller on or near [a] frontier, especially that between England and Scotland'.[1] The word 'border' comes from 'board', which stems in turn from two distinctive Germanic words, 'bordham' and 'bordhaz', meaning 'board' and 'border' respectively. To border is also to board, to neighbour, but also to colonize. If we take on board this double derivation, we can see that it fits in with what we know of borders today, and of borders in the early modern period – my period. Periodization is something that postcolonialism cannot ignore, particularly given the academic history that has encouraged it to look for the signs of empire no further back than the nineteenth or at best the eighteenth centuries, and to confine its attention to places beyond Britain, rather than those abutting England.[2] Historical borders, no less than geographical ones, demand to be crossed.

One has to take into account the historically determined institutional context out of which postcolonial theory has grown, stemming in part from the teaching of Cultural Studies in the new universities in Britain. The bias is inevitably toward the modern, and the exclusion of earlier periods means that the painful process of British state-formation is largely overlooked. Britain is naturalized, and its constituent parts taken for granted. Academic periodization is a kind of law unto itself. It dictates when things started, because we all want to be in at the inception – of nation, of empire, of individuality – therefore it all began on the cusp of our own periods. How convenient. There is a problem with such a stultifying historical periodization, the way in

31

which we glibly characterize and caricature earlier periods, inheriting a set of stereotypes as truth. It smacks of 'chronologocentrism', and of the progressivism that critics like Homi Bhabha have so eloquently attacked.[3]

Borders are boarding points, jetties, springboards. The main plank of my argument is that borders, like boards, are for treading. In the sixteenth century, the Marches of Wales, the English Pale in Ireland and the Scottish Borders marked the cutting edges of the Tudor State, its 'borderlands', to use a current historiographical term. Borders move, as Edmund Spenser proves by way of some inventive etymology in *A View of the State of Ireland*, when he derives 'pale' as in 'English Pale' in Ireland, from the Latin 'palare', 'that is to forrage or out-run, because those marchers and borderers use commonly so to doe. So as to have a county palatine is, in effect, to have a priviledge to spoyle the enemies borders adjoining'.[4] Pales, like palings, can be unearthed, uprooted, pulled out of their sockets, just as focal points can shift, for example in the upward displacement of the English Pale around Dublin in the sixteenth century to a British (Anglo-Scottish) Pale around Belfast in the seventeenth century.[5]

Sometimes crossing a border between two countries can present fewer difficulties than crossing a border within a country, an 'internal border', and it can happen that within a multination state there are a number of borders of a different order. One border that is relatively easy to cross is the Anglo-Irish border, that hyphen that separates England from Ireland. Whether taken to refer to the descendants of English colonists in Ireland, to a body of Irish literature in English, or to relations between England and Ireland, the expression 'Anglo-Irish' is divided by a border without a checkpoint. Yet it is a partition of sorts that conceals a history of violent incorporation. It is interesting to note, for example, that we do not refer to 'Anglo-Scottish' or 'Anglo-American' literature. The phrase 'Anglo-American' is used to refer to relations between the British state and the United States, where 'Anglo' includes 'Welsh', 'Scottish' and 'Northern Irish'.

Few studies of Anglo-Irish history take full account of its Scottish dimension. This is especially true of those critiques informed by postcolonial theory. The tendency is somewhat reluctantly to admit Ireland within the postcolonial domain, while dissolving Scotland into 'England' or 'Britain'. Revisionist Irish history, for instance, has shunned Scotland, remaining firmly within an 'Anglo-Irish' problematic. Cultural Materialism and the New Historicism also seem content to leave this binary opposition intact. Yet the exclusion of Scotland is not, in my judgement, theoretically or historically justified. Scotland cannot simply be inserted into a seamless English narrative or into an uninterrupted discourse on Ireland. One has to consider the matter of Britain, the matter of the British Problem, the problem of identity and difference in a multination state, the dramatic process by which Scotland and Ireland came to play Ariel and Caliban to England's Prospero. It is as though critics can deal quite comfortably with plural crossings, but must speak of borders in the singular. As well as being ahistorical, this approach stresses one kind of complicity – Scotland's with England – against another – Ireland's with England. Scotland gets lost in the hyphen of 'Anglo-Irish' history, posted through a letterbox that sustains a sterile oppositional discourse. This is a serious omission, not least of all because postcolonial theory depends precisely upon the notions of ambivalence and hybridity repressed by binary oppositions.

It is interesting to turn back to the texts of the early modern period, the sixteenth and seventeenth centuries that some people want to see as formative – strange how, as academics, we want to see our own period of expertise as formative – to turn back, and see that the incitement to discourse about Ireland conceals a repressive hypothesis. Those sixteenth- and seventeenth-century English texts on Ireland almost invariably mention Scotland. When Scotland screams out at you from almost every page of texts hitherto read, criticized, introduced and edited as concerned exclusively with Ireland, one begins to suspect a conspiracy of silence, or at least a subtle matrix of dislocation and displacement. In a relatively rare comparative article on Scottish and Irish women's writing, Marilyn Reizbaum speaks of a 'canonical double cross'.[6] I want to address a historical and cultural double cross by foregrounding a country crucified between two thieves. There are always more than two crosses, or crossings. That is the crux of the matter. More than two. Borders: plural. There is always more than one border, and the border itself is split and multiple and open, a debatable land.

In the *Novum Organum*, Francis Bacon remarked: 'Time is like a river which has brought down to us things light and puffed up, while those which are weighty and solid have sunk'.[7] Scotland, a latter-day Atlantis, did not sink without a trace, or without a struggle. One of the English objections to the Union of Crowns in 1603 was that the country would be swamped with Scots, in the same way that, as Bacon put it, 'sheep or cattle, that if they find a gap or passage open will leave the more barren pasture, and get into the more rich and plentiful'. Bacon, speaking in defence of the Union, countered this particular fear in three ways. Firstly, he suggested that Scottish migration would be limited by the fact that 'we see it to be the nature of all men that they will sooner discover poverty abroad, than at home'. So much for Scottish fortune-hunters. Secondly, he claimed 'that this realm of England is not yet peopled to the full', and could thus afford to accommodate any such prospective Scots invasion. Finally, Bacon put his finger on a key feature of the Union, its third term, as it were – the mutually profitable carve-up of Ireland:

> [T]here was never any kingdom in the ages of the world had, I think, so fair and happy means to issue and discharge the multitude of their people, if it were too great, as this kingdom hath, in regard of that desolate and wasted kingdom of Ireland; which (being a country blessed with almost all the dowries of nature, as rivers, havens, woods, quarries, good soil, and temperate climate, and now at last under his Majesty blessed also with obedience) doth, as it were, continually call unto us for our colonies and plantations.[8]

In the event, the (relative) surplus population of Scotland was planted in Ulster under Anglo-Scottish/British jurisdiction. There was a perception in English minds of Scots massing on the Borders. Ireland earthed the political energy generated by the Union, displacing its tensions and energies. Ireland was double crossed, with the Celtic Cross being supplanted by the Union Jack, invented the year the Ulster Plantation got underway.

Bacon's incisive tract reveals the colonial project that underpins the newly united kingdoms. Few histories of Anglo-Scottish Union focus on the Ulster Plantation. Few histories of the Ulster Plantation dwell on the Union. Bacon's *Certain Considerations Touching the Plantations in Ireland* (1606) brings the two together:

> And certainly I reckon this action as a second brother to the Union. For I assure myself that England, Scotland, and Ireland well united is such a trefoil as no prince except yourself (who are the worthiest) weareth in his crown.[9]

It is this 'trefoil' that intrigues me, the offspring of Anglo-Scottish union and Irish plantation, revealing the three-ply nature of the British Problem in an Irish context, a three-way struggle for sovereignty. The *Concise Oxford Dictionary* defines a 'trefoil' as 'a leguminous plant of genus *Trifolium* with leaves of three leaflets...(thing) arranged in three lobes'.[10] 'The War of the Three Kingdoms' was the name given to the

English Civil War by those who experienced it, but thinking in threes has never been popular. Scotland is foiled, wrapped in the foil of a colonial triple play, the third term, or 'Third Word', that gets lost in 'Anglo-Irish', the hyphen, hymen, suspension, or ligature that binds three nations under one heading.

Bob Purdie has argued, in 'The Lessons of Ireland for the SNP', that 'the roots of the Irish problem lay in the Act of Union of 1800'. My own feeling is that this perspective overlooks the significance for Ireland of the seventeenth- and eighteenth-century Anglo-Scottish Acts of Union. Purdie further contends that it is significant that while in Ireland the emphasis is on 'the border', in Scotland one speaks of 'the Borders'.[11] What Purdie and others fail to address is the extent to which the Borderers, those Scots who posed the greatest danger to England, were planted in Ireland by a newly-formed British polity to serve a double placatory purpose. The Borders of Scotland, the most threatening part of the country from an English perspective, as well as from a Scottish metropolitan standpoint, were effectively relocated. Just as there are three Unions – 1603, 1707 and 1800 – exerting pressure on Ireland, so there are two borders, that of partition, the one that divides the Republic from Northern Ireland, and that which separates England and Scotland. The latter may be crossed with impunity, without encountering a sentry box or watchtower, but it is no less historically constituted or politically charged, even if its troubles were postponed thanks to the joint venture in Ireland.

Current attempts to address the Scottish part in the Anglo-Irish problem are fraught with difficulty. On the one hand, there are those who prefer to speak in terms of 'Ulster and Scotland'. Whether the emphasis is on the Scottishing of Ulster or the Ulsterization of Scotland, there is an attempt to set Scotland up as a means by which Northern Ireland can maintain its links with the 'mainland', to use another anomalous term. On the other hand, there are those, like the former Irish President Mary Robinson, who have spoken of strengthening connections between 'Ireland and Scotland'. Here, one senses a move to isolate England by turning the Anglo-Celtic axis in favour of the latter term. If border crossings mean anything, they imply a breaking down of double binds and impasses.

I am not arguing for a new Pan-Celticism, although such a thing must have been on Spenser's mind when he argued that the chief purpose of the reformation in Ireland was to keep the Scots out of Ulster. Seven years later the reverse policy took hold. What we get in modern critical discussion of the British polity is the naturalization of the state through the acceptance of a single exempt member – Ireland, now Northern Ireland. Scotland is a sideshow, and, as some Irish responses to *Braveheart* showed, an irritant, a distraction from the real crux or problem which is 'Anglo-Irish' or 'British'.[12]

A 'borderline' is a 'line of demarcation', and to be 'on the borderline' means verging on obscenity or insanity. As Scotland takes its place again in Anglo-Irish history, the political codes remain heavily marked, but the overall connections being made can only be an advance on the discredited antitheses of yesterday. Border crossings ought to have no limits. All those whom Joyce called 'fullstoppers and semicolonials' might find it convenient to punctuate the discourse of postcolonialism in this way, but, in order to cross borders, we have to be able to count beyond two, to 'think two thinks at the same time'. Historical hyphens have to be negotiated, not in order to return to some unique origin or essence, but, rather, to arrive at a politics of plurality and difference rather than polarity and deference.

What, finally, are the limits of Anglo-Irish identity? One limit or horizon is that even when this term does not imply a unitary Englishness and a monolithic Irishness, even when one speaks in terms of competing forms of Englishness in early modern Ireland, or varieties of Irishness in modern Ireland, other identities, traditions, histories and ethnicities get left out of the grand oppositional narrative. The example of Scotland is salutary, but there are others. The term 'Anglo-Irish' is heavily freighted with conflictual histories. 'Hyphen' comes from the Greek 'huphen', 'together', compounded of two words, 'hupe', under, and 'hen', one. Under one. That's what it means to be hyphenated, whatever the apparent duality: 'under one'. I note that the current document on house style for Macmillan observes that 'Hyphenation is, in general, being used less frequently'. One thinks, for example, of 'postcolonialism'. A theory that has lost its own hyphen might be advised to question others.

There must always be linkage, because, as Jacques Derrida maintains in an anti-exclusionary formulation that is persistently misinterpreted, there is nothing outside the text. According to David Lloyd, 'the nationalism of a colonized people requires that its history be seen as a series of unnatural ruptures and discontinuities imposed by an alien power while its reconstruction must necessarily pass by way of deliberate artifice'.[13] For Lloyd: 'Nationalism is generated as an oppositional discourse by intellectuals who appear, by virtue of their formation in imperial state institutions, as in the first place subjected to rather than the subjects of assimilation'.[14]

In spite of all its talk of 'plurality' and 'multiplicity' much postcolonial theory depends upon a narrow dual model of positive and negative poles. 'Ambivalence' is an unashamed double bind. There is little room for a third term. 'Hybridity' can mean more than two, but that meaning is rarely thought through or worked out. Perhaps 'heterogeneity' is a better expression; otherwise we get, not only nothing but the same old story, but more of the same. It is necessary to move from one-on-one, to one-two-three.

I pointed out earlier that Ireland is allowed access to the postcolonial field through a gap in the fence, and with some resistance. Ashcroft, Griffiths and Tiffin, in *The Empire Writes Back*, distinguish between 'dominated' and 'dominating' societies, drawing on the work of Max Dorsinville. They discuss the constituent parts of the British state and conclude:

> While it is possible to argue that these societies were the first victims of English expansion, their subsequent complicity in the British imperial enterprise makes it difficult for colonized peoples outside Britain to accept their identity as postcolonial.[15]

Leaving aside the problematic status of inside and outside, terms demanding to be deconstructed, what is meant by 'complicity' here? And what is the relationship between that process of incorporation and subordination, union and plantation, conquest and colonization that saw the British state formed, and 'the British imperial enterprise'? To refuse a postcolonial passport to Scotland, to deny Scots a boarding pass, is to betray a lack of historical understanding about the formation of the British state. Again, we are back with periodization, with a starting point that naturalizes one historical domination and alienates another. In other words, we are back at the border. It could be argued that some postcolonial theorists are determined to keep the British state intact, since this monolith suits their purposes, and since they cannot tell the difference between England and Britain, and would prefer not to take the trouble to read up on the histories of the various nations of which it is composed. In the British postcolonial text, Scotland is marginalized, subliminal. It remains in parentheses. 'Parentheses', classified by Renaissance scholars as a figure of 'trespass', are, literally, borders in the text. The constant slippage between 'British' and 'English' in even those postcolonial critics most attentive to difference is troubling, as is the general insistence upon excluding Scotland from the debate. How carefully must postcolonial critics police the borders of their subject, its terrain and its time? Does it not risk, in a classic deconstructive double bind, becoming the very thing it sets out to critique?

When the Empire folds back on itself it covers its tracks. We cannot return to states of the past, even if we wanted to. But any critique of British imperialism, if it is to be thorough and consistent, has to concern itself as much with the dissolution of the state, 'Great Britain', as with the end of Empire, 'Greater Britain'. If there is something rotten in the state, then it is rotten to the core. It may be that the history of 'Great Britain' can only be properly written in a post-British context. The histories of state and empire are intimately bound up, but many modern critiques of British imperialism do not assume that the Empire begins at 'home'. Yes, there is the occasional nod in the direction of Ireland, but by and large the Union is accepted as sacrosanct, naturalized, seldom questioned.

One view of the relationship between internal colonialism and external imperialism might be that the process of conquest, plantation and union that tied Scotland, Ireland and Wales to a British state dominated politically by England was a necessary prerequisite, a dress rehearsal before the real business of Empire. First Ireland, then America. If you look at the colonial ventures of the sixteenth century, and the colonial adventurers, then you find some support for this. Drake and Raleigh were in Ireland before they foraged further afield. Purchasing power at 'home', England was then able to spend it freely abroad. By first securing its 'backyard' – the Welsh Marches, the Irish Pale, the Scottish Borders – England could then strike out for the so-called 'New World'. There are problems with this kind of chronology. For a start, when did the British state come into being? 1172? 1284? 1536? 1603? 1707? 1800? 1922? 1975? Of course, it could still be argued that no matter how fluid were the 'margins' of this state, there was a 'core' that included 'peripheries' like Ireland from the twelfth century, which allowed England to entertain thoughts of Empire. But do we credit Empire with Union or Union with Empire? Or is this a hopeless tautology that conceals a complex dialectic? The use of 'Empire' to mean extra-British activity overlooks the imperialism implicit in Britishness itself.

While Ireland has been included in discussions of English colonialism and British imperialism, Scotland is in an anomalous position. Do we see it as a colony, a colonial power, a European competitor? It had its own Celtic Fringe in the Highlands and Islands, particularly the Lordship of the (Western) Isles. It could be argued that the analogy with English colonialism in Wales and Ireland is not English colonialism in Scotland but Scottish colonialism in its own 'fringe'. One example of this was the annexation of Orkney in 1612. The crucial joint colonial project, of course, was the plantation of Ulster which followed on from the confiscation of six counties of that province in the wake of the Flight of the Earls – the Irish aristocracy – (to Spain) in 1607. Between then and 1641 some 50000 Scots settled in Ulster. This plantation sowed the seeds of the present conflict in Ireland. But Scottish interest in Ireland does not begin and end with Anglo-Scottish Union. In 1315, for instance, Edward Bruce (brother of Robert, fostered in Ireland) had invaded Ireland with an army of Scots in order to challenge the English presence there. This was the year after the Scots had defeated the English at Bannockburn. In the sixteenth century Scottish settlement in Ulster was more successful than English colonization of Munster. Both Scotland and England had long held competing claims to Ireland. In *A View of the State of Ireland* Spenser had gone so far as to say that the Irish and Scots were all one, that Ireland was 'Scotia Major' and Scotland was 'Scotia Minor'.

Recent work on the four nations that have historically formed the British state has argued for links between the respective countries, as against the traditional anglocentric or ethnocentric historiography. Modern Scottish historiography has not always recorded the interaction between Ireland and Scotland in a sympathetic way. Ireland plays a complex role in Scottish culture, often at the level of a vexing subtext. While the 'outsider's' view, and even that of many 'insiders', may be that anti-English feeling – anglophobia – is the dominant expression of exclusivity or aggressive nationalist sentiment in Scotland, religious discrimination – invariably boiling down to anti-Irishness – is arguably much more significant. There is a tendency in Scottish historiography to do one of two things: either, on the one hand, to ignore Ireland completely, except for occasional hand-wringing references to 'sectarianism' or, on the other, to blame Ireland for what is bad or negative in Scotland. Generally, critics are more often inclined to compare Scotland to Quebec, Estonia, or Catalonia than to Ireland. Ireland is too close to 'home'. However, since the peace process got underway, there has been a renewed concern with Scoto-Irish connections, which predate Union and Empire.

Reading Maurice Roche's *Rethinking Citizenship*, I was struck by his use of the term 'subnational EC region' to refer to Scotland, or rather, to Scotland in the context of the UK.[16] Should subnations be granted subcitizenship? Is the UK a national EC region or a supranational one, with its own supracitizenship to match that of the EC? Supracitizens who are subjects. Perhaps it is time for a rethink. Old ways of thinking about citizenship have to be altered in a 'postnational' or postcolonial context, but citizenship remains part of national agendas. European citizenship does not quite square with British citizenship. Europe, as a multination state, sits uneasily with Britain, itself a multination state, arguably even an amalgamation of nation states. A United States of Europe does not appeal to the United States of Britain. Any discussion of citizenship in a British context has to take into account the nature and composition of the British state.

According to Derrida, there are no nation states without frontiers:

> [E]very State-nation is based on the control of its frontiers, on opposition to illegal immigration, and strict limits to legal immigration and right of asylum. The concept of the frontier, no less than the frontier itself, constitutes the concept of a State-nation.[17]

Of course, frontiers can be linguistic and conceptual, as well as political and geographical. In a series of lectures delivered in North Carolina and published in the United States in 1960 under the title *Citizenship Today: England – France – the United States*, D. W. Brogan, Professor of Political Science at Cambridge University, opened by defining his terms:

> First of all, I must justify my use of the word 'England' in this country where the words 'Britain' and 'British' have nearly driven out the older terms 'England' and 'English'. I do not deny – with my Irish and Scottish background it would be absurd to deny – that it is often useful to say 'British' instead of 'English'. But it is often misleading, too. For what I am concerned with is a historical phenomenon of great importance of a markedly individual character which is English in its origins, not British, and has remained English even since the creation of a British state in 1707 ... A second point, not altogether trivial but not as serious as the first ... is the ambiguity of the word 'citizen' as applied to a member of the British body politic. Legally, I am not a citizen but a subject. Or, rather, I am both, for if I am a subject at home, I am, so my passport tells me, a British citizen abroad. But the normal and ancient and respectable term is 'subject'.[18]

It seems not to occur to Brogan – why should it? – for all his evocation of history in his subsequent analysis to link his status as a subject at home with the structure and sovereignty of the British state, or with the preponderance of the English nation in that bottom-heavy 'body politic'. Brogan speaks of Cromwell's failure to create a modern, middle-class state without referring to what, for Marx and others, was one of the chief causes of that failure – the conquest and subjection of Ireland, not to mention the conquest and subjection of Scotland, and certainly not to mention the conquest and subjection of England.

Policing the borders of a multination state is made easier when a theory that purports to be critical of imperialism is in reality complicit with that state. 'British citizenship' is something of an oxymoron. As Brogan concedes, the British are on the border between citizenship and subject status. They are 'Citizen Subjects', to borrow a phrase from Etienne Balibar, or 'Britizens', to coin one of my own.[19] Must every nation have a state, follow the model of the state, in its pursuit of rights and of citizenship? The era of the nation state is far from over as long as nations bereft of states are struggling for statehood. Multination states, in contrast, may well be a thing of the past. British citizenship could become part of history together with Soviet citizenship or Yugoslavian citizenship. The anti-imperialist principle of the rights of nations to self-determination challenges unequal unions and expansionist states, but national citizenship always carries with it the risk of racism and of the negation of citizenship.

Scotland, of course, was a nation state until 1707. In July 1989 *A Claim of Right for Scotland*, the Report of the Constitutional Steering Committee, was presented to the Campaign for a Scottish Assembly in Edinburgh. The Introduction stated:

> In this report we frequently use the word 'English' where the word 'British' is conventionally used. We believe this clarifies many issues which the customary language of British government obscures. Although the government of the United Kingdom rests nominally with a 'British' Parliament, it is impossible to trace in the history or procedures of that Parliament any constitutional influence other than an English one. Scots are apt to bridle when 'Britain' is referred to as 'England'. But there is a fundamental truth in this nomenclature which Scots ought to recognise – and from which they ought to draw appropriate conclusions.[20]

It may be that British subjects can only become citizens through the break-up of the British state. That is, they can only become English, Irish, Welsh, or Scottish citizens, or European citizens. Otherwise they are citizen subjects, Britizens.

Colonialism is not merely abroad. It has come aboard. It borders, and it crosses borders. In *A View of the State of Ireland* Spenser mockingly derives 'Scot' from 'scotos', meaning 'darkness'.[21] There is a skeleton in the postcolonial closet, lurking in the darkness, a skeleton that goes by the name of 'Scotland'. Those opposed to Scotland's inclusion in a postcolonial framework would prefer to keep us in the dark, and in this they display the same attitude as those early seventeenth-century opponents of Scottish naturalization who saw the Scots as 'sheep or cattle, that if they find a gap or passage open will leave the more barren pasture, and get into the more rich and plentiful', the rich and plentiful pasture in this case being that of postcolonial theory. The Irish angle is only one among many. Anglo-Irishness has its limits, its borders; so too does Anglo-Scottishness. The great Scots poet Hugh MacDiarmid, himself raised in the Borders, spoke of 'a frontier feeling', and characterized his attitude to England as indicative of 'a border spirit, where the differences are accentuated by proximity'.[22] This cuts both ways. Scotland's exclusion from discussions of English colonialism reflects a tendency south of the Border to see Scotland as an appendage of England rather than as a nation in its own right.

Finally, I would argue that the deconstructive approach I have been pursuing furnishes postcolonial theory with a useful framework for peeling back – rather than policing – the borders of a text or culture. As Derrida famously observed:

> I do not 'concentrate' in my reading ... either exclusively or primarily on those points that appear to be the most 'important', 'central', 'crucial'. Rather, I deconcentrate, and it is the secondary, eccentric, lateral, marginal, parasitic, borderline cases which are 'important' to me and are the source of many things, such as pleasure, but also insight into the general functioning of a textual system.[23]

I believe Scotland to be a borderline case whose implications are crucial for postcolonial criticism. The Scots are fenced into a defensive unionist framework, secreted in the hyphens between England and Ireland. Acting as gatekeepers, English and Irish critics – and others – are all too ready to repel borders when Scotland appears on the horizon. Is it too much to ask for an openness to those Scots who try to squeeze through that hyphen, crossing the border, claiming some affinity, some connection, a history, a context, asking that, when sheep are being counted, they be counted too?

3
The Politics of Hybridity: Some Problems with Crossing the Border

Gerry Smyth

This essay is offered as a corrective to the uncritical adoption of certain fashionable notions concerning the significance of border-crossing, or what I shall be referring to throughout as 'hybridity'. Great claims continue to be made for the project of unsettling the border, for breaking out of the prisonhouse of oppositionalist logic into some kind of radically emancipated, free-floating condition where the subject is free to move between the great dualities inherited from the Enlightenment – mind and body, culture and nature, rationality and emotion, self and other, and so on – as well as the great dualities emerging from the history of colonialism – colonizer and colonized, settler and native, active and passive.[1] As I shall go on to describe it, hybridity ranges over a number of disciplines in one form or another, emerging from the past as the lost voice of authentic modes of cultural resistance, and in the present as a strategy whereby the postcolonial critic attempts to evade his/her implication in the reproduction of neo-colonialist power. Hybridity is the *third* space which constantly rehearses and consumes its constituent parts as well as its own possibility, the principle whereby both cultural producer and cultural critic may evade the Hegelian dialectic in which traditional oppositions are resolved. Functioning perhaps as 'discourse' did in the 1980s and 'ideology' in the 1970s, hybridity is all things to everyone and anyone – anyone who, either by desire or by fate, finds herself on the margins of institutionally organized power.

I want to argue, however, that the dissolution of the border is far from unproblematic, and that although it is a typical tactic within colonial 'reverse discourses',[2] hybridity is also hegemonically recuperable, easily absorbed by those with an interest in denying the validity of a coherent discourse of resistance. This argument draws upon some of the standard criticisms levelled against the *postal* triumvirate currently dominating the academic intellectual scene – post-structuralism, postcolonialism and postmodernism. Indeed, the sub-text of this essay is that the strategy of hybridity functions as perhaps the main point of overlap between postcolonialism and postmodernism, and that such an overlap has significant implications for the former's entire intellectual and political project. For if postmodernism relies on critical/theoretical strategies which have emerged from the 'First World', and specifically from the particular phase of late capitalism into which the West appears to have moved, then this radically qualifies its claim to be the agent of resistance to Western politico-cultural practices.[3]

I

Before going on to explore some of the dangers and blind spots of border-crossing with reference to contemporary Irish cultural politics, I want briefly to describe my understanding of the operation of hybridity, its provenance and the effects it is believed to have within a range of conceptual and methodological discourses.

Most of the dominant accounts of decolonization have noted the disjunction that appears between the state-building national élites and certain modes of resistance which, as Benita Parry describes them, are not 'calculated to achieve predetermined political ends or to advance the cause of nation-building' (p. 173). Official bourgeois nationalism is concerned with a range of specific temporal and spatial discourses which it has adopted uncritically from the colonial power, organized around notions such as tradition, authenticity and sovereignty. The work of Frantz Fanon has served as the point of departure both for a thoroughgoing deconstruction of official nationalism and its attendant nativist ideology, and also as a spur to research concerned with modes of refusal which, as Parry explains, 'are not readily accommodated in the anticolonialist discourses written by the elites of the nationalist and liberation movements' (p. 173).[4]

Fanon's own thoughts were drawn towards the possibility of a post-European humanism, but most work since then has tended to focus on less 'intentional' developments. In probably the most influential account, Homi Bhabha claims that colonial cultural discourse has been produced in

> a 'separate' space, a space of *separation* – less than one and double –
> which has been systematically denied by both colonialists and
> nationalists who have sought authority in the authenticity of

'origins'...as discrimination turns into the assertion of the hybrid, the insignia of authority becomes a mask, a mockery.

(p. 120; original emphasis)

Bhabha's collection of essays *The Location of Culture* is in fact an extended exploration of the *locations* of culture, not only in the sense of the vast array of temporalities and spatializations which bear upon the production of colonial and decolonizing discourses, but also in the sense of culture's fundamental doubleness, that hybrid space which theory has opened up between signifier and signified and which allows for the emergence of dissidence and resistance. This is an 'unhomely' space (p. 10), a 'Third Space' (p. 37), 'unthought' (p. 64), 'ambivalent' (p. 92), 'uncanny' (p. 101), 'undecidable' (p. 136), and so on. Culture aims for originality and presence but is undone by its necessary repetitive and translational status, caught always and everywhere between imitation and identification: 'It is at this moment of intellectual and psychic "uncertainty" that representation can no longer guarantee the authority of culture; and culture can no longer guarantee to author its "human" subjects as the signs of humanness' (p. 137).

Bhabha's language here is reminiscent of the work of certain theorists and critics working within and against the established cultural and political parameters of the 'First World'. One strand of contemporary gender theory, for example, operates by means of a similar politics of displacement, stressing the *performance* of received categories of Western bourgeois discourse, but in such a way as to question their givenness, their naturalness, their originality. This entails a strategy of parody, not in the sense of a comic imitation, but in the sense of a disruptive, subversive deconstruction of presence, essence and identity, of the very laws of representation. Judith Butler, one of the 'queer theorists' who has been instrumental in advancing this line, writes:

The parodic repetition of 'the original'...reveals the original to be nothing other than a parody of the *idea* of the natural and the original...What possibilities of recirculation exist? Which possibilities of doing gender repeat and displace through hyperbole, dissonance, internal confusion, and proliferation the very constructs by which they are mobilized?[5]

The 'natural' gender categories can be challenged, according to Butler, by means of a parodic, disruptive repetition which reveals itself as a copy of which the 'originals' are already constructs – a copy, that is, of a copy.

One may begin to recognize here the familiar postmodernist tropes of cross-dressing, transvestism, drag, mimicry, masquerade, irony, parody, punning – all those instances in which the borders between supposedly established and essentially different categories are transgressed. Again, culture's fantasy of presence is shattered by its fatal doubleness, a doubleness which is revealed at all those points where the 'original' is repeated and translated.

Hybridity, then, is a theory for and of its time, disseminating outwards from the realms of high theory to inform a wide range of cultural and critical productions, from the undergraduate essay through artistic strategy and on to institutional policy. Contemporary Irish cultural criticism has not failed to register these developments, although those attempting to engage with new theoretical perspectives regularly confront a critical establishment entrenched by and large in what Bhabha elsewhere describes as 'image analysis', or what in the Irish context David Lloyd has called the 'narrative of representation'.[6] To date, the clearest instance of critical hybridity in action concerns Lloyd's demolition of Seamus Heaney, whose work he considers 'profoundly symptomatic of the continuing meshing of Irish cultural nationalism with the imperial ideology which frames it' (1993, p. 37).

Against both Heaney's collusive, essentialist fantasies *and* the kind of critical discourse in which these are celebrated, Lloyd develops instead the notion of 'adulteration'. This concept (compared and linked with Bhabha's 'hybridity' in a long footnote) helps to reveal not only nationalism's 'mimicry of imperial forms' (1993, p. 123), but also to recuperate those modes of resistance within Irish cultural history which, to quote Parry again, were neither 'calculated to achieve predetermined political ends or to advance the cause of nation-building' nor 'readily accommodated in the anticolonialist discourses written by the elites of the nationalist and liberation movements' (p. 173). Lloyd describes the principle this way:

> [T]he processes of hybridization or adulteration in the Irish street ballads or in *Ulysses* are at every level recalcitrant to the aesthetic politics of nationalism and . . . to those of imperialism. Hybridization or adulteration resist identification both in the sense that they cannot be subordinated to a narrative of representation and in the sense that they play out the unevenness of knowledge which, against assimilation, foregrounds the political and cultural positioning of the audience or reader.
>
> (1993, p. 114)

Thus considered, adulteration operates as an ambivalent, trouble-making discourse, evading colonialist discourse as well as the dominant forms of nationalism with its fantasies of presence and originality. Adulteration, crucially, is not a critical invention *avant la lettre* but an acknowledgement – against criticism and its focus upon intention and meaning – of the strategies and initiatives of those who have throughout history found themselves on the margins of power. Joyce's achievement, in this reading, was to textualize the incoherencies of Irish history, writing the nation's epic but organizing it around the profoundly anti-epic effects of contingency, ambivalence and adulteration.

This, then, constitutes the nature and the challenge of hybridity, a concept which functions as a history, a politics and an aesthetics of decolonization. I have been constrained throughout this opening section to speak the case *for* hybridity in a voice not always rhetorical but alive to the exciting possibilities opened up by these theories. Like many critics whose own location is thoroughly hybrid – in terms of political and cultural affiliation as well as intellectual and methodological practice – I feel the force of critiques of colonialism and the dominant forms of anti-colonialism which have emerged in postcolonial formations, critiques which in one sense speak the impossibility of criticism, or at least the radical ambivalence of the critical discourses with which I am currently engaged. Nevertheless, in the remainder of this essay, I shall try to describe briefly some of the problems which I consider to attend a strategy of resistance constituted in this way.

II

In the first place, it would seem that many critics and theorists are beginning to feel that identity politics have suffered in the wake of fierce post-structuralist onslaughts against the subject and narrative, with the result that effective resistance becomes caught up in the critique of bourgeois power/knowledge. More often than not, this amounts less to a celebration of négritude, nativism or nationalism (as the title of Benita Parry's essay would seem to imply) than a deconstruction of reverse-discourses organized around the concept of hybridity. The narrative of nationalism, as we have seen, has tended to be seen as a violent imposition by a national élite upon 'the people', an act all the more insupportable for its unproblematic adoption of the values of the European bourgeoisie. However, there are a number of problems directly relating to this critique of nationalism as an alien imposition upon the colonized population.

For one thing, the critic who rejects nationalism as a derivative discourse is incapable, as Neil Lazarus has pointed out, 'of accounting for the huge investment of "the masses" of the colonized in various kinds of nationalist struggle'.[7] The nativist is seen as a passive dupe, accepting unproblematically all that the colonizer has to offer in the way of insidious neo-colonial effects. But critiques of nationalism's damaging derivativeness seem more appropriate to specifically *post*-colonial attempts to maintain intact the broad alliance of practices and interests which had been united under the revolutionary flag. For while it seems clear that nationalism was derivative of the formation of discourses which constituted the colonized as oppressed subjects, it also seems clear that those discourses were necessarily altered when articulated to a decolonizing politics. It would be strange indeed if the highly volatile practices of self-formation foisted onto the subject population by colonialist discourse survived intact. Nationalism, especially when cross-fertilized with traditionally marginalized practices emerging from non-bourgeois sources, seems rather to represent a much more strategic form of essentialism, deployed how, when and where it is likely to be most effective.

By the same token, acknowledging the validity of native identity does not amount to an unqualified celebration of the national essence or a disparagement of extra-national effects as manifested in the cultural history of the nation. Attacks on nationalism couched in the tones of post-structuralist critiques of identitarianism by and large fail to register the struggle *within* nationalism itself with regard to the limits of the nation and the politico-cultural policies attending the discourse of decolonization. In Irish Studies in recent years, for example, a debate has emerged around the life and work of Thomas MacDonagh, the poet and critic executed for his part in the Easter Rising of 1916. On the one hand, MacDonagh is seen 'to represent the perfect, tragic fusion of literature and politics in Ireland'.[8] When the Easter Rising came to represent, as it did in the revisionist historiography of the 1960s and 1970s, fundamentalist nationalism, MacDonagh's literary critical discourse was by association implicated ('perfect, tragic fusion') in the same hyper-nationalist impulse distorting the work of other bourgeois nationalists such as Padraic Pearse and Daniel Corkery. On the other hand, MacDonagh's work, it can be argued, belies this simplistic depiction of nationalism. In the posthumous collection *Literature in Ireland: Studies Irish and Anglo-Irish*, by transferring critical attention from a 'Celtic essence' to an 'Irish note', MacDonagh insists on the authenticity of Irish literature in the English language and looks for an accommodation with Anglo-Ireland. As Luke Gibbons has argued, the issue is not one of essence at all, but of sincerity:

> We have now so well mastered this language of our adoption that we use it with a freshness and power that the English of these days rarely have... The loss of (Gaelic) idiom and of literature is a disaster. But, on the other hand, the abandonment has broken a tradition of pedantry and barren conventions; and sincerity gains thereby... Let us postulate continuity, but continuity in the true way.[9]

Here, the critic identifies and celebrates the 'freshness and power' of English as used in Ireland which allows the emergence of a Synge, a Joyce and an O'Casey, all excluded at one time or another from the nationalist canon; further, he applauds the disappearance of an effete and decadent late Gaelic tradition as itself a perversion of the 'true' Irish note. Moreover, as an abstract linguistic tendency rather than an innate racial capacity, this latter faculty is fully available to the Anglo-Irish settler community. The subtlety of this position is unrecognizable as the essentialist, fundamentalist, vulgar nationalism attacked by revisionism and post-structuralist-inspired theory.

Having acknowledged the existence of this expansive nationalist wing, we should further acknowledge its marginalization from post-1916 nationalist discourse. Pearse rather than MacDonagh became first among equals, and it was Pearsean and de Valerean nationalism, and their vision of a Catholic, peasant, anti-English state, which came to dominate postcolonial Ireland. It is this same model which has provided the target for revisionist critiques, and for the (re)entry of hybridity (and a number of variations on the theme) into Irish cultural critical discourse since the 1980s.

III

A second, related problem concerns what might be called, with reference to Bhabha, the 'location of hybridity'. Bhabha has insisted that hybridity is an effect of the history of colonialism and the myriad encounters between differently empowered subjects; but also, and more importantly, it is the condition of language itself, the 'Third Space' that opens up in any cultural moment between reality and representation, between the *performance* of the cultural text and the reality to which it refers (1994, pp. 19–39). Border-crossing as a strategy for resistance, in this reading, constitutes a dialectical movement between a radically ambivalent colonial discourse (always already self-fashioning *and* self-erasing) and a similarly ambivalent decolonizing discourse which is also always coming to terms with the differences ensuing from the colonial encounter. In other words, for the decolonizing subject both *text* and *context* are hybridized; colonial resistance is hybridized both *before* and *because of* the colonial encounter. It is the enabling, if confusing, possibilities ensuing from the movement between these two moments with which Bhabha is concerned in his work:

> For a willingness to descend into that alien territory... may reveal that the theoretical recognition of the split-space of enunciation may open the way to conceptualizing an *inter*national culture, based not on the exoticism or multiculturalism of the *diversity* of cultures, but on the inscription and articulation of culture's *hybridity*... And by exploring this Third Space, we may elude the politics of polarity and emerge as the others of our selves.
>
> (1994, pp. 38–9)

However, the subversive potential of postcolonial hybridity with its sceptical, recalcitrant attitude towards the subject and received narratives is particularly susceptible to appropriation and depoliticizing, 'not only', as another critic puts it,

> because the principle of innovation is also the principle of the market in general but also because the postmodern obsession with antimimetic forms is always on the lookout for new modes of 'self' fracture, for new versions of the self-locating, self-disrupting text.[10]

In this reading, the optimism of some commentators with regard to hybridity and its celebration of flux and indeterminacy could be said to be seriously misplaced, as such effects actually collude with the reproduction of dominant bourgeois ideology and the late-capitalist phase into which it has moved. Such a strategy, as David Lloyd has noted, has the paradoxical effect of positing minority culture as uniquely different, even as the subject of that culture is subsumed into a centralizing politico-economic sphere.[11] In similar mode, the geographer David Harvey has remarked on 'a necessary relation between the rise of postmodernist cultural forms, the emergence of more flexible modes of capitalist accumulation, and a new round of "time-space compression" in the organization of capitalism'. But, he goes on, 'these changes, when set against the basic rules of capitalistic accumulation, appear more as shifts in surface appearance rather than as signs of the emergence of some entirely new post-capitalist or even post-industrial society'.[12] As more than one contemporary theorist has maintained, then, it could be that hybridity and all its fashionable devices and effects – the 'strategic essentialism' of Spivak, Bhabha's 'Third Space', the advent of 'Queer Studies' – are merely critical rationales for the new phase of global capitalism into which we have moved rather than an explanation of the non-West's mode of resistance and survival.

The question of collusion extends to the actual dynamics of hybridity as a cultural concept. It is difficult to escape the possibility that instead of bringing about a re-distribution of power relations, destabilizing the border could instead feed into the stereotypical assumptions which helped to create the border in the first place. That is, the moment in which reality is 'blurred' is always in danger of hardening into a strategy, a badge of otherness, the very 'sign' of difference. The philosopher Richard Kearney, for example, has suggested that 'the Irish mind', as he terms it in his edited book of that name, may be seen to favour a dialectical logic of *both/and* as opposed to the orthodox dualist logic of *either/or* encoded in Western philosophy since ancient times.[13] This dialectical logic constitutes an intellectual ability to hold the traditional oppositions of classical reason together in creative confluence. For Kearney, the 'Irish mind' may be traced throughout the history of Irish writing in English – Swift, Sterne, Berkeley, Wilde, Shaw, Beckett, O'Brien, Behan, and so on, with Joyce nominated as the seminal modern exponent of this doubled discourse. In this reading, Joyce's work is simultaneously constructive and *de*constructive, keenly aware of language's role as primary site and emblem of the decentred subject. Kearney can never escape, however, the possibility that this dialectical logic (which he *opposes* to classical dualistic logic) could itself become the *sign* of Irish otherness, thus once again becoming subsumed into the oppositional, identitarian politics of traditional colonialist discourse. The 'Irish mind' becomes permanently 'hybridized' for both sides of the postcolonial divide, identified precisely by its inability to interact with reality as 'we' have defined it. 'Joyce' becomes the archetypal Irish writer precisely to the extent that his aesthetic practice is removed from reality. Seamus Deane puts it this way:

> A literature predicated on an abstract idea of essence will inevitably degenerate into whimsy and provincialism. Even when the literature itself avoids this limitation, the commentary on it re-imposes the limitations again ... The point is not simply that the Irish are different. It is that they are absurdly different because of the disabling, if

fascinating, separation between their notion of reality and that of everybody else.[14]

Just as every tactic employed by the patient to refuse the analysis can be explained by the analyst, so the refusal by the colonized to recognize the borders created by the colonizer can eventually be diagnosed as a typical colonial response, another brick in the wall forming the border between us and them. What this danger points to, I believe, is that Bhabha's 'Third Space' has to remain a *potential* rather than a *programme* if it is to avoid being re-absorbed into disabling neo-colonialist narratives. How the individual and/or the community might realize this potential is one of the most pressing questions facing postcolonial criticism today.

IV

Another point worth noting is the gap that appears to be emerging within postcolonial studies between theory and history.[15] This gap is manifested in a number of ways. In the first place, there is a problem with the effectiveness of hybridity as a strategy of resistance, or at least with the manner in which effectiveness might be gauged. Because it is the very condition of discourse, because it is an effect of incalculable relations between colonizer and colonized, hybridity appears to preclude any conscious or collective intention on the part of the colonized, and is incapable, therefore, of being deployed for sustained political purposes. Once again, the colonial subject is denied coherence and agency, colonial resistance is denied intention and effectivity. Hybridity, in this analysis, is a profoundly mystificatory notion which mimics not only the practices whereby colonialist power attempts to reproduce itself but also the practices around which a decolonizing discourse might wish to mobilize.

Following on from this, the theoretical turn towards hybridity routinely ignores the many different forms of resistance that have emerged around the world in response to a variety of forms of colonial domination. Many theorists assume that hybridity constitutes a permanent oppositional force, a panacea for the ills of colonialism that emerges always and everywhere within designated 'colonial' formations. But the notion of hybridity as the most effective reverse-discourse tends to collapse both the temporal and spatial specificities of resistance. Nationalism, we might say, is a *genre* of resistance, but every *practice* of national resistance will be unique, depending on the range of material and discursive factors obtaining in any particular 'colonial' situation. In other words, the postcolonial critic must always historicize, or at least learn to historicize, the theories through which a discourse of resistance might be conceptualized, if they wish to avoid the accusations of relativism upon which more than one 'radical' intellectual project has foundered.

This is so, moreover, not only at the level of history – that is, the political strategies employed by native and settler to empower themselves before an amorphous and fragmentary formation of colonial power/knowledge – but also at the level of the text – that is, the representations of identity which play such a crucial role in the reproduction of colonial relations and which consequently form the basis for most of the 'postcolonial' critiques organized around the category of hybridity. The discerning reader will have noticed that, throughout this essay, hybridity has been invoked more or less unproblematically in terms of political strategy *and* hermeneutic effect, and this is a reflection of the wider situation obtaining within the sphere of postcolonial studies. The deconstruction of a derivative nationalism, as we have seen, tends to take place at the level of representation where the subaltern subject is constructed as an effect both of imperial self-fashioning and of decolonization's problematic engagement with identitarian politics. It is in this context that Spivak has concluded that the subaltern cannot speak.[16] But an analysis of the absence upon which textual productions of (subaltern and dominant) identity are constructed is still some distance from historical research into the production of native agency – that is, the ways in which resistance has actually been constructed, experienced and negotiated in specific spatiotemporal locations.

Again, Ireland offers an instructive case in point for the stand-off between theory and history. Throughout its peculiar 'colonial' history, versions of the essential can be discerned alongside versions of the ineluctably hybrid, at times in competition, at other times in combination. In the Easter Rising of 1916, for example, we find Padraic Pearse combining a range of discourses and practices (aesthetic, cultural, political) to produce a form of resistance – improvisatory, body-oriented, hysterical – characterized by excess.[17] Pearse, that is, deployed hybridity in the service of a radical essentialism, producing a paradoxical form of resistance which British imperialism, traditionally so adept at defusing colonial reverse-discourses, ultimately found impossible to contain. At the same time, Easter 1916 attracts the interest of postcolonial critics for the manner in which violence as a *political* strategy incorporated a *scriptive* or *discursive* violence encapsulated within the text of the Declaration of Independence. In the sort of contradiction so beloved of Derrida, this document paradoxically initiated the revolution in the name of a pre-existing Irish nation, yet at the same time attempted to usher in the historically postponed Irish nation *by* the very act of revolution.[18] One thinks also of Yeats's alarm at being outmanoeuvred by history and his rush to formulate some kind of textual response (in his poem 'Easter 1916') which would signal not only the act of revolution but also the poet's ability to report, and ultimately to control, that act within his own terms.[19]

In other words, the theory of hybridity marks the impasse between event, agency and history on the one hand and pattern, representation and theory on the other. Contemporary postcolonial studies mark the domination of the former cluster of issues by the latter, with the result that attention has by and large drifted from the production of specific political strategies around which discourses of resistance have historically been organized to deconstructions of the universal discursive *aporia* informing both colonialism and nationalism.

Finally, a politics of resistance organized around the strategy of crossing the border between received phenomenological categories ignores what may be the most effective as well as the most widely disseminated form of resistance to institutionally organized power: silence. The subaltern may not be able to speak – the postcolonial critic may not be able to speak for her – but that in itself might represent a refusal to function as interlocutor within the colonial dialogue, signifying the subject's active withdrawal from the colonizer's discourse rather than a passive acceptance of the range of exoticized, marginalized roles on offer. As Jenny Sharpe has argued: 'The colonial subject who can answer the colonizers back is the product of the same vast ideological machinery that silences the subaltern'.[20] Silence functions, moreover, at both primary and secondary levels – functions, that is, both as a creative (cultural) force and a critical/theoretical strategy. If Irish nationalism was guilty of arrogating to itself the authority to represent the aspirations of all the people, then the contemporary postcolonial critic should not compound that presumption, either by ignoring silence as a gesture of resistance or by incorporating its deliberate, strategic incoherencies into the narrative coherence of the critical text.

V

These are just some of the problems, then, that must be faced when confronting what might initially appear to be exciting and effective ways of disrupting the borders which structure traditional, disabling systems of power and knowledge. If, with Spivak, we can define the task of the postcolonial subject as being to change from inside a situation that she is obliged to inhabit, then we are forced to accept the existence of the border as the very condition whereby effective resistance can be formulated.[21] In any narrative of resistance, hybridity can be an effective strategy, but it is less a *movement* to be supported than a *moment* to be experienced, part of a historical and material process which always risks the danger of reincorporation into oppositional, colonialist discourse.

Part II
Diasporas

4

Inside-Out: Literature, Cultural Identity and Irish Migration to England

Aidan Arrowsmith

> ...identifies are the names we give to the different ways we are positioned by, and position ourselves within, the narratives of the past...cultural identity...is not a fixed origin to which we can make some final and absolute Return. Of course, it is not a mere phantasm either. It is *something*...It has its histories – and histories have their real, material and symbolic effects. The past continues to speak to us. But it no longer addresses us as a simple, factual 'past'...It is always constructed through memory, fantasy, narrative and myth. Cultural identities are the...unstable points of identification or suture, which are made, within the discourses of history and culture. Not an essence but a *positioning*.[1]

> ...living between worlds, caught on a frontier...to come from elsewhere, from 'there' and not 'here', and hence to be simultaneously 'inside' and 'outside' the situations at hand, is to live at the intersections of histories and memories...Cut off from the homelands of tradition, experiencing a constantly challenged identity, the stranger is perpetually required to make herself at home in an interminable discussion between a scattered historical inheritance and a heterogeneous present.[2]

Ireland's lengthy colonial relationship with England demands to be viewed in its specificity, whilst also sharing many points of overlap with other such histories. Marginalizing discourses across eight centuries of colonization have positioned the Irish as an original 'other', over against whom Englishness or Britishness might be defined. But, at the same time, such representations are in tension with the Irish experience of incorporation, albeit as 'marginal Britons', the domestication of the Irish within an overarching 'British' identity which might absorb disruptive and oppositional energies.[3] Both problematically part of Britain, and its problematical colonial other, Ireland's position might be described as that of a 'metropolitan colony'.[4]

Irish migrants at the imperial centre stand at the uncomfortable intersection of these competing discourses of incorporation, marginalization and othering. Over the centuries, attempted escapes from hunger, poverty and unemployment have inevitably involved carriage across the water of the baggage of that fraught, lengthy and complex history of Irish-English relations. These migrants have been caught, to use Roy Foster's words, 'in the interstices of the Irish-English relationship'.[5] The negotiation of cultural identity in these contexts proceeds from an indeterminate place, simultaneously inside and outside both 'authentic Britishness' and the 'authentic Irishness' constructed as part of the nationalist response to colonization. In this essay, I focus mainly on twentieth-century writing in order to trace and investigate varying responses to such problematics and ambiguities of 'Irish' cultural identity in England.

I

> Peoples that span national borders are ambiguous in that they in some ways partake in both nations and in other ways partake in neither.[6]

Following Homi Bhabha, the indeterminacy, indistinguishability or invisibility of the white, western European, largely English-speaking Irish immigrant might be seen to cut back towards the disseminating centre of dominant discourse, unbalancing the already unstable binary structure of self/other, English/Irish, civilian/barbarian. For Bhabha, the colonial stereotype is inherently unstable, existing as the imperialist's projection of a denied self or unconscious.[7] And the Irish in particular have always been too close, too similar, for English comfort – an 'other' who is never quite other enough. As Terry Eagleton puts it, 'the water... is so very narrow – narrow enough to trouble the distinction between "inside" and "outside" '.[8] The Irish immigrant appears as an uncanny return, the other within the self, and, as Richard Kearney suggests, sparks a haunting of that imperial 'Britishness' by:

> the ghost of their ethnic alien – Ireland – whose very *difference* was part and parcel of their own English/British *identity*. Their other was

uncannily part of themselves, the familiar spectre hidden in strange-
ness, the original double they had forgotten to remember, the threatened *revenant* of their own repressed political unconscious.[9]

However, the inbetweenness which is celebrated in some postmodern
postcolonial theories is not always experienced as a liberated and productive space. For Jonathan Rutherford, postcolonial migrations disor-
ientate and rupture identity, remove the 'spatial and temporal
coordinates' which are 'essential for historicity, for a consciousness of
our own collective and personal past'.[10] Perhaps particularly in econom-
ically-enforced migrations, it is often return rather than assimilation
which is striven for. Ien Ang, for example, has written of such migrancy
inducing an 'existential condition' – the desire for the time before the
break, a search for a 'lost' authenticity.[11] However, the Irish quest to
reclaim the anchoring coordinates of identity which a sense of cultural
difference might supply is highly problematic. Mary Hickman and Bron-
wen Walter have particularly criticized a commonly held assumption of
unproblematic Irish assimilation within a putatively homogeneous
white Britishness.[12] The British race-relations industry, as Anthias and
Yuval-Davis note, constructs 'ethnicity' almost exclusively in colour
terms, effectively delegitimating Irish assertions of difference. This is
an ethnic invisibility which, as Walter has argued, is 'doubled' by gendering – particularly by the domestic and working roles conventionally
taken by Irish women – and which, as Mary Lennon suggests, functions
to silence.[13]

As Fanon demonstrated, nationalism in its various forms might, at
particular moments, provide the drive to reclaim devalued or subsumed
identities with a politically and psychologically important vehicle. Particularly during the decades prior to Irish Independence in 1922, the
Irish migrant search for coordinates of identity tended to fuse with the
politically current discourses of Irish revivalist nationalism. As Salman
Rushdie has argued, migrants 'create fictions, not actual cities or villages, but invisible ones, imaginary homelands'.[14] And in texts such as
John Sherman (1891), an early novella by W. B. Yeats, or Pádraic Ó
Conaire's novel *Deoraíocht*, translated as *Exile* (1910), revivalist tropes
of home and narratives of return to the source structure the migrant
characters' search for identity.

In *John Sherman*, the protagonist's existing sense of alienation from a
dominant mode of Catholic Irishness, as a member of the Anglo-Irish
Protestant Ascendancy, is compounded by his emigration to London to
take up a junior office post. His position in between Englishness and

Irishness is underlined when, encountering an old woman on the boat, he is asked pointedly, 'why don't ye stay amongst your own people' – which serves only to emphasize his inability to identify who his 'own people' might be.[15] Yeats's response to such rootlessness appears to be the active construction of a point of anchor, an 'imaginary homeland', utilizing the classical nationalist figures of the rural idyll and the maternal body – here, Ballah and Mary Carton. Binary contrast is provided by urban London and the Englishwoman Margaret Leland, who, we are told, attempts to 'culture and improve' Sherman's 'savagery and barbarianism' (pp. 38, 63). Eventually he manages to escape from the clutches of this 'civilizing mission' and return to Ballah, his (and, by extension, Ireland's) 'return to the source' being figured in the ultimate image of this returnee once again united with Mother Ireland as a child at Mary's breast.

Ó Conaire's utilization of similar tropes from a very different class position underlines their predominance. In *Exile*, Michael's migrant experience of inbetweenness is of an unremittingly, perhaps stereotypically, miserable life of homelessness, hunger and physical disability in London. Michael likens himself to 'an old forest tree laid low by the axe',[16] his rootedness now severed as a result of the 'evil' influence of British imperialism, its dynamic of incorporation and marginalization:

> London . . . ! . . . That great and terrible city that forever stretches its tentacles out towards people who are hundreds, thousands, of miles away, and draws them inexorably towards her, in spite of themselves, and remakes them in her own image, to swallow them up, to recreate them.
>
> (p. 71)

Rather than being paved with gold, Michael finds England's streets to be places of hostility and stereotyping. Sleeping in the park, he and his fellow members of the immigrant underclass are regarded as being like a virus transgressing the boundaries of the body politic, tainting the purity of a land likened to 'some huge hateful giant who was suffering from some hideous loathsome disease, a dreadful disease that was rotting his flesh, and gnawing it to the bone' (pp. 82–3). However, the immigrants' transgression of the borderlines of self/other merely provokes English reinforcement of colonial discourses of othering – and such pressurized disassociation often takes a racialized form. *Punch* magazine's infamous representations of the Irish are suggested when Michael, finally offered a job in a circus, notes his employer's striking resemblance to 'Mr Punch' himself.[17] Significantly and predictably, the circus in fact turns out to be a freak show, Michael's role being that of a deformed savage known as the Wild Man: 'all I would have to do was to double up my good leg under me so that it would not be seen, wear a wig of long black hair; paint my cheeks with fearsome colours, and put up some howls from time to time so as to terrify the public when they came to see me' (p. 65).

According to Ien Ang, drawing upon Paul Gilroy, 'the adversity of "where you're at" produces the cultivation of a lost "where you're from".'[18] Michael's difficulties in England, in combination with the rupture of emigration, drive his construction of his 'imaginary homeland', an anchor shaped from the symbols and narratives contained in the discourses of Irish nationalism. As Roy Foster has noted, Irish cultural revivalism in the early twentieth century 'performed a special function for those abroad',[19] storytelling and other exile literature serving as 'an expression, by professional intermediaries, on behalf of the inarticulate – very much in the tradition of Irish ballad poetry... providing psychological reinforcement in an alien terrain, conjuring up consoling and familiar images'.[20]

Thus, in a pub storytelling session, Michael encounters the definitiveness of Irish revivalist nationalism, and therein the material of a certain self-definition. The rural idyll, and particularly the figure of Mother Ireland, loom large. Thus Maggie the 'Big Red-Haired Woman' mourns the ravages and murders of British imperialism, tells Michael of her own imprisonment and, with the provision of spiritual and emotional nourishment as well as food and lodging, repeatedly saves him from starvation and homelessness. As Michael says, 'You would think I was a child, and she my mother' (p. 32). The politically current, unifying discourses of nationalism thus offer Michael a comforting sense of belonging, a means of locating a definite identity based in a notion of essential Irishness – race and ancestry, beyond the contingencies of geographical separation.

But this identification with the *gestalt*, as Lacan might term this seductive image of wholeness, is always a misidentification.[21] Just as that hegemonic Englishness incorporates and marginalizes, the same Irish nationalism which attracts Michael also excludes him; for example, Patrick Pearse, the leader of the Easter Rising of 1916, condemned emigrants as 'deserters who had left their posts', desiring that these 'traitors' and 'fools' 'would let *us* alone'.[22] The rootedness required for 'authentic' Irishness is gone. The migrant no longer belongs, is never one of 'us', always one of 'them', inhabiting a 'no man's land' in between two authentic cultures. As Stuart Hall puts it, 'Migration is a one way trip.

There is no "home" to go back to.'[23] And Ó Conaire figures this negation of identity in Michael's marked failure to complete his 'return to the source'. After emigration, he is no longer considered an authentic Irishman, and, when he visits his home town as part of a travelling circus, his symbolic disguise as The Barbarian renders him unrecognizable to his friends and family, who take him, appropriately, for a foreign stranger.

II

> It is suicide to be abroad. But ... what is it to be at home? A lingering dissolution.[24]

If Ó Conaire's depiction of Michael's debilitating inbetweenness suggests a critical awareness of the difficulties of essentialist definitions of identity, the majority of twentieth-century emigrant writing is explicitly condemnatory. Post-independence writers of the 1930s, 1940s and 1950s such as Patrick Kavanagh and Seán Ó Faoláin set about exposing 'home' as being far from the imagined ideal.[25] A nationalist hegemony was seen to have held Ireland in an oppressive, backward-looking trap since independence, and the insular desire to keep Ireland free from outside influence – economically and culturally – was shown actually to trigger the emigration it sought to prevent.

Leaving Ireland thus comes to be seen less in terms of enforced banishment than escape, particularly for Irish women. The rural world from which Edna O'Brien transported her 'country girls' in 1960 hardly seemed to have changed from that depicted in Kate O'Brien's 1936 novel *Mary Lavelle*. There, the gendering which Ireland and de Valera's hegemonic Catholic nationalism impose upon Mary is experienced as a 'violent and terrible Irish purity'.[26] Her dreams of getting a job are forbidden by her father, but her dreams of leaving are eventually fulfilled. She follows her desire 'to belong to no place', and finally achieves a liberation in Spain. This is overridingly a liberation of repressed sexuality, which is expressed mainly in her affair with Juanito, but also in her 'sisterhood' with her lesbian friend Conlan, another escapee.

The anti-nationalism or anti-essentialism of the mid twentieth century has perhaps its ultimate expression in Samuel Beckett's work, which develops James Joyce's attempts to liberate the self from the insular identity categories of nationalism into a fierce critique:

> What constitutes the charm of our country, apart of course from its scant population, and this without the help of the meanest

contraceptive, is that all is derelict, with the sole exception of history's ancient faeces. These are ardently sought after, stuffed and carried in procession. Wherever nauseated time has dropped a nice fat turd you will find our patriots, sniffing it up on all fours, their faces on fire.[27]

And in Beckett's emigrant novel *Murphy*, the central imagery of constriction and escape echoes the protagonist's departure from Ireland and Irishness into the freedom of exile. As one character says of a land which Beckett peoples with ridiculously zealous revivalist nationalists, 'It is always pleasant to leave this country'.[28] However, unlike his acquaintance Neary – who was admirably able to stop his heart in order to avoid 'situations irksome beyond endurance, as when he wanted a drink and could not get one, or fell among Gaels and could not escape' (p. 6) – Murphy's envisaged flight proves difficult. He is relentlessly pursued in England by Celia – who looks like the Irish tricolour with her green eyes, white skin and yellow hair – and also by Miss Counihan, through whom Beckett compares the Queen Cathleen Ní Houlihan, Mother Ireland, to a prostitute: 'For an Irish girl, Miss Counihan was quite exceptionally anthropoid' (p. 69); 'Standing in profile against the blazing corridor, with her high buttocks and her low breasts, she looked not merely queenly, but on for anything' (p. 123).

For Declan Kiberd, Beckett is 'the first truly Irish playwright, because the first utterly free of factitious elements of Irishness'.[29] However, Beckett's objection seems not merely to have been nationalist constructions of Irishness, but equally such national identity categories as 'Irish playwright' in themselves. Thus, in addition to the novel's debunking of Irish nationalism, Beckett seems equally critical of the stream of English nationalist stereotypes of clownish, idiotic Irishmen, 'not rightly human', which Murphy encounters: 'Murphy was too familiar with this attitude of derision tinged with loathing to make the further blunder of trying to abate it' (*Murphy*, p. 47). Beckett's project of demythologization thus becomes an acknowledgement of Heidegger's assertion that 'homelessness is coming to be the destiny of the world'.[30] His rejection of nationalism ultimately becomes a rejection of national and cultural identities *per se*, categories which coerce into conformity and constrain the realization of individuality. Thus, for Beckett, a position neither inside nor outside, inhabitation of a realm beyond such categorization, would be the only true liberation. And the only such realm is shown to be the life of the mind, the individual intellect divorced from the outside world. Thus the inhabitants of the mental hospital are, for Murphy, 'the race of people he had long since despaired of finding . . . He would not have admitted he needed a brotherhood. He did . . . [His] experience . . . obliged him to call sanctuary what the psychiatrists call exile' (*Murphy*, pp. 96, 100–1).

III

> I carry a brick on my shoulder in order that the world may know what my house was like.[31]

Whilst the response to migrant inbetweenness explored by Ó Conaire – that of (mis)identification with a *Gestalt* of essentialist identity – is demonstrably flawed, Beckettian anti-essentialism – an abandonment of cultural identity – might be seen to further marginalize and destabilize diasporic subjects. Recent ethnographic research has emphasized the continuing, often central, importance of a sense of cultural identity amongst the Irish, home and abroad – particularly in contemporary contexts of globalization and cultural homogenization. Breda Gray's study stresses the particular importance of cultural identity to Irish women in their resistance to 'double invisibility'.[32] Given the tendency on all sides of the 'nation debate' to overlook issues of gender and sexuality – thus Field Day's neglect of women writers in their *Anthology of Irish Writing* might be seen to replicate Beckett's failure to match his anti-national(ist) anti-essentialism with a deconstruction of gender essences – it is significant that contemporary women migrant writers are particularly engaged in explorations into the possibility of a third space, beyond both the strictures of essentialism and the nihilism of anti-essentialism.[33]

Emma Donoghue's short story 'Going Back', for example, depicts the identity confusion which might result from that wholesale rejection, and poses the question of whether going back – on your word, on your principles, to an Ireland previously rejected forever – is necessarily a submission and betrayal: anti-conservatism might itself become an intransigent orthodoxy. And Cyn, a gay Irish woman in London, holds firmly to the negative view of Ireland formed in her childhood. Having just met Lou, a gay Irish man, who refers to her as 'one of us', she replies: 'Who's us? . . . I've never felt like one of an us . . . I felt more of an exile for twenty years in Ireland than I ever have in the twelve I've been out of it.'[34] Cyn feels Irish identity to have been 'absolutely *foisted* upon us . . . Were you ever asked if you agreed to be Irish? . . . And what happens if you try to refuse it or leave it behind? Everybody freaks out as if you've dumped a baby in a carrier bag at the airport' (p. 161). Her defiance and radicalism, however, are masks for her denial of a troubling insecurity and uncertainty of identity – sexual and cultural. Whilst experimenting with heterosexuality, though, her intransigence towards Ireland remains, despite Lou's efforts and criticisms: 'What a traditionalist you are, for a deviant' (p. 169).

Gradually, however, Lou influences her with his suggestion of the possibility of more complex identities – of living as both Irish and gay in a 'grown up' Ireland apparently no longer asphyxiated by nationalist definitions of 'authentic' Irishness. Cyn's suppressed desire for home and identity – to be 'one of an us' – is allowed a limited expression and ultimately, tentatively, her concealed Irish accent begins to re-emerge.

Anne Devlin's 1994 play *After Easter* poses the problem of Irish emigrant identity, particularly that of the gendered emigrant, in terms of the final collapse of the certainties of identity associated with the nationalist Rising of Easter 1916. The search is no longer for a 'return to the source', but for the means to construct actively a stable sense of cultural identity as a counter to the neutralizing effects of emigration, anti-nationalism and globalization.

Greta's emigration from Ireland in the play had been a refusal of a patriarchal Catholic nationalism. Seeking escape from the discourses of Mother Ireland which are embodied by her sister Aoife, Greta rejects her role as mother to her new-born child at the same time as rejecting her Irishness. Although she has 'wanted to be English', England proves to be far from the anticipated liberation: 'Funny how people who leave their own country stop living, in some part of themselves, in the same year in which they left'.[35] Greta finds her identity disappearing through the interstices of various discourses of identity inscription, into the no-man's land of 'double invisibility'. None of the labels fit, and she becomes one of Fanon's 'individuals without an anchor...colourless, stateless, rootless'.[36] Her experience of this tension of categorization and identity negation is shown as one of mental ill health.[37]

Greta's inevitable desire for 'home', and her construction of an imaginary homeland, is manifested in a recurring dream of a return to the womb. But whilst Aoife's belief in rootedness, and in the idea that 'everybody should go home' (primarily, presumably, the British in Northern Ireland), has its attractions, Greta cannot resort to an anachronistic and patriarchal nationalism for definition. At the same time, the substitution of nationalism by internationalism which is undertaken by her other sister Helen – who defines herself as 'a citizen of the world' – fails to offer Greta the stability she requires in order to offset the effects of her life in England. Requiring a sense of identity formed outside the constraints and limitations of both essentialism and anti-essentialism, Greta is unable to embrace either the dogmatic certainty of Aoife's nationalism, or the postmodern uncertainty of Helen's internationalism.

Ultimately, it is her brother Manus who gestures towards a different relationship to the past and to Irish identity. As in Donoghue's story, Manus's previous rejection of Irishness was bound up with issues of sexual identity. Manus is described by his sister Aoife as 'neither one thing nor the other', and his mobile position in between the fixed authenticities of both sexual and national identities serves to emphasize the fictionality and performativity of such constructions of identity. However, such floating identities might also be experienced as the instability Greta feels. And thus, in a different context, Manus's relationship to Irishness is modified. In England he finds himself marginalized less by his sexuality than by his ethnicity and, as Ien Ang argues, in such contexts of challenged identity, 'the stress on "ethnicity" provides a critical counterpoint to the most facile forms of postmodernist nomadology'.[38] Manus's view is that 'I don't feel much like a citizen of the world when I'm treated like a Paddy and a fenian git' (Devlin, *After Easter*, p. 39). And, having previously rejected an Irish identity simplistically conflated with tribal nationalism by his father, he says: 'Now I spend all my time trying to get it back' (p. 39).

Such a reclamation recalls Richard Kearney's argument that, 'having taken one's distance from the "homeland", physically or mentally, you can return to it and find there something of immense and lasting value. Traditions of myth and music can be explored again with a new-found and non-fanatical freedom'.[39] The necessary demythologization of an anachronistic nationalism ought now, in different contexts of challenged identity, to be matched by a productive 'remythologization':

> What is required is a radical interrogation of those mythic sedimentations from our *past* and those mythic aspirations for our *future* which challenge our *present* sense of ourselves, which disclose other possibilities of being...Without mythology, our hopes and memories are homeless.[40]

Greta ultimately constructs a new relationship to her Irish identity in conjunction with a different relationship to gender identity and, in particular, to her role as a mother. Through this, she gains access to a form of stereoscopic vision – the ability to see through the eyes of her second-generation Irish-English child. And in the final scene of the play, Greta adopts the role of myth-maker, passing on to the next generation a tale of the past's presence, and of a return to 'the place where the rivers come from, where you come from' (Devlin, *After Easter*, p. 75). This, however, is no uncritical 'return to the source', but a means of cultural transmission through a strategic reclamation of those spatial and temporal coordinates necessary for a stable sense of identity.

To echo Stuart Hall, a cultural identity exists as a construction, a positioning by or within certain narratives of the past. The character of such an identity is shaped according to the various ways in which such stories, memories, fantasies, myths, might be utilized, depending upon the requirements of the moment. Both the 'essentialist' nationalism of Irish revivalism, and the 'anti-essentialism' of Beckettian modernism were vital responses to particular moments, but less helpful, even damaging, in later, changed conditions. As Devlin's play suggests, the contemporary moment requires a new conceptualization of diasporic identity – one described by Paul Gilroy as 'anti-anti-essentialist'. For contemporary Irish migrants such as Greta, the forces of anti-nationalism, of globalization and cultural homogenization, and of Irish womens' 'double invisibility' – all of which threaten to erase productive cultural memories – set the requirement for a newly wrought anchor against contemporary rootlessness, a secure sense of identity which bypasses both the strictures of essentialism and the reductions of anti-essentialism. In an echo of Gayatri Spivak's notion of 'strategic essentialism', this might be seen as a notion of identity whose constructedness and provisionality is acknowledged along with its necessity.[41]

5

States of Dislocation: William Trevor's *Felicia's Journey* and Maurice Leitch's *Gilchrist*

Liam Harte and Lance Pettitt

> Identity is changed by the journey; our subjectivity is re-composed. In the transformation every step forward can also be a step back: the migrant is here and there. Exile can be deadening but it can also be creative. Exile can be an affliction but it can also be a transfiguration – it can be a resource. I think what I am trying to say is that identity is not to do with being but becoming.[1]

The transnational movements of migrants are deeply inscribed in the discourses of Irish history and literature. Not only has emigration been a fundamental social fact for many generations, but also the Irish imagination is partly defined by its propensity to engage creatively with displacements, migrations and perigrinations, from the ancient Irish voyage tales to contemporary narratives of exile and global nomadism. Indeed, Fintan O'Toole has recently argued that the most salient characteristic of Ireland's culture 'is that it knows no borders', that 'it is porous and diffuse, that its apparent instability is maintained only at the cost of the continual export of its instabilities'.[2] It is 'the journeys to and from home [that] are the very heartbeat of Irish culture. To imagine Ireland is to imagine a journey'.[3]

Of course, not all Irish journeys are the same. 'The nature of the transition depends much more critically on the place of the emigrant within the home society'[4] and on the specific conditions presented by the host destination. Ireland's historical experience of colonization means that journeys to Britain, be they physical or metaphorical, resonate with a special significance. Suresht Renjen Bald's observation about South Asian migrants to Britain is also applicable to the Irish in Britain:

Stripped of their belonging(s), and denied their history, all migrants occupy a vulnerable position. But when the migrant is a member of formerly colonised people and the border s/he crosses marks the land of the former coloniser...the narrative of immigration comes to include not only the loss of 'continuity' and the search for 'belonging', but also the experience and negotiation of racism and colonialism.[5]

When this postcolonial migrant is a creative one, the narrative of immigration assumes additional layers of complexity, irony and ambiguity. William Trevor (b. 1928) and Maurice Leitch (b. 1933), the subjects of this essay, are two such postcolonial creative migrants. As Irish novelists who have spent most of their writing careers in England, they are located at a richly complex cultural intersection. Like many migrants who live and write 'within and between worlds',[6] Trevor and Leitch are capable of writing from a double perspective, what Salman Rushdie calls 'stereoscopic vision'.[7] Their liminality is complicated, however, by their specific location within the shifting 'interstices of the Irish-English relationship'[8] where the discourses of colonialism and nationalism confer. Within this context, their fictional explorations of dislocation and difference are informed by the particularities of their cultural backgrounds and personal journeys. Trevor's provincial Protestant upbringing placed him at an oblique angle to the dominant Catholic nationalist culture of independent Ireland, an obliquity which he found imaginatively stimulating: 'I was fortunate that my accident of birth actually placed me on the edge of things. I was born into a minority that all my life has seemed in danger of withering away'.[9] A similar preference for creative marginality characterizes his situation as an Irish writer in England, where he relishes the feeling of being foreign, dislocated, 'beyond the pale'.[10] Leitch too is an outsider in England, though his particular cultural identity complicates his migrant trajectory. An Ulster Protestant from provincial Antrim, he was forced to renegotiate the terms of his cultural and historical inheritance as a Northern Irish writer in metropolitan London. This means that he, like Trevor, productively occupies a creative migrant space in which he finds himself a stranger, involved in 'an interminable discussion between a scattered historical inheritance and a heterogeneous present'.[11]

In this essay we wish to discuss two of their most recent novels, Trevor's *Felicia's Journey* (1994) and Leitch's *Gilchrist* (1994), in which the migrant figure acts as both a disruptive presence upon the inherited identities available to postcolonial subjects and as a transformative agent engendering hybrid identities. It seems to us that the central characters, Felicia and Gilchrist, exemplify Iain Chambers's and Salman Rushdie's theories about the disruptive and transformative energies of migrancy to a significant degree. Chambers describes migrancy as a complex syncretizing process that 'disrupts and interrogates the overarching themes of modernity: the nation and its literature, language and sense of identity; the metropolis; the sense of centre; the sense of psychic and cultural homogeneity'.[12] He goes on to claim that the metropolitan migrant is emblematic of the late twentieth-century condition, of which Felicia and Gilchrist might serve as exemplars: 'The migrant's sense of being rootless, of living between worlds, between a lost past and a non-integrated present, is perhaps the most fitting metaphor of this (post)modern condition'.[13]

Salman Rushdie further emphasizes the creative and dissident aspects of migrancy in his collection of essays, *Imaginary Homelands*. The migrations of people impelled by the transnational dynamics of colonial regimes, including slavery, wars and shifting labour markets, set in motion a process of cultural hybridization which has profound, long-term ramifications for postcolonial cultures:

> To migrate is certainly to lose language and home, to be defined by others, to become invisible or, even worse, a target; it is to experience deep changes and wrenches in the soul. But the migrant is not simply transformed by his act; he also transforms his new world. Migrants may well become mutants, but it is out of such hybridization that newness can emerge.[14]

The idea that hybridity is of its nature regenerative, bringing forth fresh forms of identity, as a result of a 'transformative contamination'[15] is taken up by Homi Bhabha in 'How Newness Enters the World',[16] where he stresses the 'empowering condition of hybridity' for the migrant who exists in-between, at 'an *initiatory* interstices'.[17]

In what follows, we outline this process of hybridization at work at the level of cultural representation, where the catalyst for change is the historical fact of migration, the agent of transformation the migrant. Our postcolonial readings highlight the contingent nature of the political and gendered identities constructed within colonialism as represented in these fictional narratives. The migrant inbetweenness of the two central characters shapes their perceptions of the host culture and intensifies their sense of difference. These migrant figures do not 'progress' or 'achieve' in a traditional novelistic sense. They neither revert to nor slough off the past; nor do they become progressively accommodated within a cosmopolitan, postmodern future. Rather, they embody the migrant's capacity to mutate and survive. Bhabha is properly sceptical of the claims of some enthusiasts who see the migrant as the apotheosis of postmodernity, pointing out that 'it is too easy to see the discourses of the minority as symptoms of the postmodern condition'.[18] Our readings therefore seek to foreground a series of cultural resonances within these postcolonial narratives that are specific to the Irish-English relationship. Furthermore, while such readings are clearly set within the parameters of postcolonial criticism, we do not go so far as to interpret the novels as uncomplicated celebrations of migrant resourcefulness in the postmodern era. Felicia and Gilchrist remain in a state of dislocation, marginalized but surviving, negotiating their hybrid difference.

Felicia's Journey: a state of migrant serenity

Set in the post-Thatcherite Britain of the early 1990s, *Felicia's Journey* tells the story of a young Irish girl's travels through the post-industrial English Midlands in a desperate search for the father of her unborn child, Johnny Lysaght. Shortly after her arrival she is befriended by a middle-aged canteen catering manager, Mr Hilditch, who proceeds to assist her in her search for the elusive Lysaght. When her inquiries prove fruitless, he convinces her that abortion is the best option. His superficial altruism masks a sinister intent, however. He stalks her relentlessly, steals her money to expedite her dependence on him and pretends throughout to be someone he is not: a retired military officer with an invalid wife. As the narrative unfolds, it becomes clear that this apparently respectable, genteel bachelor is in fact a psychotic serial killer of vulnerable, homeless young girls. Trevor's depiction of the duel between deviant loner and innocent waif is marked throughout by a masterly delineation of character and a superb control of narrative suspense.

In addition to being a compelling psychological thriller, the novel may be read as a postcolonial critique of the ideologies of British colonialism and post-independence Irish nationalism. Felicia suffers a double oppression on account of her gender and nationality. In Ireland, she is a victim of patriarchal nationalism; in England, she is oppressed by the embodiment of a malign residual colonialism. She comes from a staunchly republican Munster family where the 'ancient cause'[19] of revolutionary nationalism is daily honoured by her father and 99-year-old great-grandmother who was widowed in the 1916 Rising. Felicia herself was named in honour of a female revolutionary of the Rising, a naming which is as ironic as it is symbolic, since her servile daily existence represents a travesty of the egalitarian ideals of the revolutionary generation of Irish nationalists. In a series of flashback sequences, Trevor indicts the processes of subjugation and exploitation that characterize the treatment of women in independent Ireland. Motherless and jobless, she lives as a virtual domestic slave to her father, brothers and great-grandmother until pregnancy forces her to leave. The option of return is foreclosed by the moral guardians of an abortion-free state whose harsh censure she can vividly imagine:

> Father Kilgallen will summon her if she goes back now, the Reverend Mother too, both of them intent on preserving the life of the child that is her shame. 'God damn you to hell!' her father's greeting awaits her.

(p. 69)

The crucial fact about her oppressor in England which a postcolonial reading foregrounds is that Hilditch's violent psychosis is the product of thwarted imperial ambition and psycho-sexual abuse. As a child, he idolized his Uncle Wilf who claimed to have served with the British army in Ireland during the War of Independence. It was he who fuelled Hilditch's military ambition and inculcated in him an anti-Irish prejudice: 'The Black and Tans should have sorted that island out, his Uncle Wilf said, only unfortunately they held back for humane reasons' (p. 149). But he suffered the trauma of rejection by the army as a young man and subsequently made the even more damaging discovery that his uncle's 'army tales' (p. 20) were lies invented to disguise the fact that he was having an affair with Hilditch's compulsively promiscuous mother. The devastating effect of this deceit on the formation of his masculinity was compounded by his mother's subsequent incestuous relationship with him when his uncle tired of her. The adult Hilditch has suppressed these traumatic childhood memories beneath a reconstituted self-image of imperious masculinity which impels him to befriend unsuspecting young women, in whose public company he experiences a frisson of potency. Each relationship has an 'ordained brevity' (p. 52), however, as his neurotic paranoia inevitably leads him to suspect that his companions intuit his dark childhood secrets, and so he kills them to preserve his illusory self-image.

As the first Irish girl he has encountered, Felicia activates Hilditch's suppressed feelings of sexism and racism – feelings rooted in the maternal abuse and avuncular deceit of his childhood – to a uniquely intense degree. He becomes obsessed with her exoticism from their fateful first encounter when his omnivorous gaze lingers over her dress, demeanour and speech, the conspicuous signs of her racial otherness:

> As he progresses on the tarmacadamed surface, taking his time while digesting, he notices a solitary figure ahead of him. It is a girl in a red coat and a headscarf, carrying two plastic bags. He notices when he is closer to her that she is round-faced, wide-eyed, and has an air of being lost. He doesn't recognize her; she doesn't belong. *Chawke's* it says on the plastic bags, bold black letters on green. He has never heard the name before; it doesn't belong, either.
>
> 'I don't know am I in the right place'. the girl says as he is about to pass her by, and Mr Hilditch smiles in his usual way. Irish, he says to himself.
>
> (p. 11)

With each successive meeting he grows more contemptuous of the cultural background of this 'runaway from the Irish boglands' (p. 127) whose own account of her oppressive life in Ireland confirms his inherited perception of the country as backward and stifling. When she threatens to return to her family, he imagines Ireland as a fate which is, literally, worse than death and one from which he, the enlightened colonial redeemer, must deliver her, the misguided postcolonial victim: 'She'll sink into a corner in that household where she came from, she'll dry up into a woman who waits for ever for a useless man' (p. 149); 'On her way back to nothing, he repeated to himself in his big front room, on her way to a bleakness that would wither her innocence: what good was that to anyone?' (p. 188).

Felicia foils his attempted domination of her by escaping, however, and this act of anti-colonial resistance precipitates the collapse of Hilditch's colonial identity. Unable to visualize her in his 'Memory Lane' as he can his other victims, he becomes so tormented by the image of her independence that *he* now begins to search for *her*, thus reversing the dynamics of dependence. Trevor's metaphors of invasion are highly suggestive of the postcolonial migrant's disruptive and transformative impact on the agent of colonialism: 'One morning, having fallen into an exhausted doze soon after dawn, he awakes with the eccentric notion that the Irish girl has invaded him, as territory is invaded' (p. 179). Hilditch's sense of violation is exacerbated by his encounter with Miss Calligary, a migrant Jamaican evangelist who persists in visiting his home in the hope of 'gathering' him in for Jesus. His mind eventually buckles under the twin questioning presences of Felicia and Miss Calligary, postcolonial subjects whose proximity to the former imperial centre is irresistibly disruptive. Hilditch's final act of suicide may therefore be read as the implosion of an attenuated colonialism under the impact of a migrant dissidence. But the postcolonial resonances do not end there as, in one of the most hauntingly lyrical lines of the novel, Trevor engages our sympathy for the deranged killer: 'Lost within a man who murdered, there was a soul like any other soul, purity itself it surely once had been' (p. 212). Thus, *Felicia's Journey* would seem to exemplify Memmi's description of the reciprocal iniquity of colonization: 'It diverts and pollutes the best energies of man – of oppressed and oppressor alike. For if colonization destroys the colonized, it also rots the colonizer'.[20]

For Felicia, however, the journey from the periphery to the centre is positively transformative in that it leads her to a new, migrant mode of being in the world. Though her material circumstances are grim (she has become a bag lady, continually moving from town to town), she does possess a degree of spiritual enlightenment. In the closing chapter she is shown to have achieved a kind of migrant serenity, sustained by an awareness of 'the contingency of all definitions of self and the other, and the necessity always to tread lightly':[21]

> She knows she is not as she was; she is not the bridesmaid at the autumn wedding, not the girl who covered herself with a rug in the back of the car. The innocence that once was hers is now, with time, a foolishness, yet it is not disowned, and that same lost person is valued for leading her to where she is. Walking through another morning, fine after a wet night, she accepts without bewilderment the serenity that possesses her, and celebrates its fresh new presence.
>
> (*Felicia's Journey*, p. 207)

Felicia's negotiation of her hybrid selfhood has begun. As one journey ends, so another begins.

Gilchrist: a migrant's 'pangs of displacement'

As we have seen, *Felicia's Journey* demonstrates how migrant dislocation and the articulation of difference within the heartland of the former colonizer have considerable interrogative, disruptive and transformative potential. However, while *Gilchrist* exemplifies some of the same issues as *Felicia's Journey*, it also complicates them. Whereas Felicia's socio-cultural formation is Southern Catholic nationalist, Gilchrist's is Ulster Protestant. Additionally, unlike Felicia who is doubly oppressed as an Irish woman in Britain, Gilchrist's historical and cultural identity exemplifies the ambivalent complicity which Albert Memmi calls the 'native-born colonizer',[22] whose unbearable contradiction may only ultimately be resolved by leaving the colony.[23] But for an Ulster Protestant, the 'return' to an all too proximate 'mother country', an imagined England, is fraught with problems. Gilchrist experiences a bewildering sense of otherness in England, prompting him to develop a hybrid, migrant identity. It has to be so because the 'Irishness' signified by dominant forms of post-independence Irish nationalism are historically and culturally repugnant to his social and cultural formation. Unable to bear, in Memmi's phrase, 'life [as] a perpetual compromise'[24] in Northern Ireland, and facing the impossibility of exile in England, the native-born colonizer is left with no choice: he becomes a migrant occupying the space between two worlds, at the confluence of identities.

Hence the novel opens with Gilchrist, an ex-evangelist preacher from Antrim, hiding in the anonymity of a Spanish tourist resort, fearing recriminations for embezzlement of church funds and sexual improprieties with Donna, a 15-year-old girl whom he baptized.[25] A series of extended flashbacks reveal Gilchrist's sexual humiliation as a boy and how as a teenager he ran away from home to join a travelling circus. Drifting among these outcasts and misfits, he discovers a gift for 'second sight' and, combining his visionary powers with showmanship, becomes a respected evangelist. He 'rescues' Donna from a religious refuge in Hampshire, but subsequently allows the insistent paedophile urges suppressed within his altruistic paternalism to surface, and has sex with the girl. These troubling memories are intercut with a narrative of the Spanish present in which Gilchrist meets Jordan, a shady English character living on the fringes of the expatriate British community of the resort. The significant point about Jordan is that, though younger, he is an exact physical double of Gilchrist:

> An optical illusion, but without the intervention of any mirror. The man in the lurid shirt was *himself*, some years younger, perhaps heavier, too, but very recognisably *himself.*
>
> This was no self-induced delusion either, for the girl had seen it, as had his *alter ego*, judging by the way he now stared back at him.
>
> (p. 77, original emphases)

Gilchrist's past, his heightened sense of Anglo-Iberian displacement and this invidious doubling culminate in a conflict of personalities and cultural identities between the Ulsterman and the expatriate Jordan.

Earlier in his travels, Gilchrist became aware of his racial otherness in the English heartland of 'Britishness', the countryside around London: 'they might call this the Home Counties, but not to him it isn't' (p. 210). As in Trevor's novel, an illusory 'world of Southern English order and restraint' (p. 260) is maintained through a series of potent cultural icons epitomized by the cricket match that he imagines is staged for his benefit (p. 287). While, on the one hand, Gilchrist recognizes such images are necessary to sustain the immutable superiority of the colonial self-image – 'like so many things in this country its former grandeur seems to exist more in people's imagination than in reality' (p. 230) – on the other, he is offended by the racist attitudes that underpin this mentality. For instance, Gilchrist inwardly reacts to a landlady's casual anti-Irish racism and non-recognition of his Ulster Protestantism:

> He knows he is included in her remarks about being Irish and by definition a bogtrotter. Just what makes these people behave so lordly with their pitiful pretensions to superiority, when it's obvious to anyone with half an eye that everything about them, *everything*, is one colossal lie.
>
> (p. 153, original emphasis)

The 'marginal Briton', to use George Boyce's term,[26] becomes acutely conscious that the social homogeneity of the home country is a sustaining myth riven with divisive contradictions. The imagined England is 'jolted with something foreign, unsettling, unexpected. Like a mini-bus load of Sikhs in turbans and saris shuttling past up the motor way' (*Gilchrist*, p. 286). Even in Spain, Gilchrist observes the same myth-making process at work among a group of expatriate English men (Woking Ken, Derek the cricket bore and ex-civil servant 'Diggers' Digby) who try to recreate the milieu of an imaginary England:

> all those little morsels of class, education and background which the English so enjoy picking over like monkeys combing each other for fleas. Yet it did surprise him to find it reproduced here in such a setting with such loving dedication.
>
> (p. 160)

Such migrant insights soon lead to confrontation and action. Jordan's crass colonialism sparks Gilchrist's resurgent Ulster Protestantism; the younger man's blatant paedophilia guiltily reminds him of the degenerate side of his own colonial masculinity that impelled him to abuse Donna. Gilchrist first resents and then resists Jordan's assertion that the two men are interchangeable twin 'brothers' (p. 175) or 'equals' (p. 300). In a pivotal scene, he acknowledges his violation of Donna, comparing it to the physical abuse of Angie meted out by Jordan. Thus, in Jordan, Gilchrist confronts the complicit side of his national and masculine identities, historically inscribed as they are within a residual British colonialism. Then, crucially, the realization that Jordan is a co-victim dawns on Gilchrist:

> *We did that,* he told himself, *my shadow and me.*
>
> Then he saw his own appearance reflected in a shop-window. What stared back at him was *the missing member of a trio of victims.* A sudden flicker of anger flared in him and for once was directed not inwards at himself but at something, someone else.
>
> And that someone came lurching out of an alleyway buttoning his flies, belching.
>
> (p. 297, our emphasis)

Just as Trevor evokes compassion for the wretched Hilditch, Leitch represents the postcolonial migrant extending empathy towards the ex-colonial, thus exemplifying Ashis Nandy's insight that 'victors are ultimately shown to be camouflaged victims, at an advanced stage of colonial decay'.[27]

At the novel's climax the two men fight in the sea but instead of drowning Jordan, Gilchrist not only spares the man's life but baptizes him. He then strips off his own clothes and plunges into the sea, immersing and renewing himself:

> he was swimming back home, back along those cool, dark, remembered streams of childhood, letting them wash away each stain, every accumulated transgression with each stroke he took. His troubles had been born in water. They should end there too.
>
> (*Gilchrist*, p. 309)

These final words might seem to suggest a nostalgic return for Gilchrist but in fact it is a point of revelation that leads to the assumption of a hybrid form of identity, a rebirth of the self. Rushdie points out that although there is a strong urge to remember, to look back, the migrant must accept that he 'will not be capable of reclaiming precisely the thing that was lost'.[28] And Bhabha also stresses the potentially empowering condition of hybridity as 'an emergence that turns "return" into reinscription or redescription'.[29] Gilchrist's migrant status is signified by the fact that the return here is *imagined* rather than *physical*. His migrant condition is further characterized by his capacity 'for non-stop self-regeneration',[30] producing a sense of mental composure in his dislocated state of anonymity: 'His head was a bobbing dot in the vastness – as he was – paltry, insignificant, and the thought filled him with a peace he thought he had forfeited forever'(*Gilchrist*, p. 309).

This sense of migrant equanimity is similar to that ascribed to Felicia at the end of her journey. It is important to reiterate that this condition is neither nostalgic nor naively optimistic. As Bhabha insists, it is 'to dream not of the past or present, nor the continuous present; it is not the nostalgic dream of tradition, nor the Utopian dream of modern progress; it is the dream of translation as "survival"'.[31] It is this continual state of self-translation that defines the survival strategies of the migrant transformations presented in the narratives of *Felicia's Journey* and *Gilchrist*. As works of fiction these texts may be read as examples of 'a postcolonial contramodernity',[32] interrogating and transforming the national and gendered discourses produced by colonialism: 'In the world through which I travel, I am endlessly creating myself'.[33]

6
'It's a Free Country': Visions of Hybridity in the Metropolis[1]

Geraldine Stoneham

> The barred Nation *It/Self*, alienated from its eternal self-genera-
> tion, becomes a liminal form of social representation, a space
> that is internally marked by cultural difference and the hetero-
> geneous histories of contending peoples, antagonistic author-
> ities, and tense cultural locations.
>
> (Homi K. Bhabha)[2]

> They were like the barbarians outside the gates of Rome, only
> they were already inside...
>
> (T. Coraghessan Boyle)[3]

At the American War Cemetery in Cambridge, a polished granite wall is
incised with some of the names of the thousands of American men who
died 'so that we might live in freedom'. As Benedict Anderson has
suggested, it is a truism that the imagined community can be astonish-
ingly, horribly realized in such places.[4] The story of the monument is
that of idea (nation/freedom) transformed into performance (war/
death), performance into artefact (incised granite) and artefact into
pedagogy (history). It is a narrative that is rehearsed, repeated and
performed over again within the linear time of the Western nation state.

There are contesting narratives, however, equally realized by the honour roll at the American War Cemetery. Names such as Adams, Camp-
bell, Cohen, Hogan, Isaacs, Jones, Metz, Musetti, Nigro, Ornato, Ryan,
Suomi, Wheen, Yanik, Zielenicwski simultaneously constitute the integ-
rity of the monument and attest to the hybrid and diasporic nature of
the society it represents. Yet hybridity here appears not to disrupt the
surface of the nation's history; in the context of the United States' role

in the Second World War, multiplicity and diversity paradoxically affirm the homogeneity of national identity. More recent theories of diaspora and hybridization, however, have focused on this paradox. Postcolonial discourse has foregrounded, not the 'fusion' effect of hybridity, but its equal and opposite effect, that of alienation. Homi Bhabha has identified this double effect as occurring within the discourse of nationalism. Bhabha suggests that the Nation is a state of cultural liminality – of perpetual rehearsal – always radically alienated within 'It/Self'.[5] The tension of the paradox is generated within the cultural sign of nation as 'the People'. The example of the American war memorial demonstrates a split between what Bhabha calls the authoritative pedagogical construction of the people as 'historical "objects"' (the People as One), constitutive of a continuum of events, and the people as 'subjects' of a performative function, that is, the 'living principle of the people as that continual process by which the national life is redeemed and signified as a repeating and reproductive process'.[6]

The writing on the wall is also interpreted as a doubled hybridity through the strategy of postcolonial reading. In Robert Young's phrase, the 'fixity of identity... implies a counter-sense of fragmentation and dispersion',[7] and it is this foreignness within – the clamour of the diasporic – which is read as the performative function of the narrative. Hybridity 'disarticulates authority' – that is, the authority of the homogenized sign – through the interrogative power of alienated voices.[8] More radical, however, is the present (though not retrospective) reading of the text – for the monument speaks, not just through what is there, incised into the stone, but also through the paradoxical articulation of what is absent or silent: the myriad identities of the new diaspora. Viewed from the present, it is this aspect which I intend to explore in this article: when the fiction of nation is read critically as the 'heterogeneous histories of contending peoples'. In an examination of two recent works of fiction on the subject of nation and identity, I shall consider the paradox identified by Homi Bhabha as the split within the 'narration of nation' between the 'accumulative temporality' of the pedagogical and the 'recursive strategy' of the performative.[9] How is the narrative of nation – the linear and accumulative narrative of the idea and events of nation which is both monumental and temporary – interrogated by the strategy of repetition and rehearsal through which the narrative is performed? In the narrative of migration and settlement as the escape from poverty and tyranny, how is the term 'free' in the narrative of 'the free country' repeated by the multiple and contending voices of the people with such differing inflection?

Nowhere is this double articulation more consciously interrogated than in the cross-cultural confrontation between the old and new diasporas of the United States of America. One example of this is the Indian-born American writer, Bharati Mukherjee, whose work explores just such issues of diaspora and hybridity at work at the heart of the metropolis. Her novel *Jasmine* (1989) is the story of a young Indian woman's survival of and through the process of hybridization, first in postcolonial India and then in the cultural melting pot of the United States. Jasmine undergoes multiple hybrid transformations, signalled by successive changes of name from Jyoti, through Jasmine and Jane, to Jase, each new identity reflecting her adaptation to a new set of cultural circumstances. Importantly, however, Jasmine's intervention in the life of the metropolis also transforms the people and cultures who come into contact with her, sometimes in violent and tragic ways. It is this mutuality in Mukherjee's vision of hybridity in the metropolis which is distinctive, in contrast to the apparently one-way process of colonialism, which she identifies with the 'old' postcolonial cultures.

Mukherjee's vision is therefore performative and individualist: her concept of America involves an almost continual enactment of a hybridity that 'erase[s] any prior or originary presence' of the nation-people.[10] The performative strategy takes its bearings from the 'People as One', but reinscribes the pedagogical artefact with new names, transforming the whole over time. This process alienates the pedagogic function of nation from the identity of one particular group (in this case the children of the 'old' immigrant population) and apparently opens it up to all comers.

Thus it is that Jasmine's metropolitan lover can confidently assert that 'It's a free country', invoking a founding principle of the nation, while simultaneously demonstrating the apparent accessibility of the strategies of repetition of that principle on which the identity of the United States citizen is based. That this is said while Taylor is literally teaching Jasmine to practise 'freedom' or 'Americanness', to perform as an independent citizen of the US rather than as a victimized subaltern from the Third World, through the simple use of a marker, reinforces the idea of nation as an artefact which is constantly reinscribed through its use in everyday life. It is thus possible for Mukherjee to assert that a change in performance will ultimately result in a change in pedagogy: an Indian-born woman writing the novel in America will alter the 'gene pool' of the American novel for all time.

There are, of course, other views of the doubling of both the discourse of nationalism and that of hybridization. Homi Bhabha's series of radio lectures *Letters from Chicago*[11] describes a relationship between the pedagogical and the performative within the narrative of the United States much more complex and fraught with multiple conflicting inter-pretations than Mukherjee's. Where Mukherjee indicts ethnic commu-nities within the state as a retreat from the dangers of hybridity into the inertial comforts of nostalgia, in identifying the ghettoization of metro-politan experience, Bhabha's view of US society suggests a fragmented and partial state, where the identity of nation is in constant inter-rogation by the restless hybrid encounters of disparate, marginalized cultures.

In his novel *The Tortilla Curtain* (1995) T. Coraghessan Boyle, too, explores the hybrid construction of metropolitan society and attempts by new 'immigrants' to repeat and reinscribe that hybridity. Like Mukherjee, Boyle has one of his characters utter the commonplace 'It's a free country', only this time the speaker is an illegal migrant worker from Mexico, and the phrase continues,'isn't it?' This striking variation, uttered paradoxically both abjectly and defiantly, interrogates precisely the doubled moment of articulation of the pedagogical and the perfor-mative nation. In Boyle's view (and to some degree in Bhabha's), the constant process of hybridization – both natural and inevitable – is evaluated and resisted by an intransigent, resilient pedagogical artefact that denies its own heterogeneity.

In each of these visions of hybridity in the metropolis, the split between the idea and the act, or the pedagogical and the performative, reveals the potential for political intervention or agency within the articulation of nation. The question for the reader is to interpret the nature of the intervention – its effects – and its consequences for indi-vidual and collective identity in the Western postcolonial location. Does hybridity decentre the metropolis until it becomes the metaphorical cauldron of Western liberalism, giving the same chance to all cultural interventions? Or does the concept of centre/margin simply oscillate perpetually between the nation It/Self, trapping first one then the other on the wrong side of the divide, and denying, however transiently, the fixed identity of 'the People as One'?

To begin with, Bharati Mukherjee locates herself as a writer in the tradition of US immigrant writing but she explicitly sets herself apart from the 'traditional' immigrant. These traditional immigrants – rather crudely sketched as 'the hollow-eyed and sunken cheeked', 'the black-scarfed babushkas' – were not represented at her naturalization cere-mony. In an article which begins with the words 'I'm one of you now', and which goes on to characterize the impact of the new Americans on

American life and letters, she warns the US of the faster pace of cultural change – a process which cannot help but imply catharsis for the national image:

> These new Americans are not willing to wait for a generation or two to establish themselves. They're working for themselves and their children, of course, but they're not here to sacrifice themselves for the future's sake.[12]

For the European immigrants of the past, Mukherjee implies, the American dream existed distantly in time, their progress towards the rewards was a linear process of labour and acculturation, and the present was endured for its sake. New non-traditional immigrants, on the other hand, come already equipped, by virtue of colonialism, with a double voice – a hybrid tongue which articulates the language of the self and the other. Mukherjee urges her fellow new immigrant writers to:

> cash... in on the other legacy of the colonial writers, and that is his or her duality. From childhood, we learned how to be two things simultaneously; to be the dispossessed as well as the dispossessor... History forced us to see ourselves as both 'we' and the 'other' and our language reflected our simultaneity.[13]

It is this paid-up inherence of hybridity which the new immigrant writers bring to the metropolis as their asset. As she sees it, Mukherjee's mission to 'open up the canon of American literature', to redefine the nature of *American* and what makes an American',[14] is the aim of a process of prismatic refraction of the national character through the lens of the colonial hybrid. This said, we might well then expect from Mukherjee's writing the destabilizing and disturbing effects of hybridity that Homi Bhabha describes in 'Signs Taken for Wonders':

> Hybridity... displays the necessary deformation and displacement of all sites of discrimination and domination. It unsettles the mimetic or narcissistic demands of colonial power but reimplicates its identifications in strategies of subversion that turn the gaze of the discriminated back upon the eye of power.[15]

And, indeed, there are many representations of that ambivalent and terrorizing gaze and the violence that it gives rise to. In 'Loose Ends', a story in Mukherjee's 1988 collection, *The Middleman and Other Stories*, for example, the first-person narrator, a homicidal Vietnam veteran, articulates the threat: 'Where did America go?... Back when me and my buddies were barricading the front door, who left the back door open?'[16] He responds to the threat by raping and murdering a young American member of an Indian family. Bursting in on the family as they are gathered around their evening meal, he exclaims with disbelief: 'They look at me. A bunch of aliens and they stare like I'm the freak'[17] The violence of the native/alien encounter can go both ways: in *Jasmine*, the Vietnam vet returns as Half-Face, a worker in the illegal immigrant trade, despising the merchandise and appropriating it when he can. After raping Jyoti, he is killed by her in the guise of the goddess Kali, and it is over his dead body that Jasmine finds entry to her American lives.

But it is not only in these ambivalent confrontations between dispossessed and dispossessor that Mukherjee reveals the nature of her scrutiny of the various contestants for the prize. There are confrontations between old and new immigrants which examine the self-limited horizons of the old assimilated groups against the baroque experience and hungry desires of the new. In the story 'Orbiting', the new immigrant Roashan from Kabul discomfits his lover's family by talking about his first-hand experience of torture and imprisonment and his wants for the future while waiting to be served his first Thanksgiving dinner. The family, who are themselves barely a generation away from their Italian origins, are suspicious of the new immigrant. Both confused by and attracted to his exoticism, they watch uneasily as he hijacks the holiday. Meanwhile his lover mentally remoulds him the shape of an imaginary American hero of the frontier, 'Clint Eastwood, scarred hero and survivor',[18] apparently unaware of his potential ruthlessly to transform such myths and with them her perception of America. It is this ability to record the capacity of the metropolitan to be mesmerized by the hybridized other while implying the unsettling potential of this presence which is Mukherjee's great strength and the promise of her 'simultaneity'. Her suggestion that a second-hand moral authority, the mythology of the 'white-hat' cowboy, is evidence of a society gone soft requires closer examination.

The most telling of Mukherjee's interventions into the making of Americans, however, scarcely involves the new immigrant at all. In *Jasmine*, almost by default, the heroine, now Jane, finds herself living in Iowa with a middle-aged banker, Bud Ripplemeyer, and their teenage adopted son, a Vietnamese refugee, Du. She has fled to Middle America from New York after being pursued by the terrorist who murdered her

husband back in Hasnapur. She chose Iowa because the adopted daughter of her New York lover, Taylor Hayes, was born there. The America she
finds in Elsa County is different from that in New York. It is a place
where all the dolls have yellow hair. It is a place where poor farmgirls in
trouble sell their babies to rich metropolitans so that they can have an
education. It is a place where drained and desperate farmers imagine an
international banking conspiracy and as a consequence attempt murder
and suicide. It is a place where the banker, knowing he is about to be
shot, makes the mistake of walking in front of his assailant because he
believes in 'John Wayne bravery and codes of Hollywood honor. Good
men might weaken and get pushed to the brink, but they would never,
never shoot their targets in the back'.[19]

It is in this Middle America, the location of the old myths of frontier,
Mukherjee is implying, that the apparent homogeneity of the American
myth is bogus and is cracking under the strain of its own internal
contradictions and pressures. These grandchildren of traditional immigrants – characters with hybrid names like Bud Ripplemeyer, Darrel Lutz,
Harlan Kroeger, Rindy and Cindy de Marco – are narrow-minded, fearful
of the world, and dangerously naïve; they have commitments, responsibilities, debts. They are no match for the new/old-world survivors,
Roashan and Jasmine, who are 'greedy with wants and reckless with
hope'. Yet where Mukherjee might break open the myth and expose its
contradictions as terminal, that is, call the 'free country' into question,
she uses a metaphorical sleight of hand to underpin it. Her insistence on
the failure of the traditional immigrants to practise a postmodernity
commensurate with the freedom on offer paradoxically confirms the
idea of freedom as a monument of nationalism – even if that monument
is perceived as plastic.[20] The idea is, after all, immaterial.

Mukherjee envisions the free country as a material reality. When the
diffident alien Jyoti/Jasmine blooms into the 'adventurous Jase', she
expresses her new-found freedom and unexpected riches by ordering
mail-order goods from the television. Soon she finds herself besieged
and impoverished by unwanted goods. Taylor comes to the rescue:

'America, America!' Taylor said one day... He wrote on a package in
thick marking pen RETURN TO SENDER. That's all you need to do, he
explained. If something gets too frightening, just pull down an imaginary shade that says RETURN on it and you can make it go away.[21]

Later, when Jasmine is faced with the choice between the incarnation of
Jase, the adventurous lover of the metropolitan Taylor, and plain Jane,

the self-sacrificing wife of the crippled Bud, she visualizes the shade and marks the character of Jane 'return to sender'. The sender in this case is the colonial literary canon, which saddles her with a character from a novel which she, as Jyoti the Indian village girl, was never able to read. Her choice is a deliberate rejection of the roles prescribed for the subaltern under colonialism, the female under patriarchy.

There is a moment when, in her incarnation as Jase, Jasmine catches sight of the programme *Monster Truck Madness* on the television and is transfixed:

> On the screen Cut Tire Class vehicles, frail as gnats, skim over churned-up mud. Helemeted men give me victory signs. They all plan on winning tonight. Nitro Express, Brawling Babe, Insane Expectations. Move over, I whisper.[22]

Jase, by implication, chooses the winning chance and the power that goes with it, in order to skim over the mud. But there is more to this scene. The titles of the vehicles – each driven by a man who is planning on winning – represent stages in Jasmine's incarnations. Prakesh and his bomb (Nitro Express), Half-Face and his violence (Brawling Babe) and Bud and his literary archetypes (Insane Expectations) all offer Jasmine the winning ride, and indeed she does win with all of them. Ironically, however, each of the jockeys turns up the loser. The equipment and consequently the power for this precarious ride is appropriated from the explosive encounters of colonialist legacies, capitalism and patriarchy; these encounters provide the engine for the opportunist subaltern already prepared for hybridization by the experience of cultural colonialism. For Mukherjee, this is the essence of American identity; it has nothing to do with race or colour, but with a capacity to throw off fixed roles and identities in order to take on new lives; a capacity to utilize the power machine, to make it go in *your* direction. Du demonstrates the theory in practice with his hybridized electrical appliances: the Black and Decker spliced to the Mixmaster engine creates a new hybrid power tool. But Du also has a private agenda – he is a 'hyphenated-American' with a Vietnamese identity – which strangely appears both parasitic and subversive; for Du, hybridization is a sideline. Du may be altering the 'gene pool of the common American appliance', but the pregnant Jane is altering the American gene pool, as she, it is suggested, has also been altered.[23] By the time Du leaves for his Vietnamese-American future, Nitro Express, Brawling Babe and Insane Expectations have been transmuted into Adventurous Jase waiting for her Taylor-made ride.

It has been noted in articles by Kristin Carter-Sanborn and Gurleen Grewal that Jasmine's claim for agency in her choice of what she calls her 'genetic hybridity' is suspect on a number of fronts.[24] Primarily, the violence that is perpetrated on Jasmine's selves by a succession of men in order to bring her to what Grewal calls her 'Taylor-made' dreams is a pattern of colonialist dispossession, a violence of language that turns the subaltern into the colonial subject through education.[25] Mukherjee may have her heroine reject the literary texts of the British Raj, but not before she has enmeshed her intertextually with them. Freedom is a performative act for Jasmine and for the other dispossessed, exilic and marginalized peoples who find themselves without the restraints and obligations attendant on the myths of nationalism; but Mukherjee fails to acknowledge the power of the pedagogic identity, 'the People', and the investment that there is within the discourse of nation in maintaining it. How long can the machine continue to win, and continue to throw off its paradoxical loser-rider into the mud without encountering some kind of bedrock? Perhaps the bedrock on which the myths of nationalism are inscribed? Is the articulation of freedom simply a continuation of the old struggle between the dispossessed and the dispossessor played as an all-comers game of chance?

Homi Bhabha's view of US society is a lot less encouraging for immigrants or minorities of any kind, legal or illegal. In his 1995 series of broadcasts, *Letters from Chicago*, he quotes the bartender at his local bar in the salubrious academic suburb of Hyde Park: 'Problems we have are the result of our generosity as a nation . . . This ain't no country, never were supposed to be, everywhere you go there's a new frontier to cross, somebody's territory to respect'.[26] In the obvious contradictions between the affirmation and the denial of an 'us' to oppose to 'them', Bhabha's bartender speaks from that space between the pedagogic and the performative in the narrative of nation. He exposes in this contradiction both the existence of a myth of collective identity and the denial of it: the location of the point at which the nation is divided against It/Self.

It is at this edge, where a walk to the local shop can mean the redrawing of cultural boundaries – African-American, Korean, Hispanic, Irish, WASP – that the image of nation flickers and subsides. The freedom of the country here is not the freedom of the melting pot; it is the freedom of each to be able to negotiate his or her boundary with others on a daily basis. But there is also, always, the 'us' who are the arbiters of that freedom to negotiate, the 'us/US' whose image flickers briefly between the negotiators as the transaction is made: profit, loss, violence, disrespect, envy, admiration. It is that intervention of 'us' – the United States of America, 'the People as One' however brief, that prevents that society from becoming complacent about what Bhabha calls 'cultural diversity... liberal notions of multiculturalism, cultural exchange, or the culture of humanity'.[27] Mukkherjee would surely endorse this reading of 'country' in the bartender's statement: simultaneously imaginary and symbolic, it is the negotiation point in the 'process of signification' which is cultural difference, 'through which statements *of* culture or *on* culture differentiate, discriminate, and authorize the productions of fields of force, reference, applicability and capacity'.[28]

In Mukherjee's terms the hybrid tongue is that which articulates and authorizes the field of reference, and which is empowered by it. Ghettos and boundaries are for cowards and bigots – the victims of their own incoherence, fear, rage, naïvety, infertility, boredom, moribundity. The freedom to appropriate the language of 'us' *is* the freedom of America. What concerns me is Mukherjee's confident assertion that America subscribes to this authority: It's a free country – isn't it?

T. Coraghessan Boyle's novel *The Tortilla Curtain* also explores the nature of the American, in a fable every bit as allusive and allegorical as *Jasmine*. Boyle's Southern Californians, like Mukherjee's Middle Americans, sport hybrid names like Delaney Mossbacher, which testify to their own and their country's history. In this best of all possible worlds they live lives that any would call successful, privileged, the result of generations of patient work 'for the future's sake'. And they are still pushing back the frontiers of the west, moving into areas of wilderness closer to the border with Mexico, attracting with their advance attendant predators on their privilege. Importantly, like Taylor and Wylie (the WASP wife usurped by the exotic hybrid, Jasmine), they do not produce anything, but utilize the moribund wealth with which US society is apparently soaked. Again, like the privileged metropolitans in *Jasmine*, neither are they re-productive – their physical concerns are with their own (not each others') bodies. Delaney recognizes his good fortune – he has an impeccable liberal conscience – but as the coyotes begin to threaten his pets (Sacheverell and Osbert) and the illegal Mexicans threaten his assets (including the very wilderness from which he makes his living as a writer about nature), he becomes increasingly determined to go to any lengths to protect them.

In the canyon, just outside the fence and later the wall which surrounds the exclusive housing estate of Arroyo Blanco, live Cándido and his pregnant wife América in a camp at the edge of a filthy stream. They have paid to come to work for the gringos. Like Jasmine they are illegals, and like Jasmine their encounters with Americans are frequently violent, sometimes benevolent, but unlike Jasmine's rarely so easily negotiated. As the numbers of illegal migrant workers increase, the inhabitants of the estates become nervous. A brief phone call to the authorities closes what each side in the transaction called the labour exchange, and the men who wait there for work are dispossessed. It is at this point that Boyle calls into question the story of the making of America. Like the bartender in Bhabha's account, Boyle raises the issue of generosity. A racist white character says:

> it's a question of national sovereignty. Did you know that the US accepted more immigrants last year than all the other countries of the world combined... all they've got to offer is a strong back, and the irony is we need fewer and fewer strong backs every day.[29]

At this point Boyle brings us back to the question. Standing in the pouring rain, staring at the closure of their only means of entry to the American dream, the Mexicans protest their lost heritage:

> ...looks like the *gabachos* don't want us here anymore...I don't give a shit,...I'm going to stand right here till somebody hires me – it's a free country isn't it?'
> 'Sure,' Cándido said, and the way he was feeling he couldn't hold back the sarcasm, ' – as long as you're a *gringo*. But us, we better look out.'[30]

This is the hybrid space of cultural difference, an ambivalent encounter between the pedagogic and the performative within the language of nationalism itself. This tentative assertion is the closest these immigrants get to appropriating the language of 'us'. The rehearsal of the narrative of the identity of the US only serves to emphasize the split within the idea of the nation itself. It is this split along the line of articulation of national identity that brings me into conflict with Mukherjee's vision. The ghettos of white affluent established America may be vulnerable to the ironic gaze of the new diaspora, but they have control of the marker pen and when things get too costly or too frightening, they mark the unwanted RETURN TO SENDER. Mukherjee's confidence in the power of irony to effect a change in the narrative merely through the process of repetition is challenged by Boyle's subtle interrogation of the ambivalence inherent within the narrative.

Like Jasmine and Du, Cándido and América are also new immigrants in the immigrant tradition. They, too, refuse the label of victim, they eschew the ghetto, they exploit their opportunities. But they are from that other America, whence the process of osmosis between the rich north and the impoverished south is witnessed daily. They don't find it so easy to strip away one identity to accommodate another, nor to appropriate and utilize a power which is always in the control of others. At the beginning of the novel, Delaney's first contact with Cándido is to run him over on the road. One of Cándido's most harrowing experiences comes when he and a group of fellow illegals buy a car which breaks down in a freezing winter landscape. The failure to understand and control the engine is almost fatal. His life is saved by an act of humanity by a local farmer, but even this cannot prevent him being taken by the authorities.

Boyle's answer to the impasse of powerlessness is to articulate a hybrid 'culture of humanity', even if it exists only as a figment of a naïve liberal consciousness. As Cándido puts out a hand to rescue from drowning a man who represents those who have just tried to kill him and his wife, whose children tried to destroy his possessions, whose waste has blinded his child, Cándido exercises the only freedom left: the freedom to act in humanity towards another. Boyle might suggest that this, too, is a negotiating point in the process of signification which is cultural difference. Bhabha's point about liberal notions of the culture of humanity is well taken in the context of metropolitan hegemony, but in that split-second Cándido re-enacts what Mukherjee denies: 'the John Wayne... codes of Hollywood honor in which good men... never, never shoot their targets in the back'.

What all three writers are agreed on is the liminality of the nation-space, that, as Bhabha puts it 'the threat of cultural difference is no longer a problem of "other" people. It becomes a question of the other-ness of the people-as-one'.[31] The debate lies in the freedom of the heterogeneous subjects of hybridity to interrogate the mythical homo-geneity of the hybridized nation state, but in a process which is endless and multiplicitous. Mukherjee's vision is based on a metaphor of genetic mutation rather than hybridity and as such it reinscribes the old immu-table myths of the nation with new and mutable ones. Bhabha's vision of aporial 'othering' within the narration, however, suggests that rein-scription is impossible, and that agency lies in reading the inscription for the internal contradictions of hybridization in alienation. Boyle's view is that the deep and irreconcilable contradictions inherent in the doubled narrative of the nation state are papered over by a moribund but powerful national identity, whose investment will ensure that the marginalized can exist only in the spaces and gaps between the lines of inscription.

7

I Came All the Way from Cuba So I Could I Speak Like This? Cuban and Cubanamerican Literatures in the US

Nara Araújo

I

After 1959, because of the Cuban Revolution, a permanent flood of people, of different ages, social strata and expectations left the major island of the Antilles. Most of them went to the United States, where immigration was encouraged for political reasons. Cubans started a process of conflictual and sometimes agonized adaptation. But a miracle occurred: arriving in the US, settling mainly in Miami, the Cuban community managed to become successful, first in business, later in liberal professions and even in local politics. Social scientists who have studied Cuban immigration after 1959 have stated that the causes of that 'miracle' were twofold: on the one hand, US state political interests, trapped in a hostile relationship with Fidel Castro's government; on the other, the networking abilities of the Cuban family and community.[1]

This success is, of course, relative: as with every social phenomenon, Cuban immigration is heterogeneous, and within it one can find millionaires and the working classes. Besides, later waves of immigration brought in lower educational strata from the Cuban population, people with no professional skills and, sometimes, from marginal sectors. Nevertheless, the success saga reproduced by the media has placed the Cuban exiles in a different position *vis-à-vis* the rest of the Hispanic minorities.

The Cuban diaspora not only reaches the United States, but also Mexico, Venezuela and Spain, countries linked to Cuba by language and history. It is in the United States, however, that the relationship with language changes, a change that affects all of the non-Anglo immigrant communities, and especially those who work with language and culture: the writers. Cross-culturation and hybridization of the Cuban diaspora in the US are linked to a language conflict and to an issue of identity. It is a conflict in which I also feel implicated. In 1994, for instance, I lectured in several east coast Ivy League universities. My subject was Cuban women writers, but the cultural context forced me to speak in English; and here, as in Yale, I am not sure whether to apologize for not being bilingual. But did I come all the way from Cuba so I could speak like this? I do not face an identity conflict but I have to switch to English to assure full communication. These situations help me to understand the cultural phenomenon I am trying now to approach, in English.

II

Language divides the Cuban writers' diaspora: those who left Cuba in the early stages, as adults, brought with them name, expertise, linguistic skills and works published. Some passed away in exile; others, younger, managed to find a position in the cultural establishment; all of them continued to write in Spanish. The reference of their literary discourse – poetry, essay or fiction – was the left-behind island, a lost-forever paradise. Resentment and nostalgia were two of the main issues of what continued to be considered as Cuban literature, within the Hispano-american tradition.

Analogous to the political evolution of the Cuban community, to the emergence of more liberal new generations (those who came as children to the US), a transition took place in literary works. Those who belong to the 'bridge generation' began to express the process of adaptation to the new land. As Eliana Rivero has pointed out, that generation 'share(s) only partially the historical and cultural paradigm of the elder immigrants and, what is more important, looks at the US reality with different eyes'.[2]

This process came through language: English began to appear not only as a language *per se*, but in a mixture with Spanish. A radical change had taken place, because of the emergence of a 'Cubanamerican' consciousness. In the works of Lourdes Casal, Roberto Fernández, Dolores Prida, Achy Obejas and Rivero herself, a mixture of Spanish and English, nostalgia and humour, localism and cosmopolitanism, as well as other dualities, give proof of a process that started in the late sixties and, by the eighties, was already recognized as a distinct cultural phenomenon.

This recognition was due mainly to academics such as Rivero who began constructing a theoretical discourse about the emergence of a Cubanamerican literature, quite different from the Cuban literature written in the diaspora. This inscription in a critical discourse within US academia started in the eighties and grew in opposition to another – no less valuable – attempt to recognize Cuban literature abroad, though this perspective had not considered hybridization and cross-cultura- tion,[3] nor the transition from exile literature to 'ethnic literature' (the Cubanamerican), in connection with other such Hispanoamerican hybrids as Chicano or Nuyorrican literatures.

At this point I would like to revise the use of terms describing the emergence of this new phenomenon from the broader denomination to a more restrictive one, from Hispanic literature and ethnic literature in the US, to Cubanamerican. According to Julio Rodríguez-Luis, Chicano, Nuyorrican and Cubanamerican literatures should be considered a part of Hispanic literature in the United States, as Hispanic-American Literat- ures. Born in the US context, from different roots, they receive American influence[4] but will end – depending on their strength – affecting it. Rodríguez-Luis shows some reticence *vis-à-vis* the term 'ethnic literature' which renders the ethnicity of the dominant culture invisible, although he understands the term's usefulness in describing the challenge to Anglo-Saxon culture from the ethnic cultures of minorities in the US.

In Rodríguez-Luis's argument, the broader denomination of Hispanic literatures is sustained by the possible link between Chicano, Nuyorri- can and Cubanamerican literatures, once the last has assumed an iden- tity different from both the Cuban and the American one. Consequently, Rodríguez-Luis accepts as Cubanamerican those poems and plays where subject, characters and language express an estrange- ment of the conservative positions of the first waves of Cuban immig- rants, together with a refusal of the American way of life. In his opinion there is no Cubanamerican fiction as yet, because one cannot find the same trend toward a new identity in works like Cristina García's well known *Dreaming in Cuban*, with its apparent lack of authenticity and its misleading description of Cuba.[5]

But I would suggest that this critique has more to do with Rodríguez- Luis's definition of Cubanamerican literature. In García's book, for instance, there is also an attempt to place the story in an equidistant space where both experiences – of the Cubans in the island and the Cubanamericans in the US – are portrayed, and a family link established between them. The possibility of such a space is not present, however, in Rodríguez-Luis's definition of Cuban-American (he always uses the hyphenated term) and in his emphasis on possible similarities between the three Hispanic literatures according to an ideological positioning

regarding the dominant culture. I would argue that the new Cubanamerican fiction forces us to unravel the ideological polarity inscribed in
the hyphenated term, Cuban-American.

Although Gustavo Pérez-Firmat also uses the hyphenated term, he
links the transition from immigrant and exile literature to Cubanamerican literature with that of an ethnic literature, similar to Chicano or
Nuyorrican literature. He is interested in the use of the term 'ethnicity'
to refer more to the 'non-conflictual coexistence of dissimilar cultures'
and less to the relationship with the dominant culture. However, one
could resent in Pérez-Firmat's position the ideological lack which in
Rodríguez-Luis is maybe an excess.

Eliana Rivero's own insight takes a vigorous stand against arguing for
the sustained sameness of Cuban and Cubanamerican literature. She is
particularly interested in separating them as different ways of assuming
writing. In her case, she alternatively uses the term Cubanamerican and
Cuban-American, maintaining the hyphen when she wants to focus the
idea of duality. The coexistence of these two terms points to a permanent process of self-recognition.

In Rivero's perspective the process of becoming Cubanamerican/
Cuban-American is linked to a (rather sad) sense of the loss of a centre,
the sense 'of not belonging to any place at all, whether in Cuba nor out
of Cuba'.[6] She points to the mythical image of a lost paradise which
permeates the works of those who, in the eighties, were expressing the
transculturation they went through; those functional Cubanamericans
who still resisted complete assimilation because they had become conscious of difference. Together with this resistance, Rivero also highlights
the feeling that emerges in these works of being a 'privileged' minority
within the larger minority of Hispanics.

In one of Rivero's own first poems (written in the late seventies), the
poet goes back to the first experiences of the Cuban community, arriving in Miami:

(. . .) Miss Miller who at fifty-five
swore never to rent her nice one-bedroom apartment
to another Cuban: (. . .)
    the upstairs neighbour (very proper high school
    administrator) had a visitor
    every Thursday evening and my living room rafters
    would screech with the jolts of the bed
    and middle-aged white Anglo-Saxon
    passionate Protestants making love

over my head
      another uncle of mine was married
to a Puerto Rican lady who shopped at Jordan Marsch
and scolded me for studying too much (most of all Spanish,
of all *idiotic* things) and she recited every time I was
      her captive audience   'marry a doctor
nice, Latino parents but American ways' (...)
      this is
another land of plenty where I reap and am reaped
where I deal in my words   and forget
that I ever ate surplus commodities ... and still
the two circles surround me the dual love-and-hate
relationship   my languages the mother that I rec-
      ognize
as real   legitimate and splendid and the sur-
      rogate
the tongue that lets me be two times the person
that I am.[7]

Cultural dualism, adaptation/alienation compose the fabric of this text, though the main language is already English. The lyrical persona is facing the present, the past has faded away except in the allusion to the mother language. There is no nostalgia but rather an acceptance of the ambivalent situation, also shown in the typographical disposition of the poem. The text is an example of the transition toward 'ethnic literature' which, according to Pérez-Firmat, assumes otherness *vis-à-vis* the culture of origins as well as the culture of adoption. Thus ethnicity is not interested in identity but in difference, is contrasting and challenging; it is and it isn't; it places itself in a border space, sometimes made explicit by the hyphen.

In a more recent text, written as a personal narrative, Rivero states: 'We are more US Latinos each day', but she still resents the difference *vis-à-vis* the Anglo and other 'Latinos' as well. Once again she uses the hyphenated term to describe her dilemma: 'I am not only living on the hyphen which separates the compound word Cuban-American but also in the space: in the frontier, and on the edge of the to be and the not to be.'[8]

This feeling is similar to what Chicana writer Gloria Anzaldúa has described as a survival strategy: 'To survive the Borderlands/you must live sin fronteras/be a crossroads', and paradoxically, 'you are at home a stranger'.[9] These words differ from those of Eliana Rivero in their aggressive tone, which contrasts with the former suffering voice. Perhaps this is linked to a more complete acceptance of the border situation in the Chicana than is the case for the Cuban-American. Rivero's perspective differs from Antonio Cornejo Polar's conception of the diasporic condition as that which 'duplicates (or more) the subject's space and offers or condemns the subject to talk from more than one place',[10] but both coincide in their conflictual character.

Other Cuban-American/Cubanamerican authors write about an alternative which does not convey anguish and agony but amusement. For Antonio Vera-León, the 'cultural border subject' challenges and criticizes the 'contact zone', but adopts the positions proposed by the various cultural spheres which constitute it/him. It is an 'oscillatory subject', active in several ethnicities, a subject for whom biculturalism acts as live equipment.[11] In this sense, Pérez-Firmat talks about the need to go beyond the roots, accepting joyfully the 'transplantation', because 'Cuban identity is not a matter of challenge, but of routes, we are defined by the passage, not by the staying, it has to do with the landing and not with the place where we land'.[12]

Hence, hybridization in the Cubanamerican context may well be related to conflictual decentredness (Rivero), joyfulness (Pérez-Firmat, Vera-León) or political stances (Rodríguez-Luis). This multiple perspective speaks of the complexities of a cultural phenomenon which affects and conveys identity problems. Monolithic definitions of national culture and literature are under discussion, for the current debate has made the idea of homogeneity problematical, enhancing the dialectical relationship between past, present and future and the need to constantly redraw the boundaries. This is even more conclusive when focusing what Homi K. Bhabha calls 'hybrid hyphenations',[13] because of the more explicit and visible exchange of cultural elements.

From this point of view, rather than trying to find an essence to Cubanamerican literature, one should try to think in terms of a positioning that occurs in the discourse of history and culture, in what Stuart Hall calls 'unstable points of identification or suture'.[14] Thus, Cubanamerican literature takes from the Cuban cultural matrix – plot, characters, language – but also moves forward toward integration (even if problematical) in the American mainstream language. Within this continuum, texts are produced which take a variety of forms, from the ambivalent Cubanamerican positioning of *Dreaming in Cuban* to one more conscious of marginality and oppression, like *We Came All the Way from Cuba So You Could Dress like This?*

III

Cristina García's *Dreaming in Cuban* (1992) and the book of short stories *We Came All the Way from Cuba So You Could Dress like This?* (1994) by Achy Obejas come from the Cubanamerican minority.[15] Both published in the nineties, they illustrate, in various ways and degrees, the main trends of an ethnic literature, already explicit in their titles. The authors were born in Cuba and grew up in the United States where they became journalists and writers. García's first novel was well received by the press and was talked about as a 'hybrid offspring of the Latin American school' in American literature, as an 'intricate weaving of dramatic events with the supernatural and cosmic', as containing 'ordinary magic'. This reaction shows how stereotypes find their way quickly into the media. García Márquez's and Isabel Allende's so-called magical realism has become the epitomized Latin American school. Cristina García's literary use of resurrections, transaquatic spirits and parapsychological human skills makes her fit into the cliché that the 'First World' cultural centres have built out of Latin American literature.

My purpose, though, isn't to discuss García's (probable) intention of 'fitting in', but to place her novel within the context of Cubanamerican literature. *Dreaming in Cuban* tells the story of a family which splits apart after the 1959 Revolution. Although the *dramatis personae* include both men and women, the feminine genealogy is central to the plot. Through their personal stories and different narrative voices, time is recovered by means of a non-linear structure which enhances the idea of separateness and bifurcation, but also of multiplicity. The feminine characters are grouped in parallels, in mother–daughter, conflict-ridden relationships. Celia and Felicia in Cuba, Lourdes and Pilar in the United States are pulled apart for reasons which include ideological positions, but go beyond them. If there is some nostalgia, it is related to Celia and exposed through her old letters to a former lover in the thirties. Pilar, the Cubanamerican character in the story, has grown up into liberal ideas issuing from her US experience, and as an artist she places herself in a rebellious marginality. Her idea of her native country is linked to her grandmother's affection. Pilar's mother recalls bad experiences derived from the revolutionary changes, but her most profound refusal to recognize a symbol of them – her own mother's commitment in Cuba – is related to her recollection of her mother's resistance to her birth. Nation, then, as space and time, is linked to personal, intimate and affective experiences.

García's use of words and expressions in Spanish is an example of a pertinent language. She switches to Spanish whenever it can help create an atmosphere or present a character. Although there is a difference with the bilingualism of Chicano or Nuyorrican literatures – where the intermingling of Spanish and English creates a new linguistic dimension – the switching parallels the alternate sequences of action in the US and Havana.

García's carelessness with historical and cultural facts – she writes 'Plaza de las Annas', instead of 'Plaza de las Armas'; she talks about *voodoo* (referring to *santería*); she mentions a Havana school with an impossible name, Nikolai Lenin; she refers to Santa Barbara as a black image – could be justified or explained by her particular object of focus. Hers is not a narrative of nostalgic evocation or factual recuperation – after all, it's dreaming in Cuban – but of unhappy women's lives. That unhappiness is related to the separation which may occur between mothers and daughters living in the same country.

The fact that none of the characters prevail, that the story doesn't impose a precise or unique way of understanding identity, ideology or political position, comes perhaps from an equidistant attitude which places the narrative in the border. The non-linear structure, the construction of a feminine genealogy, the idea of nation not as a territory or discourse but as an affection (not the public but the private), also has to do with writing from a gendered border.

Gender concern is made explicit in *We Came All the Way from Cuba So You Could Dress like This?* A feminist attitude is displayed by characters who are often radical lesbians. The book's title, taken from one of the short stories, appeals to the Cuban issue, but the narratives have a wider focus: the Hispanic minority in the US. The switching into Spanish, less frequent than in *Dreaming in Cuban*, can also be considered as the use of a pertinent language, for the same purposes.

Homosexuality, AIDS, immigrants, discrimination, identity conflicts and drugs are subjects that enhance the narrative's border position, its marginality. The non-identification with the culture of origins – that of the parents in the last short story of the collection – and the sarcasm about the culture of adoption make this book an example of an ethnic literature, the Cubanamerican. The border position derives from a distanced, humorous perspective which undermines both the clichés of the highly industrialized world and the nationalistic, essential self, as well. This double vision, this inbetweenness of the permanent migrant could be, as Homi K. Bhabha concludes, 'the truest eye'.[16]

In 'Wrecks' the protagonist ironically says 'I am trying to be environmentally conscious' (p. 11), and, referring to cars, 'They provide this
very cool, very American answer to pain' (p. 14); while in 'The Spouse'
an argument arises between the recent immigrant Mexican and the
adapted one: 'You are running away from your Latin self...you need
me to remember all your real feelings, to remember passion, and maybe
think about motherhood and about music and poetry too', says the
former, while the latter answers him: 'Jesus, listen to that pile of stereotypes you just spit out. Passion? Poetry?' (p. 86).

Radical activism can also be something to be seen humorously: 'It'll be
the first time in months I'll be without an antiwar demonstration to go
to, a consciousness-raising group to attend, or a gay liberation meeting
to lead' (p. 121). In this statement by the last story's protagonist,
the enumeration of those long-formulated activities undermines their
seriousness.

A shifting position speaks of the mobility of the border as a disturb-
ance of the immobile, and this would include the clichés of the commercial appropriating of the 'other'. In 'Forever', for instance, the
protagonist laughs when she recognizes in a ceramic 'the siete poten-
cias, the pantheon of gods revered in santería. But these icons don't look
African, instead they are stereotypically Native American with feathers
and tomahawks' (p. 101). Thus, African-American-Indian!

The protagonist of the last short story, which gives its title to the
book, is a Cubanamerican character. As in *Dreaming in Cuban*, she is a
rebellious daughter who has moved away from her parents' political
position. Her questions about leaving Cuba, living in the United States
and her possible other destiny – not leaving the island nor living in the
United States – do not receive ideological answers, but answers that are
personal and intimate: 'I wonder if we'd stayed in then who, if anyone –
if not Martha and the boy from the military academy – would have been
my blond lovers, or any kind of lovers at all' (p.125).

The title 'We Came All the Way from Cuba So You Could Dress like
This?' speaks of difference, shifting and interrogation, three themes of
this short story as well as of the collection and probably of the border
position. The stories told – often with a rich sense of humour – are those
of homosexuals or bisexuals who are looking for harmonious relationships. This search, although permanent and futile, seems more important than political activism or public life:

Forget hunger, equality, environmentally correct bags; let's work to
eliminate heartbreak instead. Love, coupledom, the right person –

they are as anachronistic and elusive as Puerto Rican independence: everybody's for it, but no one's quite sure what it means or how to get it.

(p. 97)

As in *Dreaming in Cuban*, the private excels the public and the thinking of the nation in terms of identity; political discourse, history, nostalgia or memory – past, present and future – are linked with the personal. As in García's novel, the splitting and shifting of plot, characters and subjects reveal a border position, an inbetweenness which derives from the intermingling of Cuban and US cultural contexts, non-homogeneous and 'unstable points of suture'. Focusing directly on the Cuban/Cubanamerican issue, *Dreaming in Cuban* moves away from dogmatism or essentialism while *We Came All the Way from Cuba So You Could Dress like This?* opens up a broad range of Hispanic issues and characters. Both belong to the cultural phenomenon of cross-culturation and hybridization.

IV

One could conclude that one of the more visible differences between Cuban and Cubanamerican literatures is the passage to English in the latter, even though Spanish doesn't (and must not) completely disappear. Bearing this in mind, one could be tempted to compare Cubanamerican women's narrative with the Cuban island's women's fiction. One could even find other forms of cross-culturation, ones that go beyond territorial and cultural borders and have to do with other categories, such as gender. This process – replacing the concepts of homogeneous national cultures, the 'consensual or contiguous transmission of historical traditions or "organic" ethnic communities'[17] – is, as Homi Bhabha points out, one of the ways in which the redefining of the grounds of cultural comparativism takes place.

Though belonging to different contexts, then, Cuban and Cubanamerican women's texts can be seen to share a predominant interest in the personal and the emotional. In the island's most recent women's texts, for instance, public and collective issues – important subjects in the seventies and the eighties – have been substituted by private ones.[18] The canonical heterosexual couple has disappeared and the harmonious relationship now occurs within the absurd, the hallucination or reverie, or it is trivialized altogether. It seems that these writers also occupy a border space, that they do not wish to exist within the sanctified order, and suffer from a saturation of the official mainstream discourse about identity, homogeneity and unity: History and Heroes.

This kind of comparative study suggests that the nation is understood by women, on both sides of the Cuban-American hyphen, in a close relationship with personal experiences and always on the border of any monolithic, public concept of nation – such as territory, government, flag and other emblems. The splitting and shifting, while responding to specific contextual conditions, may also be the cross-cultural connection between these women writers, linked to Cuba in various ways. As well as charting the process of hybridization, then, Cuban and Cubanamerican literatures can also be usefully approached by focusing on categories such as gender and race.

Maybe I will have an opportunity to come all the way from Cuba to speak like this, and about this.

Part III
Internalized Exiles

8
Border Anxieties: Race and Psychoanalysis

David Marriott

> 'Je dirais que j'attends'
> Fanon (*Pn*, p. 97, *BS*, p. 120)[1]

I

How does one begin knowing it's in there all the time, looking for a way out?

In 1952, a Martiniquan philosopher, travelling to the Sorbonne in order to complete his philosophical training, is, according to the psychiatrist Frantz Fanon, 'already on guard' ['soit sur ses gardes'] before he steps off the boat (*Pn*, p. 118, *BS*, p. 145). To begin with, he has embarked on this journey after several years spent in the pursuit of his baccalaureate, without any sign of neurotic conflict. So what has produced this feeling of anxiety about the future awaiting him in France? Is it the uncertainty of what awaits him? Does the circle begin to close because of some real or imagined persecution? If we were to run through the stages of his anxiety, would we find the traces of some forgotten trauma lying buried in his past, enclosed within without ever being noticed, waiting, in suspense, for a way out? And is the fact that he's about to disembark onto mainland France – his advance destination – an arrival merely coincident to this unfolding of anxiety, or is France the place that awaits and expects it, its narrow threshold and probable cause?

Now, what fascinates Fanon is the fact that the philosopher's neurosis is not the result of a real event or traumatism. Nor is it simply a case of a delusion. For Fanon, the important thing is to lay bare how the sense of being on guard is already constituted by a negrophobia he identifies elsewhere in *Peau noire, masques blancs* as the fate awaiting blacks in France. To address this issue, Fanon turns to Freud's 1895 article, 'On the Grounds for Detaching a Particular Syndrome from Neurasthenia under the Description "Anxiety Neurosis"'.[2] This article, together with a lecture on anxiety written thirty years later, identified 'anxious expectation' or 'expectant dread' as the condition of neurotic anxiety at the foundation of phobia. For Fanon the relation between anxiety and phobia is essentially one of time, that is, present anxieties about the future are related to traumatic memories from the past. This is a relation at the limit or border between a negation of a former self and its future loss. But why is this temporal disorder at the origin of a phobic response to blacks, why is it directed in this way?

Analyzing this *border anxiety*, Fanon insists on its dissociative nature: the arrival in France, whether at Le Havre or Marseille, is not the cause of the philosopher's anxiety but its condition, a condition which can be neither avoided nor foreseen; but it is only precipitated by the entry into metropolitan France.[3] Fanon advances the idea that this anxiety is the derivative of a childhood aggressivity which, in the wake of racial tensions in the Antilles, is converted into a somatic fantasy of the black. This is what happens when black family life and culture are dominated by French colonial projections. The black child, contrary to expectation, learns to love himself insofar as he is white. However, at a certain moment, in this sacrificial dedication to whiteness, an inversion occurs by means of racism which produces a 'sensitizing' action or somatic anxiety in the black child: 'A normal negro child, having grown up within a normal family, will become abnormal on the slightest contact with the white world' (*Pn*, p. 117, *BS*, p. 143). This abnormality implies an impassable limit for the black child coming into contact with the white world, a limit reserved for him which he can neither transgress nor decline, and one instituted at the border of psyche and culture, fantasy and the real. This limit already speaks within the black self due to the penetration of cultural racism and its resonances in erotic and phobic fantasies of black sexuality. When entering this white world the black child, like the philosopher arriving in France, has already adopted a white subjective attitude inherited from the somatic anxieties and fantasies of Martiniquan culture and the latter's deep complicity with French racism. The child will come to discover himself anew through this encounter, an encounter in which he will not recognize his former white (black) self, because it will be only after this conscious recognition of himself as a *nègre* in France that he will recognize his former self for what it was: an unconscious and cultural fantasy combining regional ontologies of racial hierarchy, of proper being, with a metropolitan mythology of civilization and savagery, foreignness and impropriety.

The black body – as sign or symbolization – thus leads to an ambivalence in the white-identified black child, for it has become the 'epidermalization' of a social inferiority at the limits of his own hostility and self-love (*Pn*, p. 8, *BS*, p. 11). The imaginary dislocations of this colonial psychodrama thus stand revealed: the black self has never been present to itself other than as white, and never will be; the black psyche is that which cannot be presented in the space of this truth, that which cannot lend itself to being beyond this denegation, this limit which is out of time, and whose 'sacrificial dedication' to whiteness has not yet been received. The philosopher will soon be made to know that his arrival is 'predestined' even though, unconsciously, he already knows it. His arrival will have the effect of a revelation of what he has been for a long time without knowing it. He knows this will be the case and he also knows why this revelation will be intolerable. In other words, the child's past fixation on being white is in conflict with the image of himself he sees reflected back. From this cultural injunction, anxiety is born. On the one hand, he knows now what he has been; but, on the other hand, he doesn't know how to deal with this new image of himself as *nègre*. Confronted with the insufferable void of black abjection, he fortifies himself with a negrophobia as a defence against anxiety: the black signifier turned devouring (in a psychic process wherein the former self is consumed, eaten, used up). Negrophobia is thus an attempt to free the self from this anxiety by reviving the original hostility and directing it onto other blacks.

Elsewhere in *Peau noire*, Fanon writes enigmatically, and almost as if in autobiographical proof of this doubling duplicity: 'Je suis un nègre – mais naturellement je ne le sais pas, puisque je le suis' ('I am a negro – but of course I do not know it, simply because I am one') (*Pn*, p. 155, *BS*, p. 191). Thus formulated, the being of the black can not be where it is but must erase itself, must vanish in the truth of a predestined negation, all the while conserved and repressed on the border of an anxiety which it can neither subsume nor resist and whose temporalization takes on the form of a deferral and adestination.[4] To be black in racist France is thus to have a psyche which is adestined, regressed and reversed; it is to have an unconscious circumscribed by an impassable border or limit. But perhaps this adestination and this (non) arrival are nothing but two differing responses to the same anxieties: anxiety about confronting the racial deliria the philosopher knows await him; anxiety about the dissolution of his ego, destined to be effaced by the phobias and imagos attached to both his heredity and inheritance; anxiety about being unable to detach himself from these primordial fantasies whose provocation consists in designating the black as always 'arriving too late'. For Fanon, this belated arrival remains a fundamental symbol of black non-being: in lines taken as an epigraph to this paper he writes: 'If I were asked for a definition of myself, I would say that I am one who waits' ('je dirais que j'attends') (*Pn*, p. 97, *BS*, p. 120).[5]

What, then, is Fanon's thinking on this pre-empted (non) arrival, and what might it tell us of the mutual imbrication of psychoanalysis and race?

The above anecdote occurs in the celebrated sixth chapter of *Peau noire, masques blancs* (1952), on 'Le Nègre et la psychopathologie'. This chapter, including as it does readings of both white *and* black phobic responses to the imago of the *nègre*, confirms Fanon's complex encounter with psychoanalytic approaches to time and consecution, trauma and symptom. Fanon's incorporation of psychoanalytic theory into his psychiatric practice is not simply a question of borrowing but one of transformation or translation. This incorporation was based on a decision: not only did he choose to question the universality of oedipal neuroses, but he also refused the rigid connection between the family and social consciousness. These two refusals consisted in an acknowledgement of the colonial influence on kinship and social ties. Anxious to understand the impact of culture on the unconscious – how racial subjects learn internal and external interdictions – Fanon was intent upon producing a psychoanalytic psychiatry of racial fantasy. Fanon's goal was to go beyond Freud or Adler by clarifying the notion of a racial or cultural unconscious in the Antilles. It was an initiative designed to 'lay bare the anomalies of affect' ('les anomalies affectives') (*Pn*, pp. 7–8, *BS*, p. 10) at the origin of white racial fears and black alienation. As such, before and beyond any judgement on Fanon's use or understanding of psychoanalysis in *Peau noire*, it is not fortuitous that he should include this anecdote on the 'neurotic fate' (*Pn*, p. 8, *BS*, p. 10) of a black entering France; or that his entire filiation to psychoanalysis should be charted with reference to either neurosis or phobia.[6]

If the unconscious dynamics of racism are linked through black anxiety and white guilt, how is one to account for the double bind of this imaginary identification with its disjunctive exclusions, loving hatreds and neurotic gifts of self? In this essay, I will be seeking to restore the question of phobia and anxiety – so crucial to Fanon – to the *via regia* or royal road of racist fantasy. This essay is therefore, in part, an exploration of the complex inheritance of Fanon's encounter with French postwar readings of Freud. In the readings that follow, and in order to lead us back to Fanon's unembarrassed encounter with phobic neurosis, my point of departure and arrival will be generated by what he says in 'Le Nègre et la psychopathologie'.

II

In this innovative chapter on what he terms 'négro-phobogénèse', Fanon cites several case histories of white phobic patients for whom blacks act as anxiety-producing, phobogenic objects. In an effort to grasp what is, in fact, at stake in this convergence of unconscious anxieties, racist fantasies and projections in which blacks recur as psychic substitutes, or phantoms absolving or defending against white instinctual conflicts and sadistic, aggressive impulses, Fanon introduces an analysis of phobia in three parts: the paralogical nature of phobic thinking, its links to imaginary aggression, and its hallucinatory and affective structure. All three elements are in dialogue with what has become known as Freud's second theory of anxiety, as recounted in Angelo Hesnard's *L'univers morbide de la faute* (1949), and Charles Odier's *L'angoisse et la pensée magique* (1947).

According to Hesnard: 'Phobia is a neurosis characterized by the anxious fear of an object (in the broadest sense of anything outside the individual) or, by extension, of a situation' (*Pn*, pp. 125–6, *BS*, p. 154). Certainly, what are feared are the temptations of forbidden ideas and the anxieties they provoke, released anxieties which the ego tries to bind by finding an external substitute or phobogenic object. In fact, the gist of Fanon's entire argument is that the onset of phobia does not simply derive from some original real traumatism ('traumatisme effectif') (*Pn*, p. 118, *BS*, p. 145), but from an inner attack by the drives resulting in the ego's inhibition of anxiety.[7] According to Freud, in regard to phobias: 'it is always the ego's attitude of anxiety which is the primary thing and which sets repression going'.[8] At the origin of phobias is thus the ego's flight from a libidinal conflict into regression, a flight which appears retroactively through the substitution of an 'outer danger' for a dreaded internal conflict.[9] In this example of what Odier terms 'paralogical' or magical thinking – representing a dissociation or splitting of affects and ideas – Fanon suggests a comparison with the 'facade' of manifest dreams, for phobias also reveal mechanisms of displacement, substitution and condensation. In the hallucinatory nature of phobic projections, internal fears – the loss of love or threat of castration – are transformed into external persecutions by real substitute objects. As Odier points out: 'the phobic patient . . . objectifies his fear of reality by projecting into reality the aggression which is the positive completive attribute of his negative affect'.[10]

Fanon would little by little discover that this aggression is brought to the fore in a racist social imaginary. Taking his cue from Freud concerning the birth of phobias in 'phylogenetic inheritance',[11] Fanon asked why blacks are the 'predestined depositories' of sadistic racial aggression, which superimposes phobic formations upon fantasmatic and real violence? What is this *fixation* upon the imago of the black body in white pathogenic fears? Is the transformation of instinctual into perceptual fears in negrophobia the sign of a more original event to which it has become falsely connected? In the course of asking these questions in *Peau noire*, Fanon reexamined racial phobias as a problem of identification, that is to say, the problem of incorporating the other inside the self via the substitution of a fear of the real by a real fear.

Two epigrams, or formulae, offer a clear sense of Fanon's development of these insights: 'Le nègre est un objet phobogène, anxiogène' ('The negro is a phobogenic object, anxiogenic') (*Pn*, p. 123, *BS*, p. 151 amended); and 'Avoir la phobie du nègre, c'est avoir peur du biologique' ('To suffer from a phobia of the negro, is to be afraid of the biological') (*Pn*, p. 134, *BS*, p. 165). At the mere sight of or contact with the imago of the black, therefore, the negrophobe undergoes an 'imaginary aggression' ('agression imaginaire') (*Pn*, p. 131, *BS*, p. 161) intimately tied to a fear or revulsion of his own drive impulses and instinctual incitements. In this imaginary identification, the ego responds to the fear or anxiety of being destroyed from within by an internal foreign body as if confronted by a malevolent object outside itself. It is an identificatory interdiction that, in the first place, operates through the expenditure of white neurotic conflict onto black substitutes, and one that allows the displacement or avoidance of repressed thoughts or traumatic memories. These projections have a cultural past, or history, incorporating blacks as symbolic representatives of the primordial (sexual) instincts. In this sense the phobic object acts as a psychic prosthesis or support within the space of the white body: it allows the pleasurable excitement of the offensive idea both to escape repression and to remain unconscious, whilst presenting a way out of ambivalence for the white subject.[12] Secondly, Fanon suggests that the fear and revulsion evoked by negroes refers to a primal impasse – scene or fantasy – in the future becoming, or future articulation of, white and black corporeal schemas. Finally, the colonial past, in the form of 'cultural impositions', intrudes and fixates upon the black body as the corporeal sign of dirt, sin and excreta, an insignia for which white phobic anxiety appears to be already destined: 'At the extreme... the Negro, because of his body, impedes the closing of the postural schema of the White' (*Pn*, p. 130, *BS*, p. 160, amended).

Perhaps the shift here is from a corporeal to a 'racial-epidermal' schema, but the point is that once there is a 'sadistic aggression' ('agressivité sadique') (*Pn*, p. 143, *BS*, p. 177) toward the imago of the black at the level of both culture and affect, this corporeal malediction cannot be simply avoided; the black body has become, 'along roads that we know, the predestined depository ['le dépositaire prédestiné'] of this aggression' (*Pn*, p. 145, *BS*, p. 179). The violent character of this sadism gives rise to anxiety and guilt. Similarly it is no longer relevant to ask whether 'Fanon attempts too close a correspondence between the *mise-en-scène* of unconscious fantasy and the phantoms of racist fear and hate'.[13] There is no mimetic relationship between white neurotic conflict and anti-black racial aggression, at least in terms of Fanon's reading of phobia, nor is the predestined nature of this imaginary aggression anything more than a container for that which infects or inhabits it. Rather, introducing the term 'collective catharsis', Fanon argues that in every society there is always a 'channel, an outlet through which the forces accumulated in the form of aggression can be released' (*Pn*, p. 118, *BS*, p. 145). This channel cannot be solely contained within a *mise-en-scène* of representation because, for the phobic, a dimension of the real superimposes itself on this internal fear by which he feels aggressed. Fanon underlines how this malformity of the black enigma or thing is experienced as a violent intrusion within the corporeal edifice of the phobic. In 'Le Nègre et la psychopathologie', Fanon not only defines the phenomenology of this intrusion but how unconscious and cultural hatred is fixed into place by the psychic work of negrophobia. Racist anxiety is frozen in the phobic symptom as a defence against the dark 'thing' that waits.

In fact, it is not the imaginary nature of this aggression, nor its corporeal embrace of neurosis and imago, that interests me the most here. In order to trace the frontier between white fantasies of somatic contagion and unconscious self-mutilation, phobic anxiety and racial guilt, the question arises in Fanon as to whether this sadism conceals a more primary masochistic impulse:

> Another solution might be this: There is first of all a sadistic aggression toward the black man, followed by a guilt complex because of the sanction against such behaviour by the democratic culture of the country in question [the United States]. This aggression is then

tolerated by the Negro: whence masochism. But, I shall be told, your schema is invalid: It does not contain the elements of classic masochism. Perhaps, indeed, this situation is not classic. In any event, it is the only way in which to explain the masochistic behaviour of the white man.

(Pn, p. 143, *BS*, pp. 177–8)

So sadistic fantasies towards blacks represent a tendency to white 'auto-castration' *(Pn*, p. 143, *BS*, p. 177) in the paralogical thinking of the phobic. The erotic components of this masochism, given the cultural symbolization of the black male as a sexual aggressor, receive direction, and become psychically effective, through the imago of the black as a phobic, genital object.[14] It is because this imaginary aggression is invariably culturally mediated – through symbolic and institutional law as well as somatic fantasies and acts of literal violence – that white imaginary self-mutilation can be insistently focused through the real spectacle of black dismemberment: 'There is a quest for the black, the black is in demand, one cannot get along without him' *(Pn*, p. 142, *BS*, p. 176, amended).[15] Hence, racial sadism is never simply aggression but an imaginary disarticulation of the self transferred onto the bodily imago of the other. Thus, to the extent that white and black anxiety represents the experience of being grasped by the force of this symbolization, and to the extent that corporeal schema can neither resist nor avoid this imposition in terms that I will go on to describe, both white and black sado-masochistic fantasies are foreclosed by the imago of the double.

III

The psychic working through of this 'aggression against aggression'[16] can be observed in two of Fanon's case histories of negrophobic white women. In the first, Fanon analyzes the fantasy of 'a negro is raping me'.

First the little girl sees a sibling rival beaten by the father, a libidinal aggressive. At this stage (between the ages of five and nine), the father, who is now the pole of her libido, refuses in a way to take up the aggression that the little girl's unconscious demands of him. At this point, lacking support, this free-floating aggression requires an investment. Since the girl is at the age in which the child begins to enter the folklore and the culture along roads that we know, the Negro becomes the predestined depository of this aggression. If we penetrate further ['pénétrons davantage dans'] into the labyrinth, we notice that when a woman lives the fantasy of rape by a Negro, it is in some way the production ['la réalisation'] of a private ['personnel'] dream, of an inner ['intime'] wish. Accomplishing the phenomenon of turning against self, it is the woman who rapes herself ['qui se viole'].

(Pn, p. 144–5, BS, p. 179, amended)

It is not easy to understand what is being solicited or incorporated here, nor why the transferential destination of a private dream, or inner wish, should be so elusively transitive.[17] At first sight, Fanon's commentary appears to be an illustration of the psychoanalytic formula for simple phobias: 'what a person fears, he unconsciously wishes for'.[18] The formula suggests that phobic fear is expressed directly in the inhibition. But the structure of evasion and containment on display here appears to be driven by something that the girl does not want, something persecutory or properly intolerable for her, and which, moreover, is the source of a failed demand to the father to take up, or liberate. Implying that the source of the girl's anxiety lies in the way the father withholds or withdraws himself, Fanon condenses several different things: an unendurable isolation linked to a need for a reassurance of paternal love, and hostility towards the father triggered by a sense of feeling rejected by him and its denial in the form of guilt. On this basis, there may be an equivalence between the flight from her own impulses and external dangers (aggression against the mother as rival, loss of paternal love), and the turn to the father as a way out of this aggressive tension. Failing to secure imaginary satisfaction for these internal instinctual conflicts, her need for a substitute arises, and one whose symbolic form is obvious both in the real and in the psyche. The evolution of the fantasy therefore demands a corporeal signifier onto which libido and aggression can be projected with the added advantage of securing the father's desire without any sanction – this fantasy demands the black male. Thus, although the fantasy comes in the wake of libidinal aggression and paternal refusal, the girl's vengeful masochism, in this instance, also derives from an unconscious demand addressed to the father.

Unfortunately what is being posted here is a transfer of persecutory anxiety onto a network of correspondences indentifying rape with black men; a postal network which contains not only introjected elements sampled from negrophobic fears and oedipal desires, but also drive-anxiety elements regarding the internal menace of too much instinctual excitation. The cultural logic that declares 'whoever says rape says negro' (*Pn*, p. 134, *BS*, p. 166) ensures that this inhibition of sexual or aggressive drives will be both contained and anaesthetized, however fatal this inner dream or private wish may prove to be for those black men who could not, without retribution, refuse this demand. In the dynamics of positionality and address which typified the sadistic staging of lynching scenes, for example, the black male's refusal was essentially oxymoronic given that the main performative of these scenes was an identification between blackness and sexual guilt. In these scenes a most extreme unity of law and dream is literally incarnated through the mutilated body of the black male.

The question is: does Fanon's reading, in its abyssal indistinction between fantasy and sadomasochistic wish, paternal refusal and unconscious demand, not reproduce an equally problematic transference onto the white girl's desire for rape?[19] And does this inversion and reversal not raise the further issue of what precisely is being sent here from the facade of unconscious aggressivity and negrophobic dreams into the traffic of cultural life?[20] To answer these questions, recent readings of Fanon have tended to focus on his own oblique departure and evacuation from those transferential adestinations, those interior switching points of unconscious anxiety and sadomasochistic wishes or aims. Thus, Bhabha writes:

> In chapter 6 he attempts a somewhat more complex reading of masochism but in making the Negro the '*predestined* depository of this aggression'...he again pre-empts a fuller psychoanalytic discussion of the production of psychic aggressivity in identification and its relation to cultural difference by citing the cultural stereotype as the predestined aim of the sexual drive. Of the woman of colour he has very little to say. 'I know nothing about her,' he writes in *Black Skin, White Masks*. This crucial issue requires an order of psychoanalytic argument that goes well beyond my foreword. I have therefore chosen to note the importance of the problem rather than to elide it in a facile charge of 'sexism'.[21]

Whenever Fanon proposes that the unconscious actually *arrives* in culture – whether as phobia, fantasy or amputated affect – Bhabha, on the other hand, disposes, proposing a time-lag of difference between the spectacle or stadia of unconscious *mise-en-scène* and the cultural states of fantasy. Bhabha's premise is this: the cultural states of fantasy will not be overrun by the imaginary amputees or imagos of unconscious aggression, for the stereotype is culture's last defence against the predestined aim of the sexual drive. But if the relay of fantasy and violence between stadia and station is *predestined only insofar as it is adestined*, that it arrives only insofar as it arrives too late, is it not pre-emptive to situate unconscious fantasy as the place where cultural forms of fantasy never arrive at all? In many ways, of course, unconscious fantasies are already possessed by the real, in the way that racist cultures can be said to arrive on the royal road of the dream, at the intersection of the imago, stereotype and *mise-en-scène*, and yet neither ahead of the dreamwork nor simply what is outside it in the real.[22]

This arrival is at the heart of Fanon's dissatisfactions with psychoanalysis for setting up an affective mimesis between family environments and individual neuroses. We have already seen the way in which European culture fixates or forecloses upon the imago of the double. In Europe, Fanon insists, it is the family circle which presents to the child, for the first time, a 'sick' discourse of the racialized black body, its instinctual danger and its contagious affect (*Pn*, p. 117, *BS*, p. 143). And it is by means of this discourse of the polluted body that European neurosis first proclaims itself. If, therefore, there is an indissociable knot between the imago of the black and the girl's negrophobic fantasy, what part does the father's desire play in her sadomasochistic desire and the libidinal satisfactions which the fantasy brings? Is it the case (and I only point this out speculatively and in passing) that the girl's phobic symptom is itself a divisible body, oedipally amputated into a good and bad body? Here, the transitivity of Fanon's own analysis seems to vacillate over whether the girl's spectatorship of the rival being beaten is something sadistic or sexual that she identifies with, or whether the idea of being beaten by the father is something from which her own sadistic and libidinal desire for the father is allowed to emerge. Better put, it is not clear where, in this scene of a sibling rival being beaten, stimulation ends and gratification begins.

This brings us to Fanon's second negrophobic case history, in 'Le Nègre et la psychopathologie', of a white adolescent girl. At the psychiatric hospital of Saint-Ylie, Mlle B, aged 19, is admitted suffering from 'a nervous disease consisting of periods of agitation, motor instability, tics, and spasms which are conscious but which she cannot control' (*Pn*, p. 165, *BS*, p. 204). It is soon revealed that this nervous condition began at the age of 10 and had become aggravated by the onset of puberty at 16. We also learn that Mlle B. has suffered intermittent periods of depression and anxiety, closely followed by a renewal of the somatic symptoms. According to the ward nurse: 'It is worst when she is alone. When she is talking with others, or is merely with them, it is less noticeable' (*Pn*, p. 165, *BS*, p. 205). Mlle B. was also often heard uttering sounds or loud, inarticulate cries which ceased when she was spoken to.

The psychiatrist in charge decides to arrest these tics by employing waking dream therapy. A preliminary interview reveals the existence of hallucinations in which the patient is surrounded by circles over an abyss. The edges of these circles contract and expand according to the rhythm of tom-toms, a syncopation that reminds Mlle B. of 'the danger of losing her parents, especially her mother' (*Pn*, p. 166, *BS*, p. 205). Furthermore, a fearful group of black men is dancing within what are now broken circles before a fire. They are threatening to burn a half-dressed white man who later disappears. Moreover, this threat consumes itself after the intervention of the dreamer's guardian angel. Mlle B. then enters into the broken circle over the abyss because she wants to 'know the chief', to hold hands with the negroes and to dance.

In his commentary on this case history, Fanon suggests that the circles represent, unconsciously and symbolically, a defence mechanism against the racial hallucinosis. Fanon takes the broken edges of these circles to denote a borderline or switching point between Mlle B.'s psychoneurotic symptom and her phobic fears. In this waking dream there is thus a circular regression from the ego and its defences to the underlying psychic conflict and infantile dangers involved. The phobic symptom that emerges betrays the essential asymmetry between these two elements of the circuit, a closed loop of discourse between the frightening sexual excitement of the negro and Mlle B.'s own persecutory fears and anxiety concerning parental abandonment and loss. Mlle B.'s response to the lure of the tom-toms suffices to awaken a need which threatens to overwhelm her; the onset of her anxiety is the result of this mental conflict, as are the bodily symptoms which signify their resistance to this excess, a resistance reconstituted and disguised, and ultimately transformed, through inhibition, into a phobic signifier projected onto blacks. It is at this point that the object of the father's desire – the tom-tom – expresses itself, radiating outwards into the black mirror of her dreams.

> When she was ten or twelve years old, her father, 'an old-timer in the Colonial Service', liked to listen to programs of Negro music. The tom-tom echoed through their house every evening, long after she had gone to bed...Lying in bed and hearing the tom-toms, she virtually *saw* Negroes. She sought refuge under the covers, trembling. Then smaller and smaller circles appeared, scotomizing ['scotomisai-

ent'] the negroes...Later, the circles appeared without the Blacks –
the defense mechanism came into play without knowing its cause.

(*Pn*, p. 168, *BS*, p. 208, amended)

This music, the sign and object of paternal desire, appears destined to
engulf or consume her; in it, she not only hears the veiled, savage
presence of the black imago, she also *sees* her own oral-sadistic fantasies
and desires unveiled, cannibal fantasies or desires which she fears will
destroy both parental objects. It seems that in Mlle B.'s waking dream,
the tom-tom is the object of a persecutory anxiety in which desire itself
becomes terrifying. Her dread of desire appears to be communicated
through the sounds of those drums and black voices gathered about
her, their loud proclamations laying siege to her, through sensual
advance and through a deluge of orgiastic rhythms. And, although it
is far from clear what the circles signify, they seem to be doing the work
of binding, inhibition and reparation for Mlle B. who 'sees' in the
imaginary speech of the drums her worst fears realized. Fanon concludes: 'Even when one concedes a constitutional factor here, it is
clear that her alienation is the result of a fear of the Negro, a fear
encouraged by determining circumstances' (*Pn*, pp. 168–9, *BS*, p. 209,
amended). No doubt it would be worth investigating more fully those
'determining circumstances' – the paternal rhythm and its signifying
pulsion in the dream; the symbolic relationship of the white man about
to be burned to the desirable (good-enough?) chief, and to Mlle B.
possessed by the drums; or that violated circular line or border between
desire and need – but one can only surmise as to their role in the phobic
projections and racial dreaming of Mlle B.

IV

What Fanon's two case histories thus allow us to reconsider is his exact
relation to psychoanalysis and the psychoneuroses. In both case histories the formation of the phobic symptom appears as an aggression
against an apparition or hallucination of the black – the black in so far as
the latter is understood to present himself as the genital, the biological,
or the rapist. To hit out at this blackness of the black in order to cure
symbolic castration, to hit out at it on the imaginary plane of the imago,
is the path the negrophobic chooses to abolish the pathogenic nature of
certain ideas, and to restore, for him or her, the paternal love object to
the primacy of desire – but at the price of a degradation of the black in
the imaginary elision of an instinctual conflict. It is in so far as the

phobic is at this precise point of ambivalence that his relationship to the imago of the double – an always metonymical object – is essentially governed by something which has a relationship to castration and which here takes on a directly aggressive form: this refusal of the black aiming both at an abolition of the black's desire, and a rejection of him as a contagious sign. And it is from this that there emerges the particular impasse of the phobic who is not at all freed from the underlying conflicts but only of the guilt and anxiety that pertained to them.

Thus, in 'Le Nègre et la psychopathologie', Fanon has tried to articulate the special emergence of the phobic symptom through an imaginary fantasy of the black, and how the meaning of this symptom takes place through an imaginary introjection of cultural elements, which is very precisely incarnated in the dream work in so far as this cryptomnesia reveals itself to analysis. It is, moreover, from this white fear and revulsion of the black that Fanon situates an entire symptomology of real fantasies ('phantasmes réels') (*Pn*, p. 86, *BS*, p. 106).[23]

To be a black subject is to be the locus of these fantasies at the precise point where the subject vanishes, no longer recognizes itself, is symbolically produced, unveiled and rendered invisible by racial phantasms. What is produced instead is the mirage of white narcissism which comes to occupy the black psyche through cultural imposition, a mirage and imposition which manifests itself in the black child as 'a sacrificial dedication ['oblativité'] permeated with sadism',[24] and, in the white, as a defusion of aggressive drives expressed through an outside situation, amid the cultural imagos of phobia (*Pn*, p. 120, *BS*, p. 147). This is why Fanon states that, for the black man 'there is only one destiny. And it is white' (*Pn*, p. 8, *BS*, p. 10). Here, in the movement of his very discourse, Fanon designates a psychic elision or caesura, an endpoint or termination, wherein the black subject disappears from view. As regards this little allegory of the signifier, *Peau noire* repeatedly directs our attention to the affects of its destiny. In the story of the Martiniquan philosopher, for example, the shadow of elision was already beginning to form itself through the birth of a neurotic symptom. At the horizon of this philosopher's experience, there was a certain fear or anxious expectation concerning his destiny, or future, and one destined to reveal the limits of himself in France. In the interstices of this delimitation, the imago of the phobic object enters into the subject, converting the trajectory of his desire from an imaginary coherence into a prosthesis, supplement or deferred affect. The symptomatic consequences of this delimitation can be traced throughout 'Le Nègre et la psychopathologie', if not *Peau noire, masques blancs*, through the figure of cryptomnesia – a decoding of loss and its psychic affect whose traces continue to affect the present and the coming future. This, then, is the etiological structure of racial neurosis according to Fanon – it represents a complicity between whites and blacks to dream only in so far as they project.

All Fanon's difficulties with psychoanalysis are resumed in this: the place of the black and the white in relation to the phobic signifier *is not the same*, but reflects a profound antinomy which psychoanalysis has been slow to address. Despite this inhibition, in his own attempts at an analysis of the mirage of white narcissism and the hallucinosis of the black, Fanon states, without reservation: 'I believe that only a psycho-analytical interpretation of the black problem can lay bare the anomalies of affect ['anomalies affectives'] that are responsible for the structure of the complex' (*Pn*, pp. 7–8, *BS*, p. 10). It is for that reason that Fanon may be considered a 'purveyor of the transgressive and transitional truth'.[25] It is at the border where all racial subjects fail to arrive that Fanon calls forth a new horizon of possibility and a new language of demand and desire, a place where Fanon's cultural politics of the uncon-scious may well be reclaimed for a new epoch.

9
Nationalism's Brandings: Women's Bodies and Narratives of the Partition

Sujala Singh

As the official Partition of India in 1947 was negotiated by 'nationalist' leaders on all sides, large segments of the population underwent violent dislocations across what was to become the Indo-Pakistani border. These journeys of Hindus to India and Muslims to Pakistan left in their wake a series of horrific mutilations suffered by people in cities, small towns and villages, in their homes and on their bodies. Women's bodies often became the markers on which the painful scripts of contending nationalisms (Hindu, Muslim or Sikh) were inscribed. In response to the mass rapes and abductions on both sides of the border, and in order to legislate a 'fair' exchange of abducted women across borders, the governments of India and Pakistan signed the Inter-Dominion Treaty in 1947 (later to become the Abducted Persons Act in 1949) 'among the first agreements between the otherwise hostile nations'.[1]

Urvashi Butalia sketches the ironies and presumptions behind these exchanges. She observes that such legislation, which sets out to rescue women and restore them into the bosom of the nation to which they 'naturally' belonged, was crucial to the very consolidation and definition of the fledgling nation states: 'For the postcolonial, deeply contested, fragile and vulnerable State, the rescue operation was an exercise in establishing its legitimacy.'[2]

The fiction written about the Partition (mostly in regional languages) is rife with the uncertainty and carnage of the times. One of the horrific symptoms of the violence referred to in the stories is the rape and abduction of women. Whether it be through rumours, a looming fear or dread about the possible threat of rape, or its actual description, stories about the Partition return repeatedly to the violence or potential violence done to women. My essay focuses on a short novella by Amrita Pritam called *Pinjar* (The Skeleton) and discusses the fraught intersections between rape, narrative, violence and nation-ness.[3] But before I move on to discuss the representation of Partition rapes and the subsequent rescue operations in fiction, I will briefly outline the various mechanisms for regulating, constituting and producing the legal parameters of women-as-subjects set forth in the acts of legislation mentioned above. I will then look closely at some critical and historiographic debates about the problems of representing and retrieving violence. These frameworks will make it possible to explore the ideological binds that produce and permeate Pritam's text.

Despite India's definition of itself as secular, Hindu and Sikh women were to be returned to India and Muslim women to Pakistan. Emphasis was laid on maintaining the equality of numbers of women to be exchanged while women's wishes in the matter were considered irrelevant. It was decided that children born as a consequence of abductions and rapes would be considered war babies and were to be left behind in the countries where they were born. For ten years after independence, the fates of these women remained an issue of debate between the two countries. Veena Das contends that 'this interest in women was not premised upon their definition as citizens but as sexual and reproductive beings'.[4] She cites as an example the paranoia in Constituent Assembly debates over the issue of India returning women of all ages while Pakistan returned only old women or little children. The obsessive legal bargaining over women's bodies highlights the anxieties of nations searching for secure self-representations, even as the nations celebrated the end of colonialism.

I

Recent articles dealing with women and Partition record the invested silences of both colonial and nationalist versions of history when they document the everyday torments of migrating populations in general, and of women in particular. According to Gyanendra Pandey, 'history tends to produce a prose of Otherness'.[5] He contends that Indian historiography often mimics the procedures and methodologies of colonialist historiography in that violence is always sidelined and relegated to the margins, the spaces of the 'Other'. There are several strands to his argument. By setting itself up as the arbiter and manager of 'native' violence and insurgencies, the colonialist state naturalized the violence of its own strategic bureaucratic legalities and counter-insurgency manoeuvres. Not only did the postcolonial states inherit this legacy, postcolonial historians too learned the lessons of writing histories of the

State in an attempt to record the progressive march of modernity and nationalism, thus perpetuating 'the violence involved in making national histories, like nations, appear natural'. Pandey comments on the rhetoric of otherness that infused the speeches of Nehru and Gandhi as they invoked, for instance, the natural proclivity to violence of rebellious tribes, and finds such prose in the language of contemporary historians describing the 'pent up forces of disorder'. While, on the one hand, Pandey charts these disturbing complicities and patterns of co-incidence, on the other, he wonders about the (im)possibilities of representing violence:

> The historian seeking to represent violence in history faces problems of language (how, for example, does one describe pain and suffering?), of analytical stance (how can one be 'objective' and express suffering at the same time?), and of evidence (for does not large-scale violence destroy much of its most direct evidence?). There is the associated question of how the moment of violence comes to be recorded by the state or by 'neutral' observers, how it becomes part of an archive, and how it is integrated into a larger history by the historian.[6]

These cogent questions accentuate the difficulties of mediating a relationship between the private and the public. Ritu Menon and Kamla Bhasin, in a more forgiving vein than Pandey, write of the 'pain' of representing private violences into the structures of public discourse:

> Perhaps it has been too painful, too difficult to separate personal experience from corroborated fact...too hazardous, at least for those who tried to record it, to claim objectivity.[7]

To the silencing operations of the State and the historiographers, Urvashi Butalia adds the silence of the survivors, the 'real' women whose memories may have helped construct an alternative history:

> Accounts of survivors mention these details only in a fairly general sort of way, for they are difficult to articulate particularly because of the stigma they continue to carry. Women will not speak of them, nor will families...[8]

The management of violence into or out of the annals of public memory is thus crucially hinged upon the separation of the sphere of its effects, the private world of the victims and agents. This partition is not just enforced by the sensitivity of the individuals who record the pain of the victims. In parallel with the managerial stratagems of the overarching community of Statehood, the families and immediate community of the violated women marshal the enunciation of such terms. Veena Das explains the necessity for maintaining these 'veils of silence', the 'unspoken censorship on speech' by communities which accepted abducted women, 'so that kinship norms of purity and honor could be strategically manipulated to allow the fallen woman's reabsorption into traditional networks'.[9]

The juxtaposition of the excesses of the rhetoric of the State against the weave of silences outlined above becomes a crucial strategy for Butalia, Das, Pandey, Bhasin and Menon, not only in locating the significant gaps in history writing but also in accentuating the difficulties of attempting re-constructions, of filling in the gaps, as it were. So what kinds of sources can these critics have recourse to in order to provide alternative ways of perceiving and recording these unspeakable, untold histories?

Besides details of the obsessive legal bargaining between the two nations, their sources include personal testimonies and memoirs by survivors and female social workers like Kamlabehn Patel and Anis Qidwai who were responsible for monitoring a fair and efficient exchange. Urvashi Butalia prefaces an issue of *Seminar* devoted to Partition narratives by stating that the interviews and memoirs 'foreground another archive and provide "another" history of this major event'. She then proceeds to outline problems of oral narrative, unreliable memory, nuances lost through transcriptions, and asks the question, 'how then does the interviewer ensure an honest interview?'[10] The dilemma of the critic in this situation thus becomes one of being caught in the double bind of the necessity of re-presentations even as she stumbles upon the impossibilities of such a project. As they foreground issues of representation, not only do these critics focus on the mediated nature of the oral testimonies they employ, they are also careful to name themselves and their stakes in the projects that they undertake, whether it be through family memories, their involvement in the women's movement or a framing from the perspective of contemporary riots. Thus, both issues of representation *and* the impossibility of definitive retrievals remain significant to their projects. As they reveal the processes that go into the retrieval, recording, collating and writing of history, processes that fail to represent the grief of the women, in particular, whether by the nature of the discipline itself, or by the agents who relate or those who record, these critics attempt to guard against authoritative universalisms in the modes of history writing that they critique and are careful to demarcate the necessary limitations of their own projects.

It is interesting to note, however, that even as they critique the closures of the historiographic narratives and recognize the absences that such accounts enforce, they seem to suggest that literature might be able to breach this repression. In a curious reversal of the traditional binarism which valorizes history as the realm of the real, of facts, removed from the world of fiction, of imaginative fancy, these scholars hail the efforts of writers to document what history has failed to document. According to Pandey:

> In part because of the way in which the historiographical agenda has been constructed, and in part because the historian's craft has never been particularly comfortable with such matters, the horror of Partition, the anguish and sorrow, pain and brutality of the 'riots' of 1946–47 has been left almost entirely to creative writers and film-makers.[11]

Bhasin and Menon hold history to be guilty of not confronting the trauma and anguish of private lives and claim that 'so far only some fiction seems to have tried to assimilate the enormity of this experience'.[12] Veena Das, too, shares a similar sympathy for the heroic role of the creative imagination in coping with the grief whose silencing is so widespread:

> although...we failed to produce a national discourse (or perhaps succeeded in repressing one from emerging), those dealing with this trauma in the imaginative mode did not fail their society and their times.[13]

Thus, in these accounts, literature has the methodology, the freedom, the form, the honesty, the daring, and is more able to cope with the grief and the excess spilled over from history's repressive agenda. However, it is striking to find how these critics, so anxious to define their positions as history's representers, slip into using fiction as 'reality'. With the exception of Veena Das, none of these scholars engage with literature in any detail in their writings.[14] For instance, after paraphrasing Manto's short story, 'Toba Tek Singh', Pandey merely comes to the somewhat trite conclusion, 'in this time of "madness", it was only the insane who retained any sanity'.[15] Urvashi Butalia retells another Manto story, 'Open Up' ('Khol Do'), only to conclude 'Sakina's story was not uncommon at the time of partition'.[16] As questions of narrative are asked of history, but not of fiction, fiction almost becomes the desired 'Other' of history.[17]

While the role of literature as a compensatory medium that dared to represent the horrors of the times is indeed interesting and full of theoretical possibilities, these have not been explored in any detail in most of the above accounts. I would like to use the theoretical and historical frameworks provided by these critics, which have been crucial to my understanding of the invested networks of silences surrounding the traumatic moment of the Partition, in order to ask questions of 'fictions'. That literature provided a space for breaking the cramped silences of history is undeniable. However, I want to explore the limitations of a position that assumes that the breaking of silences in and of itself is enough. I want to examine the necessary limits to fictional narratives that set out, however sympathetically, to represent violations enacted on women's bodies. In this context Gayatri Spivak's cautionary position is appropriate:

> What is left out? Can we know what is left out? We must know the limits of the narratives, rather than establish the narratives as solutions for the future, for the arrival of social justice, so that to an extent they're working within an understanding of what they cannot do, rather than declaring war.[18]

II

Amrita Pritam's novella *Pinjar* (The Skeleton) is about the ways in which women get situated at the crossroads of an extended array of events, norms, rites and laws which lay claims on their bodies in intrusive and invasive ways. The opening page of the novel expresses Pooro's repugnance at the visible bodily manifestation of her violation: 'She felt as if her body was a pea-pod inside which she carried a slimy, white caterpillar'.[19] Pooro views her pregnancy as a reminder of the foraging, intrusive abduction and branding of her body – as a woman at the nexus of society's clawing definition of her being. Set in pre-Partition Punjab, the novel begins with the 14-year-old Hindu girl Pooro's abduction by a Muslim man, Rashida, days before her arranged wedding. Pooro flees from her abductor, but, despite being a virgin, is rejected by her family who refuse to accept her because of the dishonour they fear from the community. She returns to Rashida who marries her and re-names her Hamida. The 'slimy, white caterpillar' in her body is conceived through this marriage. The narrative then weaves through Hamida's desires and fantasies, the estrangement between her Muslim naming and her Hindu longings; it traces violence done to other women, both before and after the Partition which encroaches into her village, precipitating rapes and forced migrations of Hindus and Sikhs to "India":

> Just as a peeled orange falls apart into many segments, the Hindus, Muslims and Sikhs of the Punjab broke away from each other. As clouds of dust float over the roads, rumours of 'incidents' began to float over the countryside.[20]

The role of rituals, habits and icons in demarcating boundaries and spaces between communities and religious identities is significant to the novel. Women's bodies are often imprinted with the visual markers which serve as declarations of their identities in relation to the communities to which they belong. The etching of 'Hamida' on Pooro's arm is only one example of this. Hamida wonders at her luck when she, a Muslim through marriage, manages to slip in and out of a Hindu camp as she rescues one Hindu woman and dramatically meets Ram Chand and learns of the abduction of Lajo (her brother's wife who is also Ram Chand's sister), without the guard noticing her give-away jewelry ('It did not cross his mind that Hindu women seldom wore silver ornaments').[21] The Hindu community which had so cruelly disowned and ousted the outcast madwoman who wanders the streets of their village makes claims on her son after her death, as a result of a rumoured visual mark on her body: 'With my own eyes I saw the sacred "Om" tattooed on her left arm.'[22]

Of course, as Pierre Bourdieu writes, 'the body believes in what it plays at: it weeps if it mimes grief';[23] the imprints on the body are not merely its external markers. According to Bourdieu, 'practical belief is not a "state of mind", still less a kind of arbitrary adherence to a set of instituted dogmas and doctrines ("beliefs"), but rather a state of the body'.[24] Though evicted from the Hindu community, Pooro/Hamida retains a phantasmatic desire for inclusion through the Hindu rituals by which she could embrace her status as daughter/daughter-in-law. Prior to her abduction, she had dreamt about her forthcoming arranged match with Ram Chand, the Hindu fiancé she had never met, through enacting the fantasy of the rituals of marriage in her mind. Her abduction by Rashida interrupts the possibility of these symbolic rites being materialized, since it banishes her from the space of a community whose rituals would have ensured her a status in a patriarchal order where men were 'booked' and sacrifices offered for the birth of a son.[25] After the abduction, Pooro/Hamida's sense of betrayal by Ram Chand is thus not founded on any relationship she had with him, but through the engagement rituals which had provided a legalized contract for a relationship to be credited in the future.

Pooro/Hamida's desires for a definition of her identity within the precincts of Hindu rites can be considered through some theories about the ideological parameters of identity formation. Louis Althusser's theory of interpellation characterized as an 'always already' constitution of the subject is mobilized through two processes: a recognition of oneself in an ideological hailing, and a *mis*recognition, an overlooking of the fact that the very act of recognition of the name creates the content one recognizes oneself in.[26] The name is then the final seal on a definition of one's identity, the only seal that ties together contingent features into a necessary cogency. Slavoj Zizek points out that the subject is certainly 'interpellated', but its subjectivity emerges at the moment when it recognizes itself as being hailed as one. It is within this 'anticipatory' mode, wherein the subject pinpoints the gesture of 'hailing' as the key moment in her subject formation that the question of agency comes into play: 'Anticipatory identification is therefore a kind of preemptive strike, an attempt to provide in advance an answer to "what I am for the Other"...'.[27]

Thus does Pooro anticipate her naming as Hindu bride in her fantasy of being incorporated and made into a subject through the rituals of a wedding ceremony. These rites are iterable customs; indeed their social legitimacy stems from this iterability. She recognizes that the seal of her identity can only be secured by her participation in these rituals that have been accorded social sanction. This naming is an act of registration within a social code and functions as a durable mark of legitimate identity. This aspired-to norm is, however, denied Pooro. Hamida, her Muslim name, which is the name inscribed on her arm, thus remains in disjuncture to her desires. So far, I have tried to give a sense of the interplay between naming and identity (both of which order subjectivity in patriarchal ways for Pooro/Hamida).

The ironies of the Pooro-Hamida divide permeate the text, but the text does not merely rest with the pathos of the divide between the Muslim appellation and the Hindu fantasy of an abducted woman. The space of fantasy does not remain stable or fixed.

Hamida's identifications do not reside only in her fantasies of Hindu bridehood. This is juxtaposed with her empathy with the conditions of other women and her rage at the violence done to women in the novel. These identifications too take place in dreams. When she discovers the dead madwoman with a child attached to her umbilical cord, she has a dream:

> She dreamt of Rashida galloping away with her lying across his saddle...she dreamt of her turning insane and running about the village lanes with a life quickening in her womb...and then giving birth to a child under the shade of a tree.[28]

This dream fuses with the memory of her abduction, her banishment from society and the pregnancy that she had found so repugnant. She wakes up to give herself the reassurance that 'she was safely installed in his house. He was a kind husband'. The irony here lies in the fact that the threatening abductor of her nightmares and the kind husband whose shelter she is grateful for once she wakes up are one and the same person.

The third-person omniscient narration moves back and forth between these two processes: on the one hand, there is a rage regarding women's violations, on the other, there are several spaces of containment that this rage cannot disperse. Hamida's potential for anger is realized through her relationships with women with whom she enjoys a sense of nurture and intimacy through sharing a knowledge of the violence – mostly sexual violence – that these women face. This shared knowledge also serves to provide a potential critique and an undermining of Hamida's fantasies. For instance, Hamida's desire for the confirmation of her identity and the securing of her self in a legitimate social space through marriage is questioned in the text through her friend Taro's voice: 'When parents give away a daughter in marriage, they put a noose around her neck and hand the other end of the rope to the man of her choice'.[29]

Hamida's dreamworld too is confined to the desired comforts of her ritual acceptance, her desires to have her identity validated and included within the community. The identification and rituals sought out in her dreams extend to other women who have been subject to violence. Yet none of the women are released from the predicaments they are in. A crucial moment of agency and decision-making accorded to Hamida appears at the end of the novel, when she turns down the opportunity to cross the border between India and Pakistan which would have reinstated her to her former Hindu status. She stays behind with Rashida and her son in Pakistan. All through the text, the narrative emphasizes Rashida's goodness and decency, and he is finally redeemed when he helps save Pooro's sister-in-law Lajo, who had been abducted by a Muslim man during Partition riots. This act of rescue is described as one which mimics the former act of abduction, and is set up in the narrative as a culmination of the cycle of exchanges of women that undermine or validate the virtue of men within the patriarchal order. The choices are restricted to different versions of normative social structures: the good one, in which men are capable of protecting their women within the confines of 'home', and the bad, which threatens the safety of this protected domain. These parallel movements demonstrate the binds of the available patriarchal orders within which Hamida is confined. Such are the choices that the narrative remains trapped within, despite the knowledge of the violations that each choice causes women to undergo.

Such regulatory domains of practice enacted on women's bodies and on their movements are crucial for the demarcation of women's identities within the parameters of the social order. In *Bodies That Matter*, Judith Butler reviews Foucault's writing on the materiality of the body in the context of the political anatomy or schema which the material body is subject to, and which subjectivizes its materiality within specific domains of intelligibility. In particular, she addresses Foucault's considerations, in *Discipline and Punish*, not merely of the materiality of the body of the prisoner, on whom the subjection of the 'imaginary ideal' and of the 'soul' is imposed, but also of the materiality of the prison which 'is established to the extent that it is invested with power'. She adds:

> The prison comes to be only within the field of power relations, but more specifically, only to the extent that it is invested with or saturated with such relations, that such a saturation is itself formative of its very being. Here the body is not an independent materiality that is invested by power relations external to it, but it is that for which materialization and investiture are coextensive.[30]

The investiture of the nationalistic contract on the materiality of women's bodies is of course put into place within the 'domains of intelligibility' of the claims to legitimacy of the nascent nations. Never before, nor since, have the violation of the rights and bodies of women come under the purvey of such an urgency of legislative redress in the subcontinent. Such interventions could indeed have been positive, as in the case of Lajo in the novel, who is returned and accepted into the fold of her family, whose acceptance, too, meets the exigencies of patriotic/ communal (self-)definition. Hamida, who had been abducted prior to the Partition, did not qualify for the official, legal rehabilitative gestures that would have required her acceptance:

> Parents had been exhorted to receive back their daughters. A sense of resentment surged in Hamida's mind. When it had happened to her, religion had become an insurmountable obstacle; neither her parents nor her in-laws-to-be had been willing to accept her. And now, this same religion had become so accommodating![31]

Hamida's ironic reflection on the impossibility of her abduction being given the same status before the patriarchal law redressing the wrongs inflicted on the bodies of women prompts us to ask questions of such an inability to materialize Hamida's subjecthood along the same lines as Lajo's.

Hamida's abduction was framed within the tradition of abductions of women in the name of the communities they belong to – a trafficking in women placed within the chain of hostilities for generations. Rashida asks her soon after her abduction, 'Did you know that our families, the Shaikhs and the Sahukars, have been at loggerheads for many genera-tions?', and informs her that he had been compelled to abduct her because 'your uncle kept my father's sister in his house for three nights'.[32] In this crucial respect of Hindu-Muslim antagonisms, the grounds of Hamida's abduction were no different from falling under the purvey of the Inter-Dominion treaty. So if we can grant, as does Hamida, that this discursive manoeuvre of legislating the retrieval of abducted women was positive in the status and rights accorded to the women, Hamida's exclusion from the domain of this 'materialization' becomes significant. If the legislation facilitates the 'materialization' of the bodies of abducted women into subjecthood as a 'positive and for-mative' investiture of discourse and power, Hamida's exclusion prompts us to ask why she does not *matter*. This leads to Butler's question:

> To what extent is materialization governed by principles of intelli-gibility that require and institute a domain of radical unintelligibility that resists materialization altogether or that remains radically dema-terialized?[33]

The fact that the bodies of women become receptacles for the branding of rival chauvinisms is not new, before or since; it is at the singular moment in time (1947) when these communities get defined in the legalized status of nation states that the legal subjecthood of abducted women needs to be captured by legislative endeavor. This opens up a catachrestical site for the rights of wronged women within the legal precincts of the nation's self-definition. Both Lajo's retrieval and Hamida's exclusion are thus paradigmatic of the conditions and limits, of investiture and exclusions that are crucial to the nationalistic discourses of subject-formation.

III

The rhetoric and framework of nationalism's agenda is seen throughout this essay as hinged on different manoeuvres that require the management of women within the space of the national-political. It is manifest in the claims of roving male violence tapping into the energy of communal hatred in order to rape and abduct the women of the Other. It emerges in the wrangling over the patriarchal propriety of the newly instituted governments of nations seeking self-definition, as they attempt to define and codify the true essence and exchange of women thus abducted. The managerial devices that impose the further violence of silencing mechanisms on the depiction or retrieval of these horrors are seen to operate in diverse ways, as has been discussed by historians and sociologists among others. We have seen that Pritam's text breaks free of some of the binds that these managerial and silencing stratagems enforce. However, in her narrative of retrieval of silenced voices and histories of women, the choices that these voices can be given for expression is limited. Women's agency thus remains locked in negotiation with the binds of patriarchal orders of the benevolent or violent type between which it is caught.

10
Internalized Exiles: Three Bolivian Writers

Keith Richards

Any inclusion of Latin America in the postcolonial debate inevitably confronts serious misgivings over the applicability of the term 'post-colonial' in this context. At the core of this controversy is the question of nominal and effective colonialism. Latin America (the region's most commonly-accepted misnomer, which will be used here) was amongst the first colonized areas outside Europe to banish the former, but argu-ably is still experiencing the latter. The truism that all colonial experi-ences are different does not invalidate a view of this region as distinct from the realities of, for instance, Asia and Africa. The persistence of an ethnically European elite and a large mixed-race population is perhaps emulated only in South Africa (a country often compared to the Andean nations for the oppression of, and discrimination against, its original inhabitants).

It is persuasively argued in many quarters that most of the continent is still suffering a hangover of colonialism and that the true 'subalterns' of the region – its indigenous peoples – are as subject now as they ever were. Jorge Klor de Alva[1] has expressed these reservations, addressing not only the nature of Spanish endeavour in the Americas but also arguing that the Wars of Independence established creole states that had nothing to do with any radical discursive change but rather embraced their European heritage far more closely than under nomin-ally 'foreign' masters. The vision of this region as twice colonized – by both Spanish 'conquerors' and creole 'Liberators' – is difficult to evade. Klor has argued that 'colonialism' and 'postcolonialism' were 'Latin American mirages', and that they dodge the issue of the persistence of ethnically-based social strata which support his notion of a region 'colonized after the fact'. Although Klor fails to take into account the collective sense of nationhood which often, if temporarily, overrides matters of class, ethnicity, etc., it is difficult to countenance the assumption that in Latin America we are seeing the aftermath of colonialism, rather than its continuation under a different guise.

Also problematic is the sheer ethnic and cultural heterogeneity of most Latin American nations, which hinders any attempt at projecting a collective viewpoint. Unlike Argentina and Uruguay, which liquidated their native populations, the Andean nations are still predominantly indigenous. The radical film-maker Jorge Sanjinés has remarked upon the envy with which sectors of the Bolivian elite view this kind of 'solution', which has been seen as the country's route into modernity and progress. Meanwhile, within examples of even the most virulent indigenous resistance to conquest are found many of the historical premises, categorizations and stigmas imposed by the Spanish as fundamental to colonial discourse. As Irene Silverblatt[2] has demonstrated, the 'Indian' collective identity which was 'made' by colonial discourse in order to achieve control, soon began to display a tendency to reinvent its own history and ethnic origins in the form of a reappropriation of colonialist dogma. A belated identification with the Incas (the pre-Columbian masters which many native peoples chose to exchange for Spanish rule) is cited by Silverblatt as an illustration of both the durability of such prevailing discourse, but also the resourcefulness of the 'subaltern' in redirecting it.

The republics of the Andes, like those of Central America and other areas where native peoples survived the conquest in large numbers, still encounter the problem of creating a sense of common identity in the face of ethnic diversity. In this question, the prevalence of mixed-race (*mestizo*) groups has been both an advantage and a drawback. This is a phenomenon which has given rise to a massive and fluctuating body of ethno-cultural theory, firstly in the form of speculative demagoguery but also developing into an impressive body of investigation into approaches to such cultural phenomena.[3] Notions of hybridity in Latin America, as Klor points out, have a great deal to do with the maintenance of a workable caste system during the colonial years and with nation-building programmes after independence. In the twentieth century the most notable development has been the notion of transculturation, a term originally coined in the 1930s by the Cuban ethnographer Fernando Ortiz[4] in order to facilitate understanding of the essentially binary ethnic and cultural legacy of colonialism in Cuba. The term was taken up in the 1960s by the Uruguayan theorist Angel Rama[5] and applied more broadly to Latin America, in particular to the Andean nations. Rama's work on the Peruvian novelist José María

Arguedas was illuminating in that it offered a means of understanding the conditions of cultural plurality conveniently ignored by the dominant cultural discourse. Arguedas, whose fiction set out to convey formally and in the use of Spanish the reality of the oppressed majority of Andeans (the Indian and *mestizo* populations) wrote partly as a response to *indigenismo*, a movement in literature, music and other arts which had idealized Indian culture and identified it with the perceived glory of Inca rule. This type of arcadianism used the symbols of the pre-Columbian past as the basis for a cultural identity required to serve the new nations after independence from Spain had been won.

Klor's ideas on the unacceptability of a postcolonialist focus on Latin America are countered by Diana Palaversich,[6] who proposes the adoption of the term as a means of conveying both resistance to various forms of oppression and a liberating self-definition. Palaversich views postcolonialism as a response to the even more problematic imposition of the postmodernist label, which is seen to depoliticize even overtly polemical testimonial and contestatory texts. She contrasts this with postcolonialism as facilitating a search by Latin American 'subalterns' for a means of forging their own image.

If it is to remain within the postcolonialism debate, then, Latin America must be treated according to factors which differ radically from those obtaining in, for instance, the ex-British colonies. The relative longevity of independent states (since the early nineteenth century), the fact of a cycle of exploitation in which Spanish rule was succeeded (albeit unofficially) by British and North American interests, the ethnic variety in the waves of immigration following the Conquest and the republican eras, these are all elements common to Latin America as a whole. In the Andean countries, though, there are more specific features. In particular there is the existence of a large indigenous population, still economically and socially oppressed, but whose cultural production is important to questions of national identity.

Most (if not all) constituent states of the geopolitical chimera that is Latin America owe their very existence to the colonial legacy. However, it is usual for the political configuration of these states to be justified, at least by natural topographical boundaries or long-standing ethnic-cultural divisions. Chile, for example, owes its peculiar geography to the parallel confines of the Pacific Ocean and the Andes. Even landlocked Paraguay can point to the homogenizing influence of the Guarani language spoken by the great majority of its inhabitants. Such boundaries and traits provide links with a common, albeit artificial, legacy. The survival of colonial centres of power such as Lima and Mexico City, whatever adverse reactions they may provoke, also offer defining characteristics. Within such limits, and faced with such conditions, even the most radical dissident or secessionist group can find a focus.

An exception is Bolivia, which has long been characterized by its very lack of distinguishing features and clearly recognizable frontiers. The absence since 1879 of a coastline has resulted, paradoxically perhaps, in a peripheral reality at the heart of a continent. The vulnerability stemming from a lack of natural topographical boundaries has made for a tenuous nationalism which clings to nebulous militaristic and pseudo-indigenist mystiques. Bolivia is an amorphous territory whose confidence, like its borders, has been eroded by rapacious neighbours. The country's geography also lends itself to regionalism and inner disunity, compounded until recently by severe infrastructural and communication difficulties. A story of the nineteenth-century president Melgarejo and Queen Victoria, recently dismissed as pure myth by a prominent historian,[7] illustrates the precarious nature of Bolivian nationalism. This tale is of a British Ambassador humiliated by Melgarejo and expelled from the country on a donkey, naked and facing backwards. As a result of this, a disgruntled Victoria is said to have summoned her cartographers and ordered Bolivia to be erased from the map. The story is nonetheless revealing as regards the nation's self-image. It was intended to be fictionalized by the historical novelist Néstor Taboada Terán, who eventually balked at the idea of consecrating a myth of such proportions and instead produced *El Capitán del Siglo* (Captain of the Century) a reference to Melgarejo's favoured nickname. This is a burlesque critique of early neo-colonialism with a solid documentary base, which considers chronologically parallel developments on either side of the Atlantic. The novel is notable for an irreverent view of British political life as subject to many of the influences – arbitrary human weaknesses – more commonly associated with South and Central America's 'colourful' dictatorships. Above all, Jack the Ripper is mobilized as an unflattering symbol of British imperialism, comparing unfavourably with Melgarejo whose hitherto unchallenged image as a carnivalesque despot has been overhauled and rehabilitated.

The novel is a useful starting point for a discussion of the sense of assimilated exile which, I suggest, is integral to Bolivia's self-image in a global context. It also serves to illustrate Bolivia's (and Latin America's) position in the postcolonial debate. Politically, as well as geographically, this is a country at once on the margins and at the centre: Bolivia was the first part of the Spanish colonies to declare independence, and the last on the mainland to achieve it. Although its position has been romanticized by tourism as the 'heart' of South America, this is a para-doxical location at the core of the periphery. Bolivia's dependency on its neighbours for access to seaports and other means of communication with the world at large has led to postures of self-disparagement among many of its writers, who have come to see their country embodying exile as an inherent condition.

As a result of the nation's marginality and low self-esteem, Bolivian literature has been largely ignored, and paid much less attention than its 'folkloric' cultural manifestations. Understandable political sympathies have led foreign scholars to focus upon ethnographic and anthropolo-gical material to the near-exclusion of urban cultural production. This is, of course, an inversion of the prejudices held within Bolivia, which privileges Western acculturation. Nevertheless, writers are hampered by a tiny readership, and need to travel or project themselves beyond national boundaries in order to be heard. This paper deals with the theme of exile, in various forms and resulting from varying degrees of compulsion, in examples of the work of three contemporary authors. All of these write according to a sense of displacement and estrangement, whether from place, cultural origin or sense of ontological belonging. I hope to demonstrate that their work is predicated on Bolivia's condition of removal from the outside world and of internal disunity.

One writer who embodies this condition is Jesús Urzagasti, whose ground-breaking novel *Tirinea*[8] was published in 1969. Urzagasti was born and raised in the Chaco, the harsh eastern lowland area shared mostly with Paraguay (and the scene of one of the most futile and devastating of Bolivia's military defeats). *Tirinea*, which, as much as a novel, is a treatise on the role and nature of literature in relation to life, exploits the relationship between real and imaginary geography which has existed since the earliest European explorations of the Americas. The title itself is an invented toponym, although Tirinea bears all the fea-tures of the Chaco (being hot, flat and underpopulated). It also appears as primeval, possibly a microcosm or conglomerate of places. Moreover, it has ceased to exist except in human minds, which have created countless versions. Urzagasti himself rejects the interpretation that Tir-inea is based on the Utopian notion of Land Without Evil attributed to the area by the Jesuits in the seventeenth century. However, it is difficult to dispel such ideas completely: this is a locus onto which all manner of perceptions and hypotheses can be projected.

Amongst these perceptions is nostalgia: Urzagasti's childhood is to a large extent located in, and represented by, Tirinea. His narrator states bluntly that the name simply represents the path of nostalgia. Yet this narrator is an old man, which raises the question of the role of time in the novel. The protagonist Fielkho (of fluctuating age) reflects on his life from all of its phases, constantly using the present tense so that these phases appear equally valid and even contemporary. The various different places in which Fielkho turns up all correspond to periods in Urzagasti's life, whether university in Southern Bolivia, Northern Argentina and Buenos Aires, research in Europe or work in La Paz. Much like death, travel is viewed as an absence even before it is undertaken.

Once it is understood that the aged narrator is at once a manifestation of Fielkho and of his creator, then Tirinea appears as a conflation of time and space. This is a feature of Andean and other indigenous South American cosmology: the two phenomena appear in Urzagasti's novel as necessary delusions, as points of simultaneous departure and arrival. The narrator declares, 'I confess that I've never felt happier than at this moment, because I haven't the slightest suspicion of where I am' (p. 38). There is a clue here to the perceived nature of Bolivia as a place of constant exile. Elsewhere in the novel Fielkho says, 'I imagine that I'm not here: then my eyes see things in their exact dimension' (p. 36).

Bolivia's geographical position nurtures this sense of displacement, of removal not only from the metropolis but also from the present moment, from immediate perception. It is a land of 'valleys and villages mysteriously sunk into the deepest recesses of memory' (p. 38).

The effect of the loss of its sea outlet (to Chile in 1879) has had a profound effect on the Bolivian psyche. Yet for Fielkho, who has only known his country landlocked and cannot imagine it otherwise, any unlikely reconquest of its coastline would lie in the realm of dream-fulfilment or revenge. For him, death is the only true outlet from this 'mediterranean' (i.e. landlocked) condition. But, 'the death of a Bolivian is no laughing matter if you take into account that most of his or her life has been spent in Argentina, either studying or cutting sugar cane, or else there may be one or two in Europe lying belly-upwards on some beach' (p. 29). Landlocked, forsaken Bolivia, Fielkho adds, might provide a comic or melancholy spectacle seen from a satellite.

Néstor Taboada Terán's eight-year exile in Argentina was a result of political persecution, but produced arguably his best work. The novel *Manchay Puytu*[9] is set in the late eighteenth century during the decline of the silver boom in Potosí. This is a city taken to illustrate a multitude of perspectives on colonialism: for the Spaniards, a proof of God's blessing for their cause; for Northern Europeans, a reminder of the Iberian decadence and cruelty of the Black Legend. The novel takes as its central theme the colonial tale, spread by native Andeans, of an indigenous priest and his forbidden love for María Cusilimay, his 'Indian' servant. This is shattered when she dies while he is on a mission to Lima. The priest, Father Antonio, cannot bear this abandonment and exhumes the corpse to make a flute from its tibia. This act echoes pre-Columbian practices and marks the priest's cultural disinheritance. The resulting music is unbearably melancholy and even terrifying for local people, who oblige the priest to play with his head and hands inside a storage jar (*puytu*). Father Antonio is also a fugitive from the Inquisition, which at any moment may visit him and find out the truth about his unholy cohabitation. Taboada's version also suggests necrophilia: the priest, moreover, has a taste for prohibited literature. Worse still is the perceived betrayal of his ethnicity and culture, at a historical moment when Spanish and white supremacy is about to be challenged by vast Indian rebellions and the Wars of Independence. Antonio is estranged from both sides of his cultural formation. Moreover he is inexorably removed from his lover, María, and his forlorn attempts to bring her back only exacerbate his predicament. The two are found to have several previous incarnations. María, for example, is evoked as an Inca noblewoman abused by the Conquistadores and Antonio as the conquistador Pizarro's interpreter, Felipillo, who was instrumental in the conquest of Peru and became a historical scapegoat on both indigenous and European sides.

Written in Buenos Aires, where it won significant literary prizes, this novel deals with a form of estrangement paralleled by the author's own experience. Like Father Antonio, Taboada found himself living a furtive existence: this was the mid-1970s, when political oppression was growing in Argentina just as in Bolivia. The secret police used by Videla's military junta at least provided Taboada with a useful model for the climate created by the Inquisition. Like the priest, Taboada had to be careful about his reading and his behaviour, and was cut off (albeit rather more temporarily than Padre Antonio) from his wife and family during this time. However, he found the experience rewarding enough to recommend travel to young Bolivian writers in order to find a perspective on the country he has called 'secret land' because of its obscurity. Taboada's novel is ultimately concerned with reconciliation and the search for a solution to Bolivia's debilitating ethnic, cultural and regional divisions. Exile, a condition opted for in his choice of political stance, has served him as an observer of his country's realities.

René Poppe, another La Paz writer, experienced a similar trajectory. Again he found himself obliged to travel by political circumstance, so as to help mining communities resist political persecution from the military. During later trips to mining areas, he spent some time working below ground: this capitalized on the trust he had earned through his political activity, and was essential in the development of his mining literature. Poppe's collection of stories *El Paraje del Tío*,[10] by narrating from below ground, breaks with a long tradition of well-intentioned but inescapably inaccurate fictions by urban writers remote from the miners' everyday experience. This marks a crucial departure from a stultifying norm, since 'interior mina' is a wholly different environment from that inhabited by either peasants or city folk. Reigning in the mine is the *Tío* deity, represented in the mine by a grotesque statue featuring a huge erect penis; this environment is a male preserve, creating an estrangement from the miners' wives who exist above ground along with inimical forces such as the military and mine authorities. Family and enemy inhabit the same stratum, and obey a distinct set of principles from that which prevails below ground.

The exile presented by Poppe, then, is essentially that of his subjects: the miners are a displaced Quechua- and Aymara-speaking indigenous peasantry, whose working lives are controlled from La Paz and beyond. In Poppe's stories they virtually come alive in the mine, whose darkness and remoteness affords the secrecy in which they can develop and sustain their own beliefs. The mine constitutes an ethnic and cultural divide, beyond which rules a set of beliefs having little if anything to do with Christianity. The miner is subject, even more than is normal in Bolivia, to a variety of oppositions and contradictions in the course of his self-definition as a social being. His identity is the product of a complex and unresolved dialectic involving ethnic background, class and gender.

Poppe's minimalist stories capture the miner, usually alone, in his elements of darkness and solitude. These basic facts of their reality are presented with an immediacy which makes no allowance for unfamiliarity: the reader is plunged into this ambience with no acclimatization. Neither is there a glossary to familiarize a literate urban audience with the miners' almost impenetrable slang, based largely on words from the Quechua language and Bolivian Spanish solecisms. Thus the experience of alienation and displacement, familiar to some extent both to the author and the characters he describes, is foisted onto the reader.

Although often depicted alone or in small groups, their solidarity is emphasized by the sense of equality fuelled by the mine environment and its levelling conditions: faced with physical danger, as well as poverty and oppression, the workers' differences are minimized. Characterization is thus kept to a minimum; instead of individual detail there are nicknames, often recurring in more than one story, which not only afford intimacy but also encapsulate distinguishing traits which are left unexplored. Prevalent instead is a crude common denominator: the imperative of extracting a living from the rock whilst remaining alive. As a correlative of this, the *Tío* deity is a protector – closely identified with the workers themselves – who may, nevertheless, at any time turn destroyer. In several of Poppe's tales the *Tío* even changes places with the men, appearing in the title story 'El Paraje del Tío' as a reincarnation of one murdered worker whose rights he assumes and asserts. Another story is entitled 'Khoya Loco' (Crazy Miner), alluding to the 'madness' which, according to the miners, is required in order to do this job. Here, a worker repairs a *Tío* figure damaged in an explosion, only to find it has taken on his own characteristics: the miner, it must be assumed, was either the true victim or else has been killed in the mending process.

Much of the potency of Poppe's fiction derives from his use of microcosm, which lends the stories coherence as an overall body of narrative. This is achieved largely through the prevalence of archetype, applied not only to the workers but to their fate – a recurring pattern of protest answered by massacre. Poppe is not the first Bolivian writer of mining fiction to deal with this cyclical nature of repression: Luis Antezana[11] has written of the phenomenon in Bolivian literature by which 'reality imitates itself...through fiction'. Yet Poppe avoids the usual functional and mimetic nature of this literature, its tendency toward denunciation, social criticism and testimony. Life in the mine, as has been said, is far more complex than its usual depiction in this genre: most exponents ultimately represent the mine as a clandestine political environment and the miners purely in terms of class interests. Although the mine necessarily politicizes the workers, they nevertheless operate according to a parallel frame of reference which allows for the influence upon their lives of divine or extra-rational, supernatural forces. Poppe's effective self-exile through political activism is echoed by the experience of the miners themselves, still in the process of crossing cultural frontiers. To read his narratives as an outsider is to undergo a similar linguistic and perceptual alienation and, particularly for a Bolivian reader, a symbolic or subliminal exile.

The three writers mentioned in this paper all tend towards distinct interpretations of the role of literature: what they have in common is a recourse to some vision of exile as a metaphor for cultural, ontological or political estrangement. Bolivia, whether seen as a 'secret' or 'melancholy' land, inexorably imposes the terms of its own marginality upon its writers.

This country, created in the wake of the demise of the Spanish colony through its simple amputation from the rest of the former Viceroyalty of Peru, named after the arch-Liberator Bolívar, nonetheless illustrates Klor's thesis. Some three-quarters of its population are doubly subaltern; their ethnic and cultural marginality is, if anything, heightened by the fact that they 'speak' through self-appointed urban representatives. Whether 'postcolonialism' is a term we can apply to such well-intentioned voices as these perhaps depends on whether these writers attempt or achieve self-definition on a collective level. Urzagasti, Taboada Terán and Poppe share a use of exile as a vantage point from which to criticize the historical legacy and current reality of their country and of Latin America as a whole.

11
Writing Other Lives: Native American (Post)coloniality and Collaborative (Auto)biography

Susan Forsyth

In December 1890, at Wounded Knee Creek in South Dakota, around three hundred Lakota (Sioux) were killed by the United States Army, an incident which became symbolic of US military aggression towards Native Americans, and which gave Dee Brown the title and final chapter of his 1970 popular history of the defeat of American Indian armed resistance to white expansion.[1] Coincidentally, the 1970s saw a resurgence of Native American resistance in the form of the political activism of the American Indian Movement (AIM), viewed as a terrorist organization by the United States government. The highpoint came in 1973 when AIM occupied Wounded Knee Village for 71 days in protest at the corrupt Tribal Council (called a 'puppet government' by the protestors) on Pine Ridge Reservation, once again drawing world attention to this resonantly symbolic site.

One of those involved in the occupation at Wounded Knee, Mary Crow Dog, a 17-year-old woman of Lakota/white parentage, subsequently collaborated on an autobiography, called *Lakota Woman*,[2] with the Austrian-American, Richard Erdoes. Although completed by the end of the 1970s, the text was rejected by the publisher who had originally commissioned it, because of its political content. In 1990, more than ten years after it was written, *Lakota Woman* was finally published after some judicious re-writing allowed it to be marketed under the heading 'Autobiography/Women's Interest'. This essay uses an analysis of *Lakota Woman* to raise questions about the production of contemporary Native American autobiographical collaborations, the relationship between subject and author, and the censorship imposed by publishers who, although apparently encouraging Native Americans to 'speak for themselves', in effect choose the subjects about which they may speak. A comparison will be drawn with the form of writing known as *testimonio* which, within the American context more generally, allows the possibility of individuals from subaltern groups conveying the immediacy of their own and their community's struggle for survival during periods of conflict or revolutionary change.

My title, 'Writing Other Lives', emphasizes the collaborative nature of many Native American autobiographies. The 'writing' in question is undertaken not by the subjects of the autobiographies but by their collaborators; the 'lives' or life stories are related to the collaborators for the express purpose of inclusion in marketable texts; and writing about cultural 'others' enhances the marketability of those texts. The title also has a larger resonance in that the course of Native American lives has always, in a metaphorical sense, been written for them: US 'Indian Policy' dictated where and how (and often for how long) they should live. Writing other lives is both a literary and an administrative process: this essay will ultimately focus on the former.

*

As, in effect, the first stage of postcolonial analysis enters a period of consolidation, the centrality of the work of Edward Said, Homi Bhabha and Gayatri Chakravorty Spivak has ensured that the Middle East and India during the nineteenth and twentieth centuries remain the most conspicuous topics and that the Americas have tended to be neglected.[3] Re-drawing the postcolonial map to include the Americas in general and the USA in particular is not a way of resolving the question as to whether contemporary American countries can be considered in some useful sense postcolonial in relation to their European 'origins'; nor is it necessarily an encouragement to postcolonial readings of American writers. However, it does serve to include on the postcolonial agenda a set of questions involving the practice of the internal colonization of Native American nations. Since the 1970s, and therefore parallel with the establishment of postcolonial cultural theory, a Native American discourse has developed which has affirmed the importance of the term 'colonialism' to describe their own history and current situation. Although originally a European colony, independence 220 years ago permitted the newly formed United States to continue unhampered the colonization of the continent and its indigenous peoples begun by Britain and Spain; this was perhaps the first but by no means the last example of the postcolonial state simultaneously acting as a colonizing force (Indonesia's treatment of East Timor comes to mind). US government policies which affected the lives of Native American people have swung pendulum-like between attempts at segregation and assimilation. They include acts enabling: Removal (1830) of tribes west of white settlement areas, involving dislocation from ancestral lands and isolation from whites; Allotment (1887) of land into individual, as opposed to tribal, ownership, thereby encouraging nuclear family structures as opposed to larger tribal communities; Reorganization (1934) of traditional tribal leadership into 'democratically' elected Tribal Councils, which allowed a limited amount of self-government on reservations; and Termination (1950) of Native American nations which encouraged further dislocation, this time to urban centres. Often enacted unilaterally or fraudulently, these Acts were driven by a desire to solve the 'problem' which the Native American nations posed to the United States: 'vanishing Americans' who stubbornly refused to disappear. The legacy of US Indian policy is that much of Native North America lacks sovereignty and continues under its original colonization whilst facing neo-colonial forces in the form of governmental and corporate appropriation of land and mineral rights.[4]

Indigenous issues were again given global prominence when the 1984 *testimonio* of Rigoberta Menchú,[5] analyzing the conflict in Guatemala as a contemporary example of a 'postcolonial' continuation of European aggression against the indigenous Maya population, led to her being awarded the Nobel Peace Prize in 1992. Writing from within the USA, Ward Churchill, perhaps the most prolific of many powerful Native American writers, sees the way forward as one of pursuing 'strategies and courses of action designed to lead to decolonization within the colonizing "mother country"'. The most spectacular of these strategies included the occupations of Alcatraz Island in San Francisco Bay and the Bureau of Indian Affairs building in Washington, D.C., and armed resistance both at Wounded Knee in 1973 and during the Mohawk struggle in New York in 1990. They should also include, according to Churchill, the implementation of 'alternative technologies leading to greater self-sufficiency (and corresponding independence from the United States)' and the recognition of Native American nations 'as fully sovereign entities within the international arena'.[6]

There are signs that postcolonial criticism has begun to pay attention to Native American arguments of this kind. James Clifford engages questions of Native American cultural self-representation in his new book *Routes*,[7] and the introduction to a recent anthology of critical writing, *Dangerous Liaisons*,[8] begins with an ironic comparison of Dorothy's fictional 'dislocation' in *The Wizard of Oz* to the actual displacement of Native American communities, a displacement which allows

Dorothy to have a sense of 'home' in the first place.[9] *Dangerous Liaisons* is the first 'postcolonial' collection to include an essay by Native American writers addressing Native American issues, thereby complicating postcolonial questions as they were originally posed: no longer concerned purely with European colonialism, the second wave of decolonization is perhaps interested in the internal position of indigenous peoples in 'settled' countries.

From early in the twentieth century until the present time both autobiography and autobiographical collaborations have been produced by the Lakota of Pine Ridge and Rosebud Reservations. These texts provide information about prevailing conditions on the reservations and in urban centres, highlight the tensions between traditional life and modernity and provide a response to US government policies and actions. Two texts published in the 1990s contain a personal account of the Wounded Knee demonstration in 1973. These are *Lakota Woman* and *Ohitika Woman*.[10] They are by the same woman, initially using her married name, Mary Crow Dog, then reverting to her maiden name, Mary Brave Bird. Both have the same collaborator, Richard Erdoes, who is well known to readers of Native American collaborations as the co-author of *Lame Deer: Sioux Medicine Man* first published in 1973.[11]

Collaborations are *conventionally* seen by critics as rooted in at least three different genres: the Native American oral tradition and two Western forms, autobiography and ethnography. When Native American oral literatures were initially collected (a function of salvage anthropology), unselfconscious authors presumed a transparency which supposedly made the reality behind the text apparent to the reader, effacing any problems of translation or lack of understanding caused by cultural differences.[12] The act of speaking their own stories indicates a strong link to the Native American oral tradition (although Arnold Krupat points out that telling the whole of one's life is a concept alien to Native Americans);[13] traditionally they would tell stories short enough to keep the audience's attention at a single sitting. So oral literatures changed considerably on collection, through a 'translation' process which was both linguistic and formal.

Western autobiography *traditionally* tells the story of one life. Although this may not be the primary characteristic of the texts under consideration here, the European format is often adopted in Native American autobiographies in terms of chronology, important turning points and answers to questions of individual identity.

Anthropology was instigated primarily to provide the history of the evolution or progress of mankind, not necessarily to furnish a thorough understanding of other cultures. When it was thought in the mid-nineteenth century that Native Americans were to 'vanish' with the approach of European 'civilization', the rush to preserve and collect oral histories, lifeways and cultural artefacts began. Traditionally a study of another culture by administrators, missionaries and travellers, ethnography was taken over in the twentieth century by university-trained participant-observers and has, since the 1970s, become a complicated affair with authors (or editors as some prefer to be known) manipulating their position to enable them to be seen to be dealing with the complex issues of representation involved in writing other lives. This self-conscious approach has meant that writers promote, to varying degrees, a co-production, which involves higher visibility for themselves as ethnographers/writers within the text, whilst at the same time allowing their informants to speak for themselves. The whole question of 'authorship' is scrutinized as writers attempt either to displace the monological production in favour of dialogical or polyphonic texts, as in *Tuhami: Portrait of a Moroccan* by Vincent Crapanzano,[14] or to transfer the authorship of all or part of the text (or responsibility for it) to the speaking subject, as in *Nisa: the Life and Words of a !Kung Woman* by Marjorie Shostak.[15]

The collaborations discussed here are produced by at least two people, one Native American or part Native American, and one white, or Euro-American. The most famous example of a Native American collaborative autobiography is the 1932 'as told to' production of Nicholas Black Elk, a Lakota, and John Neihardt (which didn't become hugely popular until the revival of interest in all things Native American in the 1970s).[16] The title, *Black Elk Speaks*, explains much about the aims of the work and the ideals it attempts to incorporate in enabling a Native American to tell his own story. It also introduces some of the complexities involved in its production: that Black Elk speaks is only the first step in a complicated process which eventually allows us to read what he has said, or an edited version of it, from the printed page.[17]

The collection process of the collaboration occurs in a variety of ways using available technology, from shorthand notes taken during interviews in the case of *Black Elk Speaks* to tape recordings collected by Richard Erdoes over 20 years. Although early collaborations, in addition, required the assistance of an interpreter, he or she, despite being a pivotal part of the process, is almost always totally effaced in the text. More often than not autobiographies contain material selected and edited by white writers as being of interest to a white audience, in this way changing the point of view from that of the Native American storyteller to the white author, although the extent of any editorial interven-tions in the form of promptings, questions and diversions remains on the whole unspecified. The notes and recordings are then transcribed and rearranged by the collector prior to publication, to conform to European conventions of chronological order. David Brumble lists six 'distinct kinds of preliterate autobiographical narratives',[18] which turn up regularly in Native American autobiographical texts and are incorpor-ated into the overall life story. These are coup tales, tales of warfare and hunting, self-examinations, self-vindications, educational narratives and tales of acquisition of powers. Despite the collaborative effort involved, these texts are often presented as first-person narratives, referred to as 'a pleasing fiction' by Brumble,[19] since the degree of editorial intervention at all stages is rather larger than admitted.

It appears that the development of Native American collaborations has in some aspects followed a path similar to that of ethnography: initially the desire to know another culture in order to enable us to understand our own, followed by more recent attempts to enable the subject of the text to tell his or her own story. In 1981 R. D. Theisz published an article entitled 'The Critical Collaboration: Introductions as a Gateway to the Study of Native American Bi-Autobiography'.[20] In his examination of several collaborations he indicates six points to look for in introductions to these texts: namely the manner of the collabora-tion, the meeting of collaborators, the reason for the existence of the book, the cultural phase and the cultural/geographic region, the type of narrator and the subsequent treatment of the original account. Some of these elements are also included in personal narratives or introductions by ethnologists to 'authorize', give authority to, their productions. They perform the same service in each case.

To this hybrid oral/autobiographical/ethnographic literature should be added what John Beverley calls *testimonio* – 'a new postfictional form of literature with significant cultural and political repercussions'.[21] By *testimonio* Beverley means

> a novel or novella-length narrative in book or pamphlet (that is, printed as opposed to acoustic) form, told in the first-person by a narrator who is also the real protagonist or witness of the events he or she recounts, and whose unit of narration is usually a 'life' or a significant life experience.[22]

A component of 'resistance literature', *testimonio* 'coalesces as a new narrative genre in the 1960s and further develops in close relation to the

movements for national liberation and the generalized cultural radicalism of that decade'.[23] It is normally a collaboration, because in many
cases the narrator is 'either functionally illiterate, or, if literate, is not a
professional writer or intellectual';[24] nevertheless, one characteristic of
testimonio is the fact that 'the intentionality of the *narrator* is para-
mount', not that of the recorder. Also

> [t]he situation of narration in *testimonio* has to involve an urgency to
> communicate a problem of repression, poverty, subalternity, impri-
> sonment, struggle for survival.[25]

Less concerned with one life, *testimonio* is interested more in the
collective social situation of the narrator and those she or he lives
alongside; the narrator must therefore be representative of the community and able to speak for or in the name of them. The best-known
example of this form is probably *I, Rigoberta Menchú*, which opens with
the claim that her story is 'not only my life, it's also the testimony
of... all poor Guatemalans. My personal experience is the reality of a
whole people'.[26]

Native American collaborations often share characteristics of *testimonio* – particularly a politically aware and active narrator who is representative of (that is, indistinct from) a community whose collective situation
is one of struggle against repression, poverty and imprisonment. John
Beverley and Marc Zimmerman argue (when comparing two works by
the same author at different stages of revolt) that once a movement has
been successful the subsequent literature 'covers much the same ground
... as a leisurely and reflective autobiographical memoir, without the
pain and urgency of the earlier book'.[27] He concludes, therefore, that
'*testimonio* seems better adapted to express a process of struggle than of
revolutionary consolidation or counter-revolutionary destabilization'.[28]
This conclusion may be tested by examining the texts by Mary Crow
Dog/Brave Bird and Richard Erdoes. The problem historically has been
the impossibility for Native Americans in the USA to make themselves
heard during times of crisis because of the lack of immediate access to
publishers. Clearly it was the intention of this narrator to have her story
published at the time when she was also making public demonstrations
and speeches against oppression on the reservations in South Dakota
and against the wrongful arrest and imprisonment of AIM activists.
Erdoes clearly was supportive of this aim but was thwarted at that time
from publicizing Mary's story; the moment was lost. The circumstances
of its subsequent publication would indicate that Mary's story had to be

considerably modified in order to be published at all. The intentionality of the narrator was perhaps sacrificed in the intervening years to the desire of the publishing house.

*

Ohitika Woman, the second book by Mary, has an introductory chapter in which Richard Erdoes relates the story of the production of the *first* book, *Lakota Woman*, following the conventions of ethnographical introductions and covering the points raised by Theisz. *Ohitika Woman's* introduction contains a short autobiography of Erdoes, including an account of his meeting with John Fire/Lame Deer, which led to his first collaboration with a Native American in the 1970s. In fact, *Lame Deer* was his first book, as Erdoes was by profession an artist, not a writer: we are told that Lame Deer badgered Erdoes into writing his life story. We discover that Erdoes was born and raised in Vienna, where he had been a member of the anti-Hitler movement. We have to go back to the Epilogue to *Lame Deer* to discover more of the story, and we find that it is one of displacement, alienation and finally exile, as Erdoes has to leave Europe altogether. He describes his experience in Europe:

> Wherever I had been so far, I had belonged to the wrong religion, spoken the wrong language and behaved in a strange and therefore wrong way. To the Germans I was a sloppy Austrian, to the Austrians a *"Sau-preuss"* – a swinish Prussian. To the Hungarians I was the son of Habsburg oppressors. The Bosnians called me a *"Schwob"*, a chauvinistic Hungarian overlord. Frenchmen called me the little Boche... None of this was intended as a compliment.[29]

Erdoes admits to being 'culturally still more European than American',[30] and, perhaps because of his own experiences in Europe and the USA, he can sympathize with Mary's expressed feelings of alienation, sometimes from white society, sometimes from the native community, because of her mixed Lakota/white parentage. Erdoes and his wife, Jean, became 'heads of a defense committee for Leonard Crow Dog and a few other Lakota friends who were indicted for strictly political offenses'.[31] Since the 1960s Erdoes has been a frequent and welcome visitor to South Dakota and maintains many Lakota friends. These moments of sympathy help to authenticate Erdoes's credentials as a suitable recorder of Mary's story. Erdoes, at the time of collaborating with Mary, fitted Beverley and Zimmerman's description of an 'interlocutor who is a journalist, writer, or social activist'.[32] Despite these favourable credentials, Mary, because she had had nothing but bad experiences of whites (in boarding school and on and around the reservation) found it very difficult to 'accept' him but they finally did 'become close friends'.[33] This is also often the pattern which emerges from ethnographic accounts, leading to what James Clifford calls 'rapport'.[34]

Because of the popular success of *Lame Deer*, Erdoes was asked by one of his publishers to write something else 'in that vein'.[35] During 1976 and 1977, Mary Crow Dog was living with the Erdoes family in New York so that she could be close to her husband, Leonard, who was in prison nearby because of his political activities at and following Wounded Knee,[36] so Erdoes's response to his publisher was that he 'would like to help her write an autobiography'.[37] His use of the words 'help her' is indicative of the complications of a collaborative venture. The hybrid nature of the resulting production could easily conceal an unequal power relationship between the collaborators, so we ought to be concerned with whom ultimate control of the text lies. There are few clues given here, and perhaps nothing to cause great concern in the initial production. Mary and Erdoes worked 'on the taping and transcribing of her story', and then, when Leonard was released and the couple went back to the reservation, Erdoes 'put the manuscript together like a jigsaw puzzle out of a huge mountain of tapes'.[38] This is the only published reference to the actual writing process. In *Ohitika Woman* Mary talks of 'going over this [*Ohitika Woman*] manuscript with Richard for the last time for final proofreading'[39] in September 1992, indicating that the collaborative venture, with regard to that book at least, continued to the final stages before publication; but there is no mention of this in relation to *Lakota Woman*. The most interesting period in the life of *Lakota Woman* begins after the manuscript was completed in 1978/9.

Lakota Woman was not published for over *ten years*. Now this might give us cause to consider that perhaps the political struggle in which the narrator was engaged was not so urgent after all. On the contrary, the reason for the delay justifies the contention that the nature of the text is, or was originally, highly political. The publisher in question decided that the book was much too *radical* and told Erdoes: 'The political climate had changed. This radical shit is out. Mysticism is "in". Make her into a female Don Juan! Make her into a witch. Make her fly through the air!'[40]

The publisher appeared to be shying from political content and radicalism generally, in favour of an exotic combination of fantasy and sexual adventure rather than harsh reality. Perhaps he thought that the success of the re-released *Black Elk Speaks* with its hallucinatory spiritual 'flights' and visions of the 'other world' could be emulated. The publisher certainly seemed uninterested in realism and perhaps was intent on supplying a demand at that time for other-worldly or alternative lifestyles for a disillusioned post-Vietnam War generation.

Erdoes's reply to his publisher is revealing. He said, 'Mary is ... for real, not something out of my fantasies. If I faked her story she would come after us with her skinning knife, and rightly so'.[41] The nineteenth-century stereotype depicting an encounter with a primitive and threatening yet exotic Native American woman is indeed the stuff of white male fantasies, but its use is a disappointing episode in a text which purports to present a modern-day Lakota woman who has fought against such dated stereotypical labelling. However, Erdoes seems to be concerned to give an accurate portrayal of Mary and so does not feel free to tamper with her narrative to suit this publisher's understanding of market demands. In 1990 there was, apparently, another climate change and women, especially 'American Indian women', were 'in'; *Lakota Woman* was distributed by a different publisher, became a bestseller, and procured a movie contract.

Prior to its eventual publication in 1990 an epilogue was added to *Lakota Woman* to bring the reader up to date with events, since the narrative proper ended in 1977. Despite there being no mention of editing or re-writing in the epilogue to *Lakota Woman*, or in the introduction to *Ohitika Woman*, and despite Erdoes's assertion that the new publisher 'loved the book',[42] on closer examination it is obvious that *Lakota Woman* has undergone substantial revision to the main text. The introduction to *Ohitika Woman* said that Leonard and Mary went home and Richard Erdoes put the manuscript for *Lakota Woman* together and 'delivered it a year or so later'.[43] It is fair to say, therefore, that anything which appears in the book relating to events which happened after Mary's return to the reservation in 1977 is an addition or alteration made probably at the request of the eventual publisher. There are many changes, including descriptions of both a celebration on Leonard's return to the reservation and 'a giveaway feast in 1989',[44] indicating that rewriting did take place just prior to publication. This prompts the question of whether there was not so much a climate change as a change in emphasis in the text from political activism concerning the community as a whole to women's issues, a change which was consolidated in the 1993 *Ohitika Woman*. The demands of the original intended publisher were not pursued in 1990. Mysticism, witches, flying and sex do not seem to have been on the new agenda. Also, realism was not an anathema in the 1990s, and women's issues were of more interest than those of an ungendered political nature as the stirrings of an interest in feminism had become apparent in a few native comment-ators.

Lakota Woman is very strong in its condemnation of both US govern-ment policies towards Native Americans, such as forced sterilization of women and 'judicial double standards',[45] and the Pine Ridge tribal council's 'reign of terror' between 1972 and 1976, during which around seventy AIM members and supporters were killed and many more injured. Mary rages against the poverty, drunkenness and domestic violence which she sees as the legacy of US 'Indian policy'. But she appears to withdraw her wholehearted support for the AIM, which, in the 1970s, was viewed by the US government as a communist, terrorist, anti-American organization and was under constant investigation and infiltration by the FBI.[46] In the chapter devoted to Mary's first contact with the American Indian Movement, there is clear indication of sub-stantial re-writing which indicates a change of attitude to the AIM. She says '[m]eeting up with AIM for the first time loosened a sort of earth-quake inside me', and we feel her sense of excitement and anticipation; but then she continues, 'I am thirty-seven now but feel as if I have lived for a long time – I can see things in perspective, not subjectively, no, but in perspective'.[47] Mary was 17 at Wounded Knee in 1973 but she talks of being 37 in 1990 (which would make her 20 in 1973), and this confusion points perhaps to a rewriting of the chapter. The question of Mary's age, however, is less important than the 'things' she claims to see 'in per-spective'. The AIM and her relationship with it have been redrawn. Her statement that 'movements get used up and the leaders get burned out quickly',[48] suggests a perception of the impotence of the movement. An alternative to this view might be that the defeat of the AIM was brought about by an imbalance of power, further 'judicial double standards' and unethical FBI operations. The subjective, supportive perspective, which is what has made the book seem so urgent and passionate to this point, is replaced by a retrospective, oppositional objectivity, and the narrative loses its edge. In loosening her ties with the AIM, her 'community' in 1973, the text is at this point less of an urgent, immediate *testimonio* and resembles more a leisurely, reflective memoir. In effect there are two texts, although only one was published: the 'first' text, written during the AIM's struggles against repression, is *one* 'work' and the re-written, published *Lakota Woman* is *another*, ideologically separate, work. The 'first' conveys the immediacy and urgency of the situation of the 'com-munity' formed within Wounded Knee in 1973. The 'second' text is reflective, distanced from, and even dismissive of, the AIM community (as already shown) in a manner which would not have been possible in the heat of the moment. The element of retrospection makes *Lakota Woman* resemble the later *Ohitika Woman* which is more reflective and, because of this, detached and critical about some native elements. Interestingly *Ohitika Woman* is marketed under the heading 'Memoir/Native American Studies' and follows Mary's lone struggle to raise her children outside the reservation community.

It seems, then, that adjustments were made to the original text to make it more palatable. Erdoes wrote that 'back in 1979 . . . women, especially Indian women weren't "in" at the time'.[49] This is a little surprising when compared to the interest in things Native American and the upsurge in feminist writings during that period. It is more likely that AIM and organized political activism were not 'in', particularly as there were legal appeals ongoing which originated in the three-year 'reign of terror'. By 1990 it appears that communal political issues were still not marketable subjects, implying that the viewpoint of the original publisher ('this radical shit is out') still held true; but a higher value was placed on individual feminist issues than in 1979. In addition by 1990 the book would have received a more favourable response from a publisher because by then the defeat of the American Indian Movement as a national body had been achieved with many of its leaders serving long jail sentences, not simply 'burned-out' and 'used-up'. The popularity of *I, Rigoberta Menchú* may have made a book by a Native American woman within the USA an attractive prospect to a publisher, but, in the USA, Native American women were only 'in' if they fitted the desired image of a feminist radical, not a political radical.

The change in emphasis to women's issues is perhaps best illustrated by a short review of the book's two 'beginnings'. The first is:

> I am Mary Brave Bird. After I had my baby during the siege of Wounded Knee they gave me a special name – Ohitika Win, Brave Woman, and fastened an eagle plume in my hair, singing brave-heart songs for me. I am a woman of the Red Nation, a Sioux Woman. That is not easy.[50]

This is followed by a potted description of the birth of her baby during a Wounded Knee firefight, her treatment by the 'Feds' after Wounded Knee, the killing of her friend Annie Mae Aquash, her sister-in-law's death from beating, her sister's forced sterilization, her own whipping at the boarding school which she attended, her rape at age 15 and a general discussion about the harshness of life as an Indian and especially a woman: 'Among Plains tribes, some men think that all a woman is good for is to crawl into the sack with them and mind the children.'[51] These two pages concentrate on the conditions which are tolerated by women growing up on the reservation and their treatment by men, both native and white. There is then the second start:

> To start from the beginning, I am a Sioux from the Rosebud Reservation in South Dakota. I belong to the "Burned Thigh", the Brule Tribe, the Sicangu in our language.[52]

Mary is a 'Sioux' not a 'Sioux Woman' in this, the second, 'beginning'. The first 'beginning' can be viewed in at least two ways. It could be that it is a technique attempting to portray the oral tradition where speech does not necessarily follow a strict chronology but tumbles out in order of importance or impact, ranging over a series of different events and times. These different stories are then described in detail during the remainder of the text. Alternatively, the two pages comprising the first beginning may have been added prior to publication in 1990, along with the other rewritings already mentioned. The emphasis of the material on women and important women's issues raises the suspicion that this is so, particularly as the rest of the first chapter does not return to these issues.

We can only speculate whether these adjustments to the text prior to publication were required by the publishers or suggested by Erdoes. The rejection by the original publisher is clearly an example of the 'containment' of texts written by individuals from marginalized and politically powerless movements. A change in emphasis at the demand of the publishers is perhaps not so out of the ordinary if compared to normal practices: publishers are there to try to give the public what they think the public want. If the re-editing was by Erdoes (or even by Mary at Erdoes's suggestion), that could indicate an imbalance of power between the white European writer and the native narrator. Of course, if changes were instigated by Mary, this establishes the former discussion as speculative but advances the argument that Mary was seeking to distance herself from her previous political activism in order to promote an image of an independent woman struggling against the oppressions of a male-dominated society, an image which may have enhanced the book's acceptability to US publishers whilst increasing its appeal to a white female readership.

*

As the 'second wave' of demands for decolonization is heard from the internally colonized indigenous populations throughout the world perhaps it is appropriate that the 'second stage' of analysis should begin to untangle the complicated relationships not only of resistance and conflict but also of collaboration and hybridity which have developed. The hybridization of modern culture is often viewed within postcolonial discourse in a very positive light and certainly as preferable to a complete assimilation (and therefore loss) of one culture to another as promoted in nineteenth- (and early twentieth-)century USA. This is certainly so in this instance where the combination of the native traditional oral literature with autobiography and ethnography has produced a new, hybrid form of 'collaborative' or 'bi-autobiography' which allows a Native American to participate in the telling of her own story even though this includes voicing resistance to oppression. Within this hybrid form, however, there exists the possibility of unequal power relationships both between the two collaborators and between the collaborators and the publisher, where a certain degree of persuasion or coercion could be applied in order to shape the narrative in a way not originally intended by the storyteller.

The phrase, 'writing other lives', resonates with interwoven actions and ideas, from colonial administrations writing policies which affect the lives of Native American communities to textual representations of the lives of individual Native Americans undertaken by outsiders. *Lakota Woman* is intriguing because it portrays the lack of political autonomy which Mary and her community had over their lives during the Wounded Knee siege and its aftermath, and at the same time illustrates Mary's possible loss of authority over the textual representation of her own life.

Lakota Woman, if published in 1977, would have powerfully portrayed the urgency of the political circumstances in which it was written – a *testimonio* to the struggle of her community. The full extent of the rewriting of *Lakota Woman* for the 1990 publication was not admitted in the text and is, therefore, unknown. In any case, the re-editing process was not comprehensive and Mary's outspokenness and obvious anger at the experiences of Native Americans at the hands of the US government remain. Feminist issues on a personal level have perhaps been emphasized in the text at the request of the eventual publishers, but this has not eliminated entirely the powerful illustration of Native American political activism which occurred during the 1970s, only brought into question Mary's continued defence of it. What degree of control was imposed by market demands on the indigenous narrative is something we can begin to work out. How much more vibrant the text was as an anti-colonial *testimonio* prior to re-editing is something we can only surmise.

12

'The Limits of Goodwill': the Values and Dangers of Revisionism in Keneally's 'Aboriginal' Novels

Denise Vernon

In his critical analysis of Aboriginal writing in Australia, Mudrooroo Narogin challenges Thomas Keneally:

> If a Patrick White, a Thomas Keneally, a Dorothy Hewett decides to write about Aborigines, after they have done with them, they are discarded. The fringe after all is but a subject for their literary skills, it is not the reality which confronts them each and every day.[1]

Narogin's statement raises valid questions about the potential for tokenism and cultural plunder in Keneally's writing and rightly challenges the assumption that a privileged white Australian writer, a writer culturally foreign to his subject matter, can 'know' what he hasn't experienced. However, I am going to argue in this essay that Keneally's approaches to Aboriginal material are more complex than this statement would suggest. Keneally has consistently addressed Aboriginal issues through the 1970s, 1980s and 1990s, and during this period he has shown a marked shift in his representation of the Aboriginal world. These works of fiction and non-fiction form a fascinating record of a white liberal Australian's attempts, however flawed, to come to terms with a period of marked socio-political change for Australian Aborigines – a period that saw the development of an increasingly assertive, confident and self-determining Aboriginal voice in Australia.

Any attempt to write anti-colonial criticism from a colonial/settler position is, of its nature, compromised, but, as Stephen Slemon has suggested, examination of such writers and their shifting and ambivalent positions has much to offer the postcolonial theorist:

The Second-World writer, the Second-World text, that is, have always been complicit in colonialism's territorial appropriation of land, and voice, and agency, and this has been their inescapable condition even at those moments when they have promulgated their most strident and most spectacular figures of post-colonial resistance...the ambivalent, the mediated, the conditional, and the radically *compromised* literatures of this undefinable Second World have an enormous amount yet to tell 'theory' about the nature of literary resistance.[2]

In *The Making of the Aborigines*, Bain Attwood describes the historiographic endeavours, from the sixties onwards, to recover Aboriginal history in an attempt to redress the neglect in earlier Eurocentric and racist histories. He identifies three overlapping movements: the oppositional, the revisionist and the Aboriginal.[3] I intend to demonstrate that Keneally's fictional writing has changed in parallel with these historiographic developments and reveals both oppositional and revisionist traits.

Keneally's novel, *The Chant of Jimmie Blacksmith*, published in 1972, and the subsequent film, brought Keneally into the arena of Aboriginal affairs. Controversy followed – questions were raised about the creation of a violent Aboriginal protagonist and the negative racial image it could reinforce. The novel dealt with the taboo issue of miscegenation and the particularly sensitive issue of a marriage between a white woman and an Aboriginal male. Keneally was also accused of paternalism. However, the controversy did not prevent Keneally returning to the arena of racial tensions in the following years, in an intellectual climate that was becoming increasingly sensitive to the politics of representation in a colonial space, and was therefore critical of privileged white interpreters of Aboriginal affairs.

Why does Keneally continue to return to Aboriginal culture as a source for his material, especially in a climate where white writers on Aboriginality are almost automatically suspect? Firstly, he has a genuine fascination for a culture that he cannot fully know, despite his seemingly tireless research methods and his voracious search for knowledge. In *Outback* he confesses that 'it is a fascinating but sometimes baffling exercise to try and interpret the relationship which tribal people ...enjoy with the rock' (Uluru/Ayers Rock).[4]

Secondly, Keneally is a writer who is drawn to scenes of conflict, especially where that conflict leads to the exploration of individual conscience and action. The racial tensions in Australia allow Keneally to place his protagonists, especially his guilt-laden white protagonists, in situations of moral crisis where the courage to act and the rightness of action may be explored in a contemporary and pragmatic way.

Thirdly, each of the texts I intend to examine functions as an apologia for white Australia's racist past and liberal Australia's failure to address adequately the consequences in the present. The early works, *The Chant of Jimmie Blacksmith* and *Bullie's House*, are overtly apologetic in tone, and this is reinforced by the tragic consequences of contact with European culture for the Aboriginals involved. The later works, *Outback, Towards Asmara* and *Flying Hero Class*, generally avoid images of Aborigines as helpless victims, perhaps in response to the criticism of 'fatal impact' scenarios.[5] The white protagonists in these 'Aboriginal' texts become the author's alter egos, stumbling well-meaningly, but misguidedly and patronisingly, into the complexity of contemporary Aboriginal affairs. Like their author, they demonstrate 'the very gulf between values of the two races . . . the way tragedy can arise not only from malice but from the limits of goodwill'.[6] It is perhaps significant that Adam Shoemaker's criticism of Keneally's approach to Aboriginal material is couched in the same tones as Keneally's sympathetic criticism of the black and white characters in *Bullie's House*. He identifies Keneally as a member of 'the school of concerned conscience (often motivated by guilt)'.[7]

For Shoemaker, Keneally's failings in *Bullie's House* are 'a result of ethnocentricty rather than malice'.[8] But ethnocentric colonial images of Aborigines since the settlement have fostered and concealed demeaning and genocidal programmes, whitewashing both the missionary and state-run assimilationist policies. As Slemon indicates, the Second-World writer's position is 'radically compromised', is inescapably complicit in the process of territorial, cultural and political appropriation, 'even at those moments when they have promulgated their most strident and most spectacular figures of post-colonial resistance'. Aborigines have only recently been allowed to represent themselves politically and culturally, and the act of self-determination is inextricably linked with the growing assertiveness of their own voice. Aboriginal campaigners and writers like Maureen Watson are demanding 'black mirrors' for 'black faces'.[9] In these circumstances, a white Australian writer must be sensitive to the dangers of false representation of Aboriginal characters, and, as we shall see, Keneally has revealed a developing sensitivity in his approach to Aboriginal issues, and also a growing wariness about appearing to represent or to explain fully the Aboriginal mind.

In 1991, during an interview for the BBC's *Third Ear*, Keneally stated:

> I don't have the bravado any more to write from the inside. I'm amazed that I had the arrogance ever to do it, to write from inside of the Aboriginal race. But I do think it is valid to write about what a white observer, McCloud, learns from travelling...with these people.[10]

In 1972 he had created a full psychological profile of an Aboriginal protagonist in *Jimmie Blacksmith*, but by 1991 he felt that this was naïve and patronizing. It seems a white writer may observe and explain his observations from his own cultural frame of reference, but he should not speak as an Aborigine. Trinh Minh-Ha would recognize this moment of revelation, and also its dangers:

> Many have come to tolerate...dissimilarity and have decided to suspend their judgements (only) whenever the other is concerned. Such an attitude is a step forward; at least the danger of speaking for the other has emerged into consciousness. But it is a very small step indeed, since it serves as an excuse for their complacent ignorance and their reluctance to involve themselves in the issue...[and she warns] they will not fail to fill in the blanks on your behalf, and you will be said.[11]

Keneally was involved in the issue of Aboriginal rights in the late eighties; as a member of the Constitutional Commission, he was examining, amongst other things, the exclusion of the Aborigines from the 1900 Federal Constitution. Nonetheless, following on from Trinh Minh-Ha's comments, we need to ask ourselves whether Keneally the writer is guilty of 'complacent ignorance', and of a tendency to 'fill in the blanks' on behalf of Australian Aborigines, even as he claims a new reserve in approaching Aboriginal culture.

In parallel with other civil rights movements during the sixties, Aboriginal Australians campaigned actively for improved rights and self-determination. There were key victories – voting rights, legislation on equal pay and an emerging pressure for land rights. It was in this campaigning atmosphere that *The Chant of Jimmie Blacksmith* emerged, a novel about an Aboriginal who is destroyed through contact with European culture. Keneally was not in the vanguard of the campaign, but the national and international success of the novel and film certainly alerted a wider audience.

Bain Attwood identifies this period of historical writing as 'oppositional'.[12] *The Chant of Jimmie Blacksmith* shares some of the perspectives
of the oppositional historians that Attwood discusses: an interest in
addressing the misrepresentations and injustices of the past, recording
the dispossession and destruction of the homogeneous and idyllic indigenous culture, and focusing on the interface between European and
Aboriginal culture.

Keneally's interest in history had drawn him to the story of Jimmy
Governor, a missionary Aboriginal, infamous for his massacre of
white farmers and their families at the turn of the century. This story
offered a chance to explore the nature of white racism by addressing the
destruction of an individual, indeed a culture, through cultural arro-
gance, territorial appropriation and assimilationist policies. He links this
past racism with the present in the final section of the novel when
Jimmie's execution is deferred so that it doesn't mar the Federation
celebrations or remind the good citizens that at least one section of
the population has no rights of citizenship, rights which it would not
attain until 1967.

Jimmie Blacksmith is presented as a fully initiated Aboriginal. There is
a powerful and poetic description of Jimmie's tribal initiation at the
beginning of the novel, which is important in establishing the richness
and the validity of the culture that Jimmie loses. He is dispossessed by
his life in the missionary camp, and he is further dispossessed when the
well-intentioned Reverend Neville promises progress and respect if he
embraces European values. Jimmie Blacksmith's faith in these idealistic
promises, which do not reflect the attitudes of the wider European
community, make him complicit in his loss of Aboriginal culture, and
this complicity is an important factor in the self-destructiveness of his
subsequent actions. He rejects the camp and fringe Aborigines who are
wasting away through disease and alcohol abuse and sets out to prove
himself to the white community which he perceives to be superior. The
hypocrisy and racism of the white settlers is emphasized, as is their
culpability in Jimmie's downfall. He is abused, mocked and rejected,
the more so because his ability to absorb European manners and expectations threatens their claim to racial and cultural superiority. Jimmie's
ability to learn and his natural intelligence challenge the European
treatment of Aborigines, for Jimmie cannot be dismissed as a primitive,
fossilized in the evolutionary process.

But Jimmie excites the most primal eugenic fears when he marries a
white woman. The white settlers, in particular Miss Graf, feel obliged to
separate the couple. This act finally triggers the explosive violence of

the first murders. Jimmie, disillusioned, rootless, psychologically and spiritually broken, declares war on the white settler. There is a clear irony here; Jimmie is himself a 'half-caste', a product of an illicit but common union, yet the possibility that an Aboriginal male could be attractive to a white woman is seen as both abhorrent and threatening to the eugenic order.

The Reverend Neville's assimilationist ideal is overtly criticized, and ultimately he accepts responsibility for his folly and its consequences. He is presented as a broken man as he faces the victim/monster created by his programme. This is another of Keneally's links with contemporary Australian racism. The policy of assimilation had been actively pursued in Australia, and the forced adoption of 'half-caste' children was still being pursued in the sixties. Ironically, Narogin feels that the ground-breaking Aboriginal writers who emerged in this period were often victims and consequently overt critics of assimilationist policy. They, like Jimmie, had found themselves in 'a no-man's-land between Black and White'.[13] Keneally was therefore addressing an important contemporary issue for white and black Australians.

So far we have a laudable, oppositional reading of white racism and its tragic results; but, in retrospect, with an understanding of the shifting positions of the Aboriginal political voice over the last twenty-five years, the novel appears to be disturbingly fatalistic in its treatment of the protagonist and of Aboriginal culture. Jimmie's descent into violence and self-destruction, the inevitability of his fall, the soul-destroying alcoholic life in the camps and on the fringes of the town may be powerful indictments of white racism, but they are also negative, degenerative images of Aboriginal culture. The Aborigines are presented as tragic victims, and there is no evidence in this novel that the Aborigines can survive European contact and modernity and remain psychologically and spiritually whole. It is this degradation, this 'social Darwinism',[14] that Mudrooroo Narogin has criticized in the novel. The mood of the novel denies the qualities of endurance, self-awareness, self-determination and humour that were central to Aboriginal writing and culture in the late eighties and early nineties. Jimmie is also the first of a number of Keneally's Aboriginal characters through whom he almost exclusively highlights the problems of cultural hybridity at the expense of the potential benefits of cultural exchange. However, the spirit of the novel is one of 'oppositional' redress, and it remains a strong indictment of past and present white racism. In addition, Keneally had succeeded in bringing a complex, intelligent and empathetic Aboriginal protagonist to a wide Australian audience.

Bain Attwood records a shift in focus in historical writing in the early eighties, and he names this period 'revisionist'. There was a new emphasis – a rejection of guilt-laden readings of the oppositional movement and a recognition that Aboriginal perspectives could be recorded. Aborigines are presented as active rather than passive: indeed, when the revisionist historians record the meeting between European and Aboriginal cultures, they focus on reciprocal influence. Revisionist historians actively sought an understanding of the subtle nuances of Aboriginal culture. There was also a recognition of the diversity of Aboriginal culture and experience and a new wariness about the potentially false conclusions that might be drawn by treating the Aborigines as a homogenous group. Aborigines also started to tell and record their own 'history', a movement that Attwood labels 'Aboriginal', and it became apparent that Aboriginal priorities and techniques are different from those of Western historians.

Keneally's next literary work with an 'Aboriginal' focus was the play *Bullie's House*, which was performed in 1980 and published in 1981. We return here to the 'oppositional' territory of *Jimmie Blacksmith*, for the protagonist is a missionary Aboriginal, living on a missionary camp in the 1950s. He is another victim of assimilationist policy. He has been taught to admire European culture and this leads him to question aspects of his Aboriginal identity. Like Jimmie, Bullie's search for the 'mysteries' of white Australian culture prove tragic and fatal.

However, although Bullie is confused by his attraction to both cultures, he is presented as a more positive figure than Jimmie, for his Aboriginal allegiance is a much stronger part of his psyche. Bullie does not reject his Aboriginal identity; indeed he initiates the play's crisis by revealing the tribal *ranga*, the sacred totems, because he believes them to be invaluable. In revealing the deepest Aboriginal secrets he feels sure that the white community will reciprocate by revealing the basis of the white cosmos; then, through this act of good will, the world will be in balance, and Bullie will be psychologically and spiritually at peace. So we have a 'revisionist' hero, active, self-determining, rooted in Aboriginal culture.

The white community has nothing equivalent to offer. The hapless anthropologist Cleary, already cynical and doubtful about the value of his work, is left with the impossible task of persuading the government of the significance of Bullie's act. He seems a powerless and comic figure when he struggles back with library books as a reciprocal gift. He is humbled in the presence of the Aboriginal offering, and white culture seems spiritually and symbolically deficient in its inability to match Bullie's gift.

A pattern is emerging in Keneally's Aboriginal narratives. While it is important to note the way the Aboriginal characters are being presented, it is also important to examine the presentation of the well-meaning, paternalistic and fundamentally misguided white characters who become a consistent part of the symbolic structure. These are figures of confusion, who try in a variety of ways to expiate past and present racial crimes, but who become overwhelmed by 'the very gulf between the values of the two races'.[15] These figures are Keneally's alter egos, consciously struggling to expiate racial guilt and the anxieties of privilege. Reverend Neville was an idealist; Cleary is initially a cynic, who sees anthropology as 'another white industry'. He is aware that in recording Aboriginal culture, he is ultimately assimilating and transforming that culture for Western consumption. He therefore embodies valid criticism of the role of the scientist in the colonial process.[16] Significantly, it is Cleary who is shamed and 'transformed' into action by Bullie's offering. Cleary becomes the apologist for the deficiencies of Western culture and the defender of Mallie, the Aborigine who kills Bullie for persuading the elders to reveal the sacred *ranga*. However, in providing us with these essentially sympathetic, guilt-laden white characters, to what extent is Keneally deflecting more direct criticism of their actions, particularly their involvement in the process of acculturation, and to what extent do we become 'occupied with the Savior's concern'[17] at the expense of the victim? And in highlighting the needs of the Aborigines through these white protagonists, could Keneally be caught in the 'compulsion to help the needy, a noble and self-gratifying task that also renders the helper's service indispensable'?[18]

Keneally and his publishers were clearly aware of Aboriginal sensitivities. The published play is prefaced by three essays which attempt to explain and justify the play's subject matter and its white author. Keneally's essay compares *Jimmie Blacksmith* with *Bullie's House*. Keneally stresses that Bullie is a more autonomous and self-possessed character than Jimmie. Bullie is neither passive nor dismissive of the value of his culture. Bullie offers the sacred *ranga* as an act of reciprocity, for he feels that 'white society desperately needs the sacred objects'.[19] The director defends the play by asserting that 'Keneally's triumph is in creating a play in which Australian Aborigines are the protagonists'.[20] Bob Maza, one of the Aboriginal cast, reveals his initial resistance to the text because it was written by a white writer. In discussion with other Aborigines he came to accept it: 'If it's true and it's about our people, does it matter who writes it, it's about us – about our ways'.[21] For Bob Maza and those involved with the project, Aboriginal approval was important.

Why should those involved feel so defensive? By the early eighties, Aboriginal writers and campaigners were directly challenging white writers who assumed they had the expertise to write about Aboriginal experience. Aboriginal writers' appeal to authenticity is exemplified in Jim Everett's statement: 'we are the real experts of our own cultural beliefs'.[22] Keneally faced a key test in Aboriginal notions of authenticity, the test of witness and lived experience. Two of the actual protagonists from Elcho Island were alive, and Maza tells us that 'in a meeting back in their country they voted unanimously against the play'.[23] And Adam Shoemaker records Keneally's admission that he had been 'taught...great lessons', when he discovered that the man who originally presented the *ranga* was alive and the recipient of an MBE, and that his version of events did not fit Keneally's own '*creative distortions*'.[24] Shoemaker feels that this play, in its distortion of its anthropological source, a monograph by R. M. Berndt, and in its misrepresentation of the lives of the real protagonists, 'best illustrates the risks of misinterpretation which befall even the best intentioned European writer'.[25] Few writers of documentary fiction would pass the witness test, but this account does illustrate the pressure on a writer to authenticate material when he is writing from a colonially privileged position about another culture, particularly when that very privilege rests on his ability through publishing houses to explain Aboriginal culture to a wider audience and 'to fill in the blanks on [the Aborigines'] behalf'.[26]

After this embarrassing encounter with the dangers of faction, and with the assertive Aboriginal voice, Keneally turned to journalism. In 1983, he researched and published *Outback*, a journalistic account of the people who live in the Northern Territory. The research for this book also provided Keneally with a detailed, relatively complex account of contemporary Aboriginal life and issues. This research would also be used in *Towards Asmara* and *Flying Hero Class*. Like the revisionist historians, Keneally was acknowledging the complex nature of Aboriginal culture. In *Outback* he is at pains to stress the increasingly autonomous and 'different' political voice that was emerging from Aboriginal communities. The foreword provides us with a clue to Keneally's new position on Aboriginal culture:

This account also attempts to enter that tribal cosmos of the Aboriginals, that other Australia of the Aboriginal mind, so different from the Australia of the European as to be another continent, another planet.[27]

This emphasis on the 'otherness' of the Aboriginal mind and culture governs the next two novels under discussion that focus on Aboriginal concerns. As a narrator Keneally is far less willing to explain or rationalize his Aboriginal characters' psyche. The stress on otherness may reflect a new humility in a culturally privileged author, but otherness also sets traps for the complacent. Trinh Minh-Ha points out the advantages of conferring otherness or 'difference reduced to identity/authenticity' on a marginalized group – '[it] serves to reassure the conscience of the liberal establishment and gives a touch of subversiveness to the discourse delivered'.[28]

As Ashcroft, Griffiths and Tiffin argue, to label a culture 'Other' can be an act of linguistic colonialism, for it is the voice from the centre that constructs the label, and such labelling is therefore an exercise of power over the marginalized group, not an offering of difference on equal terms. The 'Other', of course, is being defined in terms of the self. It therefore becomes another way of examining the privileged self at the expense of the marginalized Other.[29] Perhaps it is significant that when Keneally begins to doubt that his humanitarian, liberal goodwill is universally applicable and welcome, the Aborigine becomes 'the Other'.

An intriguing aspect of the narrative voice in *Outback* is Keneally's apparent insecurity about bringing his liberal city values to what he perceives to be the frontier of the cultural divide, where racial conflicts and compromises are dealt with on a day-to-day basis. This shows admirable self-awareness, though there is evidence that he developed this particular reflex from the white northern settlers who mock him for his patio liberalism. It could be argued that this new anxiety prevents him from being critical when criticism is needed. George Melly, in his review of *Outback* for *New Society*,[30] suggests that he has carefully selected his white subjects for their sympathy and tact in dealing with Aborigines; as a result he creates a landscape with remarkably few racists. White racial crime *is* recorded, and he reveals how complex is the process of satisfying the different world views of both cultures when he deals with the issues of land claims, mining rights and judicial practice. However, the subtext of *Outback* is Keneally's desire to demonstrate that both cultures can and do live together through compromise and mutual understanding. Nonetheless, there is a link between the racial subtext of *Outback* and the later 'Aboriginal' novels which deal with contemporary Australia. As I have suggested earlier, Keneally focuses on the well-meaning white Australian who seeks to help but is baffled by the gulf between the two cultures. These 'liberal' white men, who acknowledge racial guilt and who attempt redress and expiation, are important literary contributions to the racial debate in contemporary Australia, for these men of conscience are responsive to the Aboriginal claims for justice. But Keneally does not create the irredeemable, overt white racists that populated the nineteenth-century world of *The Chant of Jimmie Blacksmith*. He seems less interested, or is perhaps less happy, in addressing, the overt white racists that do exist in contemporary Australia. And, although he may deal with contemporary racial issues similar to those with which Aboriginal writers are concerned, his tone is very different from the generally campaigning, politicized voice of the Aboriginal writer.

Towards Asmara sets the Aboriginal subplot in contemporary Australia. Keneally is critical of the liberal white protagonist, who both idealizes and patronizes the Aborigines he seeks to serve. Keneally is also prepared to be critical of Aboriginal tribal culture, which is not simply presented as a repository of metaphysical truths that are absent in European culture. He is clearly more circumspect in his exploration of the Aboriginal psyche. Darcy, the central character, wishes to reject his white Australian culture, with its Eurocentric vision, and he therefore embarks upon two pilgrimages in search of the clarity and purity of tribalism. One takes him to the Australian outback, the other to the war zone of Eritrea. He leaves the outback disillusioned and humiliated, and he dies in Eritrea. Darcy exemplifies a new breed of white Australians, criticized by Nicholas Thomas in *Colonialism's Culture*, who cherish what they see as 'primitive and archaic' Aboriginal culture.[31] This becomes the unquestioned touchstone for all that is originary, socially simple and natural. Aboriginal values are read through a modern New Ageism, and are seen to represent spiritual truths that humanity has otherwise lost. Darcy becomes a volunteer legal advisor for urban Aborigines. His wife is a social worker, and over suburban dinners they decide they are tired of dealing with the crimes of urban Aborigines and seek the clarity of tribal culture. This rejection of urban Aborigines as tainted and impure, Thomas suggests, is one of the most negative by-products of this new romanticism. The rejection, together with a fetishization of tribal values, would freeze Aboriginal culture in an essentialist timewarp.

Darcy is presented as a victim of his own white liberal egotism and foolishness, for he assumes he can understand Aborigines and become a part of Aboriginal culture. He feels he will become a necessary and subtle mediator able to bridge the gulf that divides the two cultures. With characteristic irony, Keneally has Darcy face the truth at the height of his delusion. He has been taken to sacred sites and he assumes that this means he is now fully accepted. When he returns, he is in turn rejected because of his wife's deliberate desecration of a male sacred site. It is a challenge by his wife, and a challenge that he fails to meet, for he allows her to be tried in an Aboriginal court. After this fundamental betrayal, his wife leaves him to live in Darwin with an urbanized Aboriginal, a rebel that the tribal group finds hard to control. Darcy is forced to leave as well, and ironically begins to write articles for *The Times* as an expert on Aboriginal affairs. Keneally's narrative encourages criticism of Darcy, whose interventions have been naïve, self-interested and ineffective. Darcy's crime seems to be his middle-class naïvety, and the severity of Keneally's criticism perhaps reflects Keneally's own anxieties about patio liberalism. The writer of *Bullie's House* and its embarrassing aftermath would surely sympathize with Darcy's plaintive cry: 'I'd thought that because I was passionate about something as alien to me as the tribal cosmos, everything would be forgiven me'.[32]

A worrying feature of the novel is the absence of a positive image of urban Aborigines to counterbalance Darcy's disillusion with urban Aboriginality. This absence is clearly problematic, because the author could be accused of the very fault that his protagonist commits – a problematizing of the culturally hybridized, complex Aboriginal community in the city. The Bicentenary celebrations of 1988 were marked by Aboriginal political activism. Alongside the pressure to place Aboriginal rights on the political agenda was a desire to celebrate contemporary Aboriginal achievements. Cultural hybridity became a basis of urban self-assertion – proof that the Aborigines were a race who could endure and deal with the modern world on their own terms. Nicholas Thomas provides a pertinent illustration of this in his survey of the highly acclaimed musical featuring an Aboriginal cast, *Bran nue dae*. 'Ich bin ein Aborigine', proclaims the Aborigine son of a German missionary, fostered by white Australia during the forced adoptions of the fifties and sixties.[33]

While Keneally has revealed himself to be sensitive to the changing debates around Aboriginal representation, he does reinforce the 'authenticist' divide between tribal and urban Aborigines. Like Thomas, Gareth Griffiths is clear about the dangers of what might seem an unfortunate but understandable liberal reflex. It positions the urban and 'tribal' Aborigines 'as disputational claimants to a territoriality of the authentic'[34], and therefore represents Aborigines as divided along lines designated by Western voices. Most importantly it undermines the arguments for social justice and equality from vociferous urban pressure groups.

In 1991, *Flying Hero Class* was published, and it was during Keneally's promotional tour for the novel that he questioned his audacity in attempting to enter the Aboriginal mind. This new uncertainty about speaking for the Aborigine is clearly a reflection of the complex personal and literary journey Keneally has taken since the publication of *The Chant of Jimmie Blacksmith*. Having travelled so far, it is perhaps surprising to trace problems in Keneally's representation of Aborigines in these later novels. But, however well-meaning and courageous the attempt, a 'Second-World' writer is likely to trigger new racial sensibilities even as he attempts redress.

Flying Hero Class is a novel that places an Aboriginal dance troupe and their white Australian manager, McCloud, on a plane that is hijacked by the PLO. Keneally's claim to remain outside the Aboriginal psyche is in part self-deceptive. The psychological crisis of Bluey, an Aboriginal actor who has had prolonged contact with urban and cosmopolitan culture, is extensively explored. Indeed, we are in familiar territory. Bluey, like Jimmie and Bullie, is a culturally hybridized character drawn to his Aboriginal roots but 'buggered up' by Western culture. He therefore embodies the familiar theme of cross-cultural tensions. Significantly, Keneally chooses Bluey to be the Aboriginal character who allows himself to be manipulated by the PLO. The unconscious authenticist in Keneally leaves the 'tribally focused' Aborigines largely unexplored and 'Other'. For example, Philip Puduma is introduced as both a tribal elder and a Christian, and once his symbolic function is fixed, that is, as an Aborigine who can reconcile Christian faith with Aboriginality, he remains a cipher. Whitey, the leader of the dance troupe and moral touchstone of the novel, is a mysterious figure, cloaked in the powers of prophetic dreaming and the fearsome judicial responsibilities of the Featherfoot. Importantly, no member of the dance troupe apart from Bluey succumbs to the PLO's demand for denouncement and violent redress.

McCloud, the manager of the dance troupe, is accused by the PLO of betraying the troupe and the Barramatjara by removing key Aboriginal negotiators at the time when a mining company is about to push for mining rights. For Aboriginal Australians the corporate and political pressure to relinquish land is an important contemporary issue, an issue that Keneally had researched in *Outback*. McCloud is in fact innocent of conscious betrayal, but he acknowledges his professional and personal failure in accepting the mining company's sponsorship at face value:

They could depend on my lack of genuine interest in what they were up to... I've been a part of the plot. I've been to the Barramatjara country to write about sand paintings and dancing. But my interest never went so far as to asking whether or not some geologist had found promising core samples there.[35]

This is one of the many pertinent comments Keneally has to make on the intellectual and moral failings of the Western liberal in the arena of racial politics in the novels and play under discussion. These moments of insight and honesty, these recognitions of 'the limits of goodwill', are significant contributions to the racial debate in Australia.

In contrast to McCloud's self-deluding paternalism, the calmness of the dance troupe during the tour and the hijack, and their willingness to listen to the PLO but not necessarily be swayed by the emotive appeal, leave the impression that this Aboriginal troupe can handle the contemporary world, however sophisticated the pressure. They are not helpless victims like Jimmie, they are not tragic heroes like Bullie and they have no need of mediators like McCloud. As such they exemplify Keneally's ackowledgement of Attwood's 'Aboriginal period', which recognizes Aborigines' demand for autonomy of voice and culture.

Ironically, in his efforts to avoid paternalistic explications of another culture in the later novels, Keneally has become more ethnocentric in his focus. Both *Towards Asmara* and *Flying Hero Class* feature the struggles of the white male protagonist, and the Aboriginal characters have largely become symbolic cyphers. Darcy and McCloud bring their professional skills to the Aboriginal world, and, like Jimmie and Bullie, they want to be 'initiated' into another culture to replace the vacuum created by their own self-doubt and unease. Keneally has his questing knights limp away from their encounter with Aboriginal culture, humiliated but wiser, and since 1991 their creator seems to have done the same.

The Second-World writer is inescapably complicit in the political system that places his cultural values above those of other races. Even as he becomes a sincere and insightful critic of/apologist for his culture, even as he criticizes the imbalance of power and the asymmetries of representation, he will be necessarily blind to the machineries of power that sustain him. Over the last twenty-five years or so Keneally's 'Aboriginal' writing has reflected the shifting and developing patterns of race relations in Australia. These novels have served as acts of confession and expiation for the guilt-laden liberal voice, and as such they have a different political agenda to the campaigning Aboriginal writer. The subtle changes in the well-meaning, but ethnocentric, authorial voice are indicators of racial progress in Australia, but also suggest one of the reasons why those reforms are slow and limited. Keneally genuinely believes in a fair go for all, but the effort to acknowledge and surrender intellectual, political and cultural privilege is an ongoing struggle, requiring constant vigilance.

Part IV

Versions of Hybridity

13
The Trickster at the Border: Cross-Cultural Dialogues in the Caribbean

Patricia Murray

The Caribbean has occupied an ambivalent place in postcolonial studies, contributing key critics and ideas to the field but, nevertheless, dislocating many of its favourite themes and categories. Historically, geographically and linguistically it problematizes the borders of academic study, and constantly reappears in different guises – the Antilles, the West Indies, the Americas. In this context, the Amerindian has had to be the most expert of all shape-shifters, confined, as s/he often is, at the corners of critical inquiry. In this essay, I will look at a short story by an anglophone Caribbean writer, Wilson Harris, which specifically engages with Amerindian perspectives, and in a context of pre- as well as post-1492 cross-culturalities. I hope to show the relevance of these dialogues to current debates about Caribbean identity and to argue a case for the Caribbean as central to our definitions of hybridity and postcoloniality.

I

The significance of the Caribbean as an island bridge which connects North and South America, as well as the various traces of old-world points of departure, cannot be underestimated. Critical works as early as Fernando Ortiz's *Cuban Counterpoint* (1940) or Louis James's *The Islands in between* (1968) were keen to highlight the dynamics of location and the complex locutionary positions such dynamics produced. As Antonio Benítez-Rojo has written more recently (1989), the Caribbean is a repeating island, a meta-archipelago which has no boundary and no centre:

> Thus the Caribbean flows outward past the limits of its own sea with a vengeance, and its *ultima Thule* may be found on the outskirts of

Bombay, near the low and murmuring shores of Gambia, in a Canto-
nese tavern of circa 1850, at a Balinese temple, in an old Bristol pub,
in a commercial warehouse in Bordeaux at the time of Colbert, in a
windmill beside the Zuider Zee, at a cafe in a barrio of Manhattan, in
the existential *saudade* of an old Portuguese lyric.[1]

As well as the diasporic nature of the various, and overlapping, Caribbean cultures, Benítez-Rojo is also calling attention to the fact that
'every intellectual venture directed toward investigating Caribbeanness
is destined to become an unending search. It doesn't matter where
you've left from, it doesn't matter how far you've gone, it doesn't matter
which ideology you profess, Caribbeanness will always remain beyond
the horizon' (xi). Or, as Stuart Hall argues in 'Cultural Identity and
Diaspora', using a Derridean perspective, Caribbean identity is constantly *deferred*.[2] There can be no easy path through the island bridge,
no avoiding the paradoxical and bifurcatory spaces produced out of
multiple and conflicting cycles of conquest and colonialism, however
urgent the need to assemble a coherent resistance in the face of continued oppression and destruction.

This is the dilemma which sits at the heart of Caribbean cultural
debate, and which finds immediate resonance in contemporary discussions within postcolonial studies; how to embrace the multiplicity and
diversity of cross-cultural heritages, and ever increasing cross-cultural
futures, whilst continuing to challenge the rapacious system of colonial
desire that produced such hybridity in the first place. This is not (or not
always) confined to the manic violation of the black colonized by the
white colonizer, though the traumas of the Middle Passage and the
Plantation economy are still evidenced in Caribbean society today;
and certainly any discussion of the creative aspects of cross-culturalism
would have to take place within the context of unequal power relations
that enabled (and continue to enable) the colonial machinery to
enslave, obliterate, eclipse and fragment those cultures that it has irrevocably displaced. A focus on the different forms of colonialism experienced in the Caribbean since 1492, and the different forms of inequality
institutionalized by them, begins to illuminate the contrasting local
situations of, for instance, Cuba, Haiti, Jamaica and Guyana. Cuba
already had an emerging creole population (the Spanish colonizing
power distracted by European feuds) by the time the Caribbean colonies
belonging to England, France and Holland began to exploit the land
through the vicious savagery of their slave plantations. That continental
Guyana experienced this period of slavery much later than the more

accessible island of Jamaica, relying instead on the large numbers of indentured labourers from Asia typical of a later period of colonialism, constitutes both its greater relative freedom from the trauma of slavery, and the unresolved racial tensions between Indo-Guyanese and Afro-Guyanese that continue to debilitate the country today. The different forms of colonialism experienced in the Caribbean, where most nation states have been produced out of multiple invasions and periods of conquest (Jamaica, for instance, still bears the history of an earlier period of Spanish colonialism in its runaway maroon communities), have produced different challenges and contrasting perspectives in the contemporary postcolonial context, and the notion of hybridity or a *creative* cross-culturalism is not something that can be articulated or guaranteed in the same way throughout the area.

Nevertheless, the Caribbean has a long history of cultural critics who have rejected the perceived hegemony of the colonizing powers and the eurocentric categories left behind, and have focused instead on local forms of resistance and imagination that have endured, developed and interacted. Ortiz's development of the notion of *transculturation* in the thirties and forties, emphasizing the ability of subjugated or marginal groups to select and invent from materials imposed by the colonizing metropolis, has enabled later theorists (such as Angel Rama and Homi Bhabha) to focus more rigorously on the reciprocal forms of cultural exchange which have been elided by the rhetoric of colonialism, and which also reveal the colonizer to be irrevocably cross-culturalized by its contact with the colonized. This latter insight may seem obvious to anyone living in London or Paris today, or familiar with the hybridized cultural products of contemporary British, French or Spanish societies. It is important, however, that we recognize this form of dynamic cultural exchange not just as a phenomenon of contemporary postcolonial cultures but as present, in however frail or subtle a form, in the very moment of colonization. In her work on travel writing and transculturation, for example, Mary Louise Pratt refers to this space of colonial encounters as the 'contact zone' and emphasizes the need to 'treat the relations among colonizers and colonized ... not in terms of separateness and apartheid, but in terms of copresence, interaction, interlocking understandings and practices, often within radically asymmetrical relations of power'.[3] Fanon's work is a key example of this, vividly portraying the ruthlessness of colonial exploitation in Algeria (the legacy of which is still writ large today), while at the same time emphasizing the fierce and organized resistance that accompanied each stage of that colonialism and providing interesting examples of what Pratt goes on to define as 'autoethnography'.[4] In a more theorized reading of the contact zone, Bhabha has extended these insights to suggest the powerful potential for counter-domination that emerges, even before any intentional agency on the part of the colonized, in the very act of mimicry imposed on them by the colonizing mission.[5]

But however stimulating and complex his analyses of strategies for decolonization, Bhabha has been criticized for appearing to produce an overly-homogeneous notion of the colonial subject, and we must be careful not to do the same. Mention of Fanon, though, immediately reminds us of the multiplicity of the Caribbean location for postcolonial studies and the difficulty of tracing even the simplest of its critical genealogies without crossing the borders of academic study. For the Caribbean is centrally located in the intellectual journeys of both the Black Atlantic (linking the three continents of America, Europe and Africa) and the cross-cultural Americas, encompassing major writings in Spanish, Portuguese, French and English and producing important comparative work and dialogues between different moments of colonialism, as in C. L. R. James's analysis of Haiti in *The Black Jacobins* and the influence Eric Williams drew from the nineteenth-century writings of José Martí. The challenge and opportunity presented by such cross-culturality is not lost on the writers and critics in the region, indeed forming the abiding theme of creative and theoretical work by Edouard Glissant, Wilson Harris and Roberto Fernández Retamar. Unfortunately, some of these critical overlaps and historical relationships have been lost in the institutional compartmentalizing of a 'postcolonial studies' into departments of English and Modern Languages, and the disproportionate focus on the process of post-Second World War decolonization.[6] It is hoped that as the relatively new field of postcolonial studies becomes more interdisciplinary and more comparative, and includes the Americas in a more systematic and consistent way, the Caribbean will re-emerge, through the fields of hispanic as well as francophone and anglophone cultural theory, as central rather than peripheral to the field of study.

II

It is not simply the case, however, that a cross-cultural perspective emerges with the arrival of Europeans in the Americas, and the subsequent movement of displaced and migrant peoples. If we are to talk of a cross-cultural dialogue in the region then it must also take account of what Harris calls the 'live absences' or 'endangered presences' of the

Amerindian. Harris's terminology is appropriate not just in the context of his native Guyana, to which I will return in this essay, but also in relation to the wider 'statistical ghetto' and 'documentary stasis'[7] suffered by Amerindian cultures at the hands of post-Columbian cultural commentators. As Gordon Brotherston forcefully points out in the prologue to his *Book of the Fourth World*, the eclipse of native America has no parallel even in the long history of colonialisms:

> In not one of its nation-states is the dominant or official language effectively an indigenous one. Rare are the educational systems that consistently relate surviving indigenous peoples to the deeper past of America, insofar as this can be known through literature and archaeology. Rarer still is the historiography that seeks to excavate its premise locally rather than blindly corroborate imported versions of this planet's story. In short, America is the only one of the four worlds to have undergone thorough dispossession.[8]

Though Amerindians have been the object of study for a variety of disciplines, including theology, anthropology and ecology, they are repeatedly imagined as if frozen in time – in either the glorious past or the destitute present. Surviving indigenous people are thus denied a route into their own history, which becomes instead a fantasy of 'otherness' around which Western epistemologies can preen. Brotherston highlights an example of this in the debates between Lévi-Strauss and Derrida over the value and function of speech/writing amongst Amerindians, specifically the Nambikwara. Although Derrida successfully critiques Lévi-Strauss's fantasy of the pre-literate Amerindian, and argues for a 'grammatology' that cannot simply be reduced to speech or writing, he does not then give voice to that grammatology but bypasses the variety of Amerindian media in favour of his own chosen historical source, the master text of Judaism. As Brotherston concludes:

> Denying the denizens of his New World their material-historical existence, Lévi-Strauss will refer for example to the vast sweep of the Algonkin language family from Massachusetts to the Rockies as if they were still there, as if nothing had happened and yet more to the point, as if nothing was now happening every year and every day. With his genealogical Old World obsessions, Derrida likewise denies the native Americans their historicity and, by ignoring their master texts, reproduces on an intellectual plane the very hegemony he

would claim to be combating. Hence fantasy and fatalism: equals our disease and our guns.[9]

Of course, there is much that is useful in the work of both Lévi-Strauss and Derrida, and Brotherston's intention in reading them against the grain of their own (eurocentric) obsessions is to show how each subjects the other to a translation in order to suggest a new synthesis, a grammatology (Derrida) of America (Lévi-Strauss). It is this potential for translation or transformation which Bhabha defines as the revisionary force within critical theory, even as he acknowledges its institutional containment to date:

> Montesquieu's Turkish Despot, Barthes's Japan, Kristeva's China, Derrida's Nambikwara Indians, Lyotard's Cashinahua pagans are part of this strategy of containment where the Other text is forever the exegetical horizon of difference, never the active agent of articulation. The Other is cited, quoted, framed, illuminated, encased in the shot/reverse-shot strategy of a serial enlightenment. Narrative and the cultural politics of difference become the closed circle of interpretation. The Other loses its power to signify, to negate, to initiate its historic desire, to establish its own institutional and oppositional discourse.[10]

Though Bhabha is talking specifically about the limits of critical theory, and in a language typical of metropolitan academic discourse in the nineties, his words echo many of Harris's earlier concerns about the 'documentary stasis' that is produced out of an apodictic methodology. Speaking in Georgetown in 1970, Harris argued that many intellectuals in the anglophone Caribbean were falling victim to that same 'exegetical horizon' and, in attempting to contain and marginalize 'bewildering' cultural manifestations such as limbo, vodun and vestiges of Amerindian legend, deprived themselves of folk and native resources that may articulate 'a profound art of compensation':

> Insufficient attention has been paid to such phenomena and the original native capacity these implied as omens of re-birth. Many historians have been intent on indicting the Old World of Europe by exposing a uniform pattern of imperialism in the New World of the Americas. Thus they conscripted the West Indies into a mere adjunct of imperialism and overlooked a subtle and far-reaching renascence. In a sense therefore the new historian – though his stance

is an admirable one in debunking imperialism – has ironically extended and reinforced old colonial prejudices which censored the limbo imagination as a 'rowdy' manifestation and overlooked the complex metaphorical gateway it constituted in rapport with Amerindian omen.[11]

Harris goes on in this paper to explore some of the fables and myths, especially of the Carib and Arawak peoples, that point to such 'omens of rebirth' and their capacity to act as a 'complex metaphorical gateway' between cultures. In Harris's analysis, the native host regains 'its power to signify, to negate, to initiate its historic desire' and unsettles, rather than closes, grand eurocentric theories. But it is in his fiction that this dialogue takes place most productively; and it is to his fiction, and to the specific context of Guyana, that I now turn.

III

At the time Harris was working on 'History, Fable and Myth in the Caribbean and Guianas' he also wrote two collections of short stories, or Amerindian fables, entitled *The Sleepers of Roraima* (1970) and *The Age of the Rainmakers* (1971). In these stories he refers to Carib, Arawak, Wapishana, Patomona and Makushi peoples amongst others, reflecting the diversity of Guyana's Amerindian groups and the rich heritage they bring to the contemporary Guyanese imagination. Harris is aware, however, that these people are practically invisible in the representational practices of the Caribbean and that, even for most Guyanese, this cultural heritage still lies buried in the rubble of the past. Part of the problem is that the colonial demarcation of nation states in the Americas has caused Guyanese Amerindians to be historiographically cut off from their neighbours in Spanish- and Portuguese-speaking lands. So whilst a significant number of Latin American writers have drawn creatively on Amerindian sources (such as Carpentier in Venezuela, García Márquez in Colombia, Guimarães Rosa in Brazil) and the plight of Amerindians in Brazil is made at least partially visible in the Hollywood-ization of their story and its appropriation by occasional travelling pop stars, the Amerindians of Guyana and the rest of the Caribbean are popularly believed to be extinct, sometimes conjured as romantic figures in the remote past but not understood as a contemporary demographic fact. Thus, even the massive cyanide spill at the Omai Gold Mines dam in August 1995, which threatened vital water supplies to Amerindian communities in the Guyanese interior, received little publicity outside of Third World and ecological action groups, and this despite the resonance of a previous mass cyanide poisoning in the area by the Reverend Jim Jones and his followers in November 1978. Of course, the oppression of Amerindians by colonial (and then multinational) corporations in search of gold began in the Caribbean, and it was their decimation in this area which instigated the colonial traffic in new supplies of labour. Nevertheless, recent ethnographic surveys have found that Amerindian birth rates are the highest of all ethnic groups in Guyana, as throughout the Americas, reversing the widespread prediction at the beginning of the twentieth century that indigenous populations were on their way to extinction.

In 1993 Guyanese Amerindians were estimated to number 48 859 persons, comprising 6.81 per cent of the national population of 717 458 persons.[12] They are measured as the fourth largest ethnic group, after the East Indian (49.49 per cent), African (35.63 per cent) and Mixed (7.05 per cent) ethnic groups. Significantly, Guyana has a racialized geography, with the non-Amerindian majority concentrated on the narrow coastal plain which makes up about 5 per cent of the total land area. Guyanese Amerindians thus comprise the majority population in the vast interior, their settlement patterns of geopolitical importance throughout colonial history and still significant today as the Venezuelan state continues to lay claim to the Essequibo territory. Although the location and names of many of the Amerindian villages today are the result of Anglican missionary organization, which has also resulted in English superseding Amerindian languages, it is still possible to identify distinct language groups, broadly separated by natural environments in which the challenges facing riverain communities still differ from those confronted in the savannahs or mountainous regions. From these locations, colonial borders are often uncertain, or fluid – the people of the Rupununi, for instance, are largely cut off from the Atlantic Coast, speak Portuguese, and trade at Brazilian prices; Venezuelan helicopters have, in the past, landed within Guyana's border and distributed T-shirts telling the villagers that the territory belonged to Venezuela and encouraging interior residents to register as Venezuelan citizens.

From an Amerindian perspective, this process of being named (as Christian, as Guyanese, as Venezuelan), which is also an attempt to draw boundaries, goes back a long way. Even the terms Carib and Arawak were not Amerindian self-ascriptions but the product of a series of colonialist mishearings, misreadings and attempts to create polarized stereotypes out of a complicated pattern of various and often interconnected tribal groups.[13] Although these categories gradually became constitutive of Amerindian identity, so that people now self-identify as Carib or Arawak, they do so in their own historical context of continuously shifting communities, in which hybridity and miscegenation is the norm. It is this practice, this strategy of reinvention out of previous incarnations, through which no cultural legacy can ever become truly extinct, that Harris explores as an important subaltern voice and creative resource in his Amerindian fables. Born a coastlander (New Amsterdam), of Arawak, African and Scottish parentage (one of the many Amerindian descendants who would not have been identified as such in the demographic statistics outlined above), Harris recreates the multiple border crossings and trickster-like shape-shifting of Amerindian narratives to suggest the possibility of dialogue through legacies of colonialism.

IV

The story of 'Couvade' is the first of Harris's Carib trilogy entitled *The Sleepers of Roraima*. We are told in the author's note that Roraima, which is said to possess the highest mural rock face in the world, is a sacred mountain for the Amerindian and overlooks Brazil, Guyana and Venezuela. The setting of the story is immediately resonant of the kinds of cross-cultural perspectives Harris wishes to explore in his investigation into Carib, and Caribbean, history and identity. Geographical location immediately reminds us of Guyana's interior landscape, always metaphoric of psychological interiors and ancestral inheritance in Harris's writing, and the Spanish and Portuguese-speaking neighbours with whom Guyana shares these cultural legacies.'Couvade', like the other stories in the collection, tells of a 'sleeper' of Roraima, a buried voice or latent space in the Caribbean psyche which, once explored, may enable us to see, like the spirit of the sacred mountain, beyond the categories and borders imposed by colonialism.

The title of Harris's story refers to a birthing ritual common amongst Amerindians in the region and documented by Walter Roth, for instance, in relation to Carib, Arawak, Wapishana, Makushi and Warrau tribes.[14] The birth of a child was intimately connected with the birth of creation, and the whole community took part in this 're-birth' of their land and culture. Harris's note tells us that the purpose of this ritual was to hand on the legacy of the tribe to every newborn child:

All ancestors were involved in this dream – animal as well as human, bird as well as fish. The dust of every thing, cassava bread (the Carib's staple diet), the paint of war, the cave of memories, were turned into a fable of history – the dream of *Couvade*.[15]

According to Roth, the Carib term for this practice was 'Kenonimáno'[16] and involved great courage and fasting on the part of both parents, the male parent being constituted through the ritual as equally responsible for giving birth to the child. Even after the child's birth, part of its spirit was still said to follow the father and certain rituals had to be maintained[17] until the child could fully emerge out of its association with both parents into a self-identificatory being. In this way, the first crucial months of the child's life remained part of the birthing ritual and the conception of identity which emerges (*plurally* of both parents, *collectively* of ancestral community) is very different from the Lacanian model of the damaged subject.[18]

But it is significant that Harris refers to this birthing ritual using the French word that has replaced the various indigenous terms – 'Couvade' from the verb couver meaning to brood, to sit on (eggs) and indicating a 'hatching'. For Harris is aware that there is no way back to a pre-European Amerindian consciousness, that any native myths and rituals are 'all overlaid by European skeletons and archetypes as well'[19] and he is keen to expose this process of translation and mediation in which he is also inevitably involved. As a contemporary writer, he cannot enter the mind of the fifteenth-century Carib and he argues instead for a narrative method which 'borders upon a confession of weakness',[20] aware of its own partial perspective and seeking to avoid the predatory closure of the colonizing gaze.

The story begins in mid-conversation:

> The name you bear,' the old Carib said to Couvade his grandson, 'means *sleeper of the tribe*'
>
> (Harris, 'Couvade', p. 15)

where Couvade, 'this uncertain child of the future' (p. 15), is trying to understand the riddle of his name. He and his grandfather are two of the last surviving members of the 'fishermen of night' (p. 16), an ancient tribe who were attacked by the 'huntsmen of night' (p. 17) when Couvade was only six weeks old. Asked about his lost parents, and about the law of *couvade* that they are said to have broken, his grandfather will only reply:

> 'You will find it recorded – this dream – on the rocks and in the caves.'
>
> (p. 16)

This is a direct reference to the timehri of the Carib,[21] a series of ancient petroglyphs which Brotherston refers to as part of the complex grammatology of the Americas that is still to be deciphered.[22] As he sleeps that night, Couvade returns to the cave where his parents had hidden him and becomes aware of these rainforest signs which he cannot yet grasp:

> The walls of the cave were painted with many curious creatures. Birds. Fish. Men and women who were half-bird, half-fish. Scenes of the hunt. There were two figures in particular that fascinated him and they seemed to be coming alive on the wall of the cave... Though they were actually coming alive on the wall of the cave and Couvade felt that all he had to do was reach out and touch them, he had the sensation that they were still far removed from him. Divided from him by water, light, and other elements.
>
> (Harris, 'Couvade', p. 18)

The pre-Columbian visual language of the timehri is overlaid with contemporary images – the guacharo bird now wears American sunglasses, like Couvade 'had seen fall from the sky in the wake of a passing aeroplane' (p. 18) – and the child who is attempting to decipher their meaning also becomes an increasingly composite character. We are told that 'news had trickled through to the last members of the tribe that the great world beyond the great forest, beyond the Carib sea, was at war' (p. 18), and this signals both the imminent moment of conquest and colonization as well as later twentieth-century European wars.

The story proceeds as a journey through the multilevels of Couvade's dream in which two main narratives unfold simultaneously. In the central narrative, Couvade travels ever deeper into the cave of ancestors in an attempt to reunite with the spectre of his lost parents. This dream is then constantly interrupted by another, in which Couvade's grandfather is urging them to flee from enemy tribes and move forward to the next safe dwelling. Each journey is structured through a series of circular movements and the insistence on a cyclic, rather than a linear, trajectory is emphasized as we move through the various chapters of the story. Chapter 3 is the longest section of the story and the one in which the various dreamscapes most sharply coalesce, activating the same images and recurring themes. This is surrounded by two shorter (Chapters 2 and 4) and then two even shorter (Chapters 1 and 5) chapters or sections. As Mark McWatt has noted, the story is thus structured to suggest three concentric circles, each deeper and more complex as you move toward the centre, suggesting images of the whirlpool or vortex, and, in attempting a linear progression of the story, the reader experiences a cross-section of the whirlpool.[23] In this way, Harris is attempting to recreate the myth and ritual of couvade in the very form of his writing, for Amerindian myth, as well as expressing a sacred narrative, always has a strong performative element. The knowledge it reveals is not an external, abstract knowledge but one that can be experienced ritually, either by ceremonially recounting the myth or by performing the ritual for which it is the justification. As Lauri Honko explains in his definition of myth:

> The ritual acting out of myth implies the defence of the world order; by imitating sacred exemplars the world is prevented from being brought to chaos. The re-enactment of a creative event, for example, the healing wrought by a god in the beginning of time, is the common aim of myth and ritual. In this way the event is transferred to the present and its result i.e. the healing of a sick person, can be achieved once more here and now.[24]

This healing takes place on many levels in Harris's story. The ritual of couvade, as outlined by Roth above, is clearly the 're-enactment of a creative event' through which the newborn child inherits the legacy of the tribe. But in Harris's story the child has not been fully birthed. His parents fell sick and broke the law of couvade and so their child, too, is suffering a kind of sickness – fragmented and disoriented, trapped within the dream of couvade. The child – Couvade, the sleeper of the tribe – must relive his tribe's birthing ritual in order to be hatched/ parented anew and so emerge fully into consciousness. This requires him to re-connect with the parts of his spirit that have still been attached to his parents, and to reacquaint himself with his ancestral heritage.

The paintings on the wall of the cave provide Couvade with his first clues. He wears the two disguises of half-bird, half-fish in an attempt to fly and then swim across to the shadowy figures he can see there. When both of these fail, Couvade realizes that he must go to them in his own form and so removes the disguises:

> He carefully restored the head-dress, spectacles, feathers to the ground of the cave, the scales and eyes of the fish to the wall where they shone now like stars and constellations.
>
> (Harris, 'Couvade', p. 19–20)

Only when he exposes himself to his ancestors, becomes susceptible to them, does the bridge of souls appear to carry him across to the other bank of the stream. That this has been a symbolic, an imaginative bridge, is made clear in the obvious reflection of this other bank:

> No one was there to greet him but he saw that they had left their sunglasses suspended from a branch. Their head-dress too and the scales and eyes of a fish like a starry cloak which shone in the water against the trees. Couvade was glad. It was as if they wished to surrender to him all their disguises as he had surrendered his to them on his side of the cave.
>
> (p. 21)

It is not that Couvade has crossed physically to another bank but that we (through him) have *altered* perspective. Through these journeys, these changes in perspective, Couvade becomes a part of the cycle which deconstructs polarities of hunter and hunted, friend and enemy, which haunt the last remaining Caribs in the parallel dreamscape.

Chapter 3 begins as Couvade is being woken from one dream into another, and as his grandfather is packing their few belongings ready to move on. Each of their belongings signal important legacies of the past:

> First of all the sunglasses which had descended one day from the sky over the jungle in the wake of a passing aeroplane. Next – the head-dress of feathers, a relic of the past belonging to the old man's vanished son (Couvade's father). Then – scales and eyes of a fish – a kind of dancer's cloak – belonging to the vanished woman his mother.
>
> (p. 23)

As well as the twentieth-century signs which point to more recent elements of transculturation and hybridity, we learn that Couvade's father (huntsmen of night) and mother (fishermen of night) came from different tribes. This reflects the Carib practice of taking wives from the tribes they conquered and points to a cross-culturalism in the child (Couvade) who embodies both self and enemy. It also suggests why the Caribs seem to be decimated in numbers. As McWatt notes:

> They were the fiercest warrior tribe who conquered all enemies and were exterminated by their own domestic arrangements, so that their

enemy tribes flourished all over the landscape while they survived only in a few pitiful remnants.[25]

The colonizing Carib is not only cross-culturalized by its contact with the colonized, but almost obliterates its own identity in the process. As Couvade accompanies his grandfather on their journey through history, the name of their tribe changes many times, until Couvade begins to wonder if they were all 'one and the same – the cruel tricks and divisions of mankind, the cruel ruses and battles of mankind' (Harris, 'Couvade', p. 24). He begins to understand that the disguises he had tried to inhabit at the beginning of his journey had failed, because both were necessarily partial. He is the hybrid product of both parents, as his culture is the product of both colonizer and colonized, and these polarities have to be reconciled in the ritual of couvade. Thus, although Couvade is initiated into the motherhood of the tribe first, one of the most poetically rendered scenes of the journey:

> He shook himself now – the dust of stars – as if he too danced to the music of the river. In fact his feet began to move and spin. Ballet of the fish. Dance of the fish. Song of the river. Net of the river. He said to his grandfather in an ecstasy of happiness, 'I have caught her. My mother. She sings and dances in my net, in my heart. Song and dance of the fish painted on the wall of the cave.'
>
> (p. 27)

it is in the complementarity of male and female energies that the journey reaches its climax:

> The fish-net of his mother, which was no other than the bird-cloak of his father, whirled and danced in the sky, then settled itself into the bridge of dawn. Couvade felt the presence of both his lost parents crossing and re-crossing the shimmering bridge.
>
> (p. 31)

This recovery of identity is one element of the healing process of the myth, the 'profound art of compensation' which Harris had argued Amerindian myths and fables could offer the contemporary Caribbean. But Couvade's wish to integrate – with his parents, with ancestry – and the conception of cultural identity that he wishes to consolidate are constantly interrupted by his grandfather's more shifting perspective. At the point when Couvade feels he has found his mother's tribe, for instance, his grandfather intervenes:

> '[H]ush! it's a trick to make you sleep, then the enemy will take you away, make you her prisoner. *Their* prisoner. Believe me, Couvade, I tell you truly.'
>
> (p. 27)

The grandfather insists that Couvade remain mobile, recreating and reinventing himself out of their *various* histories, and reminds him that the bridges he crosses are not final, but intermediary, border crossings. According to the grandfather, there can be no illusion of integration, no final resting place:

> 'But why can't we rest here?' said Couvade. 'I'm very tired.'
> 'Impossible,' said the wrinkled lizard face of his grandfather. 'We must change our address. Change our colour. We must move on.'
>
> (p. 24)

Couvade had been guided through his earlier dream by a benevolent ancestral lizard, a shape-shifting talisman who had enabled him to journey through spaces of memory:

> Couvade followed the lizard as it moved along the wall of the forest. It kept changing colours all the way – sometimes it looked like a star or a fish, sometimes like a feather or a leaf. It was as if the colours it created were a bridge – an endless bridge spanning all the tribes, all the masks of ancestors.
>
> (p. 22)

By Chapter 3 it is clear that this lizard is one of the many transmutations of the trickster/grandfather who guides, cajoles and shadows Couvade throughout his journeys. Resembling the 'half-trickster, half-shaman' figure who appears in the tribe in times of crisis and whose role, according to Harris, 'is an indispensable creative attempt to *see* through or break through a hang-over of the past',[26] Couvade's grandfather is both the source of continuity and the dynamic through which historical rupture is replayed.

In this way, the tension that is set up in the story resembles, and could be said to prefigure, Stuart Hall's paradigm for understanding Caribbean identity:

If identity does not proceed, in a straight, unbroken line, from some fixed origin, how are we to understand its formation? We might think of Black Caribbean identities as 'framed' by two axes or vectors, simultaneously operative: the vector of similiarity or continuity; and the vector of difference and rupture. Caribbean identities always have to be thought of in terms of the dialogic relationship between these two axes. The one gives us some grounding in, some continuity with the past. The second reminds us that what we share is precisely the experience of a profound discontinuity... [27]

Harris's story reinscribes the Amerindian 'barely knowable or usable past'(Hall, p. 235) into Hall's sense of 'the empty land' (p. 234) of America, for in rewriting the dream of Couvade Harris challenges the conventional view that the Caribs have disappeared without trace. The historical moment when the Caribs are invaded is transfigured in Harris's story to illuminate the freedom and evolution also present in that cross-cultural encounter, as Couvade, the ritual dream of the Caribs, crosses 'the bridge of relationships' to become an important imaginative resource for the future Caribbean. According to Harris, the 'metaphorical gateways' that enabled Couvade to better understand the nature of his hybrid Carib identity are still available to his modern Caribbean descendants, if they can grasp their connection. Like Couvade, Harris does not underestimate the task:

Uncertain that the battle of idols, camouflage and armour, was over. Uncertain of the figures coming alive on the wall of the cave. Uncertain there was not a long hard way to go before the idols and paintings would truly melt, truly live, birth of compassion, birth of love.

(Harris, 'Couvade', p. 35)

14
Between Speech and Writing: 'La nouvelle littérature antillaise'?

Sam Haigh

Écrire 'la parole de nuit': la nouvelle littérature antillaise[1] is a very recent text from the Francophone Caribbean whose avowed aim is to celebrate the burgeoning literary tradition of the Antilles. However, this is not, as one might expect, a collection of extracts from the novels, poems and plays which make up the Antillean literary tradition – it is not simply an attempt to define a corpus of Antillean literature as such. Rather, it is a collection of previously unpublished pieces by well-known Antillean writers, a collection which aims, it would seem, to celebrate the radicality of this growing tradition, to attest to its constant capacity for self-renewal. It is an attempt, as its title suggests, to bring together examples of 'la *nouvelle* littérature antillaise', of *new* Antillean literature, and it raises interesting questions about the precise character of this 'new' Antillean literature – indeed, about the very notion of a 'new' literature for, or in, the Antilles.

This text – and it is by no means the only such recent example – is in fact a collection, mainly, of short stories. 'La nouvelle littérature antillaise', it would seem, is 'la nouvelle' – a notion which is in itself rather radical, for the short story is a genre which, apart from such notable exceptions as Joseph Zobel's *Laghia de la mort* (1946), has never enjoyed very much popularity within the Antillean literary tradition. From the first examples of 'racially aware' writing by black and mulatto Antilleans, which appeared in the early twentieth century, to the literature – principally poetry – of the négritude movement of the 1930s and the 1940s, to the flourishing novelistic tradition of the 1950s and the 1960s, poetry and, perhaps especially, the novel, have been the predominant genres of the Antillean literary tradition. And this is a fact which, it would seem, has everything to do with the relative 'prestige' attached to various literary forms.

Although the short story, within the French tradition, has certainly known periods of relatively high prestige as a literary form – during the early and the late nineteenth century, for example – the *nouvelle*, especially in the twentieth century, has never gained the prestige of the novel or of poetry.[3] Rather, as Clare Hanson suggests, it may be seen as a 'form of the margins, a form which is in some sense ex-centric, not part of official or "high" cultural hegemony'.[4] At the same time, as Frank Connor suggests, it is a form which often takes as its subject the marginal figure: the exiled or the alienated, 'the outlawed figure wandering about the fringes of society'.[5] Added to this, or perhaps consequently, the short story may often also appeal to writers who are themselves marginal in some way, writers who are not part of the dominant political, cultural and literary frameworks of their society. All of these associations, as far as the nascent literary tradition of a colonized culture is concerned, are of great significance, for black Antillean writers have typically written in order to gain entry into dominant – that is, French – culture, not in order to exclude themselves more surely from it.

Such issues of prestige and acceptance are relevant also to the recent interest in short-story writing in the Antilles, a phenomenon which may be seen to have everything to do with a gradual movement on the part of Antillean writers of the last few decades towards *asserting* their marginality and their difference, proclaiming their position on the borders of dominant culture. Faced with the failure of previous attempts at cultural 'belonging', either to Europe or to Africa, a different response has clearly proved itself to be necessary – a response, moreover, which has not simply entailed a search for yet another Western, if marginalized, literary form with which to experiment. Instead, the recent shift in genre may be seen to have entailed much more of a 'return' to an Antillean tradition which is itself much older than the *nouvelle*; indeed, to a form which Western literary scholarship has in general perceived as preceding the *nouvelle* as a genre – the oral *conte*, or folktale.

The folktale, more even than the *nouvelle*, is at once a marginal(ized) genre – decoded as a somewhat 'primitive', 'childish', 'pre-literary' form from which the *nouvelle* has had to distance itself in order to gain any small measure of literary credibility or acceptance – and a genre of marginals, of the exiled, of the outlaw. While, in the West, folktales have become associated almost entirely with children's stories or fairy-tales, and have lost much of the social or moral function that they may once have had, in the Antilles folktales have always, from the days of slavery and before, been told by adults to adults, and they have always performed an important social function. They have constituted a means of building and maintaining a sense of community, for example, or, more importantly, been a form of clandestine resistance associated with the cover of night, with the time after a day spent working in the fields, with all-night vigils and wakes, with tales of rebellion and revolt.

It is a desire to return to this, to traditional Antillean cultural and literary forms, which may thus perhaps be discerned in the recent publication of collections of short stories from the Antilles. That is, a desire to return to what existed 'in the beginning', to the Plantation, to the vital role of the oral storyteller, whom Patrick Chamoiseau and Raphaël Confiant describe as the 'father' of the Antillean literary tradition.[6] This is a desire which is apparent in the form of several of the stories in Ralph Ludwig's collection, but it is nowhere more evident, at least upon a first reading, than in the final story – Sylviane Telchid's 'Mondésir'.

Telchid's story is the only text in the collection to have a Creole version as well as French, and it both resembles, and can be read as, a traditional folktale rather than a *nouvelle*. It begins and ends somewhat formulaically, for example, opening both with a question and with a series of remarks which resemble and recall the riddles with which Antillean folktales traditionally begin (remarks which, interestingly, do not seem to be present within the Creole version of the story, as if to suggest that, when spoken, one or more riddles would indeed take their place). It then closes in an equally conventional manner, with the words 'From that day forward . . .',[7] words which leave us in no doubt that there is a lesson to be learnt from the events recounted, while the substance of the story itself, moreover, also fulfils what Ina Césaire and Jolle Laurent, in the introduction to their own collection of Antillean folktales, see as the key role of the *conte*: 'that of representing, in symbolic form, social reality'.[8] For Telchid, as she implies in her essay at the end of this collection, this 'reality' would seem to be that precisely of the changing place of 'la parole', of the spoken word, even of the oral tradition itself, in Antillean society.

According to Telchid, there are numerous Antillean folktales and proverbs in which the word 'parole' is of central importance, which thematize the positive aspects of speech and of the spoken word, and which may even characterize it as the power to 'change the world'.[9] For Telchid herself, 'speech is the essence of life', and its opposite, silence (about which she can find no Antillean proverbs, only French), is to be associated with death.[10] And in 'Mondésir', it is precisely the 'death', or loss, of the spoken word, and the dangers attending it which, in the first instance at least, may be seen to be thematized. Here, silence and death – the loss of 'la parole' – are associated with that other opposite of speech – writing.

'Mondésir' tells the tale of two brothers, Ptit Georges and Mondésir, and a woman, Titine, to whom Ptit Georges is about to be married, but whom Mondésir, jealous of his brother, decides that he, too, would like to marry. From the beginning, the brothers are positioned in an antagonistic, rivalrous relationship, one which is symbolized by the opposite associations attached to each of them. While Ptit Georges is described always via his relationship with 'la parole' – with the jokes that he is always ready to tell or with the part that he plays in vigils and wakes (p. 96) – Mondésir is described always via his silence, his lack of speech, his relationship with 'the sheets of paper which he filled with marks and drawings' (p. 96). While the thoughts of Ptit Georges are almost always expressed in direct speech, Mondésir, until the very end of the story, never speaks.

Titine, with whom the story opens, is associated, like her fiancé Ptit Georges, with the spoken word. Indeed through her very name she is associated more specifically with the oral tradition itself, for 'titim' is the Creole word for the riddle with which Antillean folktales traditionally begin. Her function in the text, it would seem, is to choose between the two brothers, between the two extremes of speech and writing – a function which, coupled with her symbolic status as 'riddle', raises several questions, to which we shall return shortly, about the function of women in traditional Antillean literature. What is initially significant, however, is the symbolic value both of the way in which Titine's choice is complicated, and of the outcome of the final choice that she makes.

Just before her wedding, Titine disappears: she is taken to the bottom of the river by the mythical river woman, Manman Dlo, who tells Ptit Georges that she can only be retrieved by a man who is able to write down the names of her 12 brothers and sisters. Ptit Georges is unable to write – indeed the very concept is alien to him – and so Mondésir, upon hearing about the challenge, completes the task and goes to claim Titine for himself. Manman Dlo, like Ptit Georges, is associated with 'la parole', for when Titine emerges from the water we are told of the revitalizing effects of her contact with the river woman, as 'a stream of words ["paroles"] poured from her mouth' (p. 101). That Titine, upon discovering that it is Mondésir who has come to claim her, decides to go back to the bottom of the river to live with Manman Dlo, can thus be interpreted once more as a choice of 'la parole', of 'speech-as-life'.

However, her choice of Manman Dlo becomes even more significant when we discover that she is regarded by many as perhaps the most ancient mythological figure of the Antillean cultural imagination, a figure inherited, it would seem, from the Carib Indians of before slavery. Titine's final choice thus becomes that not simply of the spoken word and all it represents – as, perhaps, her choice of Ptit Georges may have been seen – but rather it becomes, more widely, a choice of the precolonial. What is more, such a choice is even more significant when it is remembered that it entails the concomitant rejection of Mondésir, and of what he represents. Not simply writing, but what writing itself has often been seen to represent within colonized cultures – the dangers, the destructive potential, of the West, of Western cultural values and, specifically, of Western individualism.

For Edouard Glissant, writing and the idea of the individual are indissociable, Western phenomena. As he explains: 'In the West, the movement towards the transcendence of writing in relation to primal orality, was accompanied by a simultaneous and parallel aspiration towards being'.[11] For him, writing – that which is undertaken in solitude as well as in silence – represents nothing less than the sedimentation of the idea of the individual – of the idea of imagining oneself as 'I'/'je' – in the West. In Glissant's formulation the writer is typically preoccupied solely with himself, while the storyteller 'never says "me"'.[12] In the oral tradition, as Telchid explains, it is not the speaker, but the spoken word, the way in which it develops as it is transformed by the collective effort of both teller and audience, which is important. 'The pleasure of the folktale lies in being *in communication*'.[13]

Thus in Telchid's story Mondésir, whose very name is marked by self-possession, is left wandering the banks of the river, 'tirelessly repeating: "I can write, I can write"' (Telchid, 'Mondésir', p. 101). His attention is turned entirely in upon himself, upon writing, and upon himself as writer, while the attention of Ptit Georges is finally turned outward, for he is left 'murmuring: "Titine, Titine"' (p. 101). As in the proverbs described elsewhere by Telchid, writing does indeed seem to signal silence as death, the death of the traditional values of community and collectivity which the oral tradition itself represents. Thus Titine, as she emerges from the river to find that it is Mondésir who has rescued her, asks: 'if you knew how to write, why didn't you teach him [Ptit Georges] how to do it?' (p. 101). That is, she tells him that rather than remaining silent and solitary, guarding his knowledge selfishly in order to use it as a weapon, he should have shared it, put it to the service of the entire community.

However, herein lies a fundamental contradiction, for if the written represents little more than the death of traditional, communal values, the merits of spreading it throughout an entire community would surely be rather questionable. Indeed, this is not the only 'flaw' within such a reading of Telchid's text. Rather, it is one of a whole series of apparently minor contradictions which may lead us to what is ultimately a more satisfactory reading of 'Mondésir'. For example, Titine's choice – of traditional over modern, precolonial over Western, of speech over writing – is one also which leaves her paradoxically silenced: she disappears forever. At the same time, both Ptit Georges and Mondésir, though representative of apparently binary opposites, are left on the edge of 'madness', wandering around, homeless. It is with textual ambiguities such as these that it becomes apparent that the opposition between the spoken and the written – and, as we shall see, in the Antilles especially – is perhaps not quite as straightforward as it may at first have seemed.

Such contradictions and ambiguities are of course present also in the very form of 'Mondésir' as written text, in the very undertaking of 'Mondésir' itself, as of other written collections of folktales. How is it possible, within Telchid's own terms, to utilize that which represents silence and death – writing – to 'give life' to speech, to that which for Telchid represents life itself? Of course, such a 'contradictory' undertaking can in fact be seen to be quite logical. That is, as an attempt to create a specifically Antillean written tradition out of specifically Antillean oral origins. Not only is the folktale typically assumed to be the precursor of the *nouvelle* but, more generally – as several Antillean writers and critics have themselves pointed out – the oral, in Western literary scholarship at least, is seen to be the precursor of the written.

As Edouard Glissant points out, it is usually assumed that the oral and the written exist in a relationship of progression, that the latter developed out of the former. More particularly, that written literary forms grew out of a desire to write down and to preserve those oral tales which, together, could be said to constitute an origin myth for a given culture.[14] Indeed this is precisely how Ralph Ludwig, in his introduction to this particular collection of stories, describes their aim: to 'preserve' the founding oral texts of a culture which may be said never to have had an 'authentic' literary tradition of its own, by writing them down.[15]

Such an undertaking is not, however, unproblematic. First, there is an inevitable danger, no matter how strenuous the attempt to remain faithful to the oral text may be, that the very act of transcription will entail the loss of precisely that which one is intending to preserve – the text's 'orality'. Far more problematic than this, however, as Glissant points out, is the very belief that the oral can in some way be recovered in its 'pure' form, and then reproduced and transparently re-represented via the written word. This assumes that the relationship between the oral and the written in the Antilles is the same as that which, itself not unproblematically, has been assumed to exist between the oral and the written in the West: that the oral exists in some manner behind and before the written.

Perhaps one of the most important issues at stake here is that Antillean folktales cannot, as Glissant points out, be seen to constitute a myth of origin. For him, Antillean folktales function much less as attempts to explain origins, and much more as *reactions* against the effacement of origins, against the brutality of slavery, as strategies of resistance and revolt.[16] And while they certainly constitute the collective memories of a given community, these are memories not of origins in the sense of creation myths or myths of genesis, but rather they are memories of contact between different cultures and communities, each with already-existing myths of origin: Carib, African, European, Indian, for example, of which disparate remnants and pieces may remain. While the residues of Carib and African mythologies exist in oral form, in folktales themselves, European and Indian origin myths exist in already written form, and have always done so since their arrival in the Antilles. Thus the oral can in no way be seen to precede the written, nor is the latter a progression from the former. Instead, both have existed, been handed down, and have developed simultaneously – side by side.

The Antillean situation is thus one in which literary forms have not been successive, but have been parallel (though obviously not equal in status), a fact which is highlighted by the ever-significant issue of language. The oral tradition – tales, proverbs, songs, riddles – exists in Creole, while the overwhelming majority of the written tradition exists, and has always existed, in French. Despite the increasing amount of written literature also in Creole, the written, in whatever language, has in no way superseded or replaced the oral. In rural areas particularly, folktales continue to be told today, as they have always been, to large and adult audiences. If it is not one of progression, then the relationship between the oral and the written, especially in the Antilles, may perhaps better be described as one of 'rupture': a relationship characterized not by absolute scission but, as Raphaël Confiant suggests, by the idea of a 'space' or a 'gap' in which two intimately linked languages and cultures may be seen to 'rub' against each other.[17] Having existed side by side, neither the oral nor the written is unmarked or uninformed by the other: like Creole itself, and like the French spoken in the Antilles, both traditions have grown out of the colonial encounter.

In such a way, the Antillean literary tradition – indeed, Antillean culture itself – is in fact neither oral nor written, neither Creole nor French, but characterized rather by 'Creoleness', by what Bernabé, Chamoiseau and Confiant describe as '[this] interactional or transactional aggregate of Caribbean, European, African, Asian and Levantine cultural elements, united on the same soil by the yoke of history... [a] Creoleness... wrongly and hastily reduced to its mere linguistic elements'.[18] Indeed for Chamoiseau and Confiant, elsewhere, it is the folktale itself which has enabled this 'Creoleness' to be kept alive through centuries of obsession with seeking cultural and literary purity.[19] If the folktale is at the origins of the Antillean tradition, it is so only in a very ambivalent and ambiguous – a very Creole – manner.

The contradictions within Telchid's short text may therefore come to signify in a quite different way. That Titine is apparently paradoxically silenced rather than enabled by her return to the precolonial, or that both Ptit Georges and Mondésir are left in a state of dispossession by the end of the story, can be seen as an indication that 'Mondésir' is perhaps not simply a naïve attempt to call for, or to practise, a return to the precolonial as pure oral origin. Throughout Telchid's text we are in fact shown neither the pre-eminence of the oral, nor that of the written, but rather the dangers of a too-exclusive investment in either and, more, the impossibility of separating the two. The fundamental assumption that writing is an appropriate means of rescuing Titine from Manman Dlo, from the 'precolonial', for example, is never questioned: writing is simply shown to have been put to the wrong use by the wrong person. Similarly, it is writing, in the end, which finally prompts Mondésir to speak, as he repeats: 'I can write, I can write...' (Telchid, 'Mondésir', p. 101).

The inextricability of 'speech' and 'writing' may be seen also to operate at the level of language use itself, for when Ptit Georges is told that he must *write* the names of Titine's mother's 12 children, he exclaims 'Write? But what does that mean ["signifie"]?', and we are told: 'it was the first time that he had ever heard such a word ["parole"]' (p. 99). Similarly, when Mondésir himself succeeds in writing the names of the 12 children, Manman Dlo's first and only exclamation is: 'une parole, c'est une parole': 'a promise is a promise' or 'my word is my word' (p. 100). In both of these examples, the choice of the word 'parole' – rather than the more general 'mot', in the first example, or the more specific 'promesse' or 'serment' ('oath') in the second – is informative, for the effect in each case is that writing itself becomes just another spoken word. That is, that 'l'écriture', writing, becomes part of 'la parole', part of the oral tradition itself for, as Telchid points out, in Creole 'la belle parole' is used to describe not only the spoken word but also the whole tradition of oral communication. Finally, and relatedly, even Titine's name, which as we have seen would seem to be associated with the oral tradition itself, only *sounds* like the word 'titim'. When written down, it has undergone a transformation which, however slight, may be seen to render Titine herself not simply symbolic of the spoken, but rather a *creolized* figure.

But the ambivalence of Telchid's text – and indeed of the oral tradition in general – becomes most evident in the figure of Manman Dlo herself, a figure in fact much more complex than it may initially have seemed. First, because though she may indeed have been passed down from surviving Carib Indians to the first slaves to arrive from Africa, it is of course impossible to recover the 'original' Carib figure upon which she may have been based – not least because of the already creolized, Franco-Carib language 'baragouin', through which this transmission can only have taken place. Second, because she is by no means specific to the islands of the French Caribbean. Rather, she is similar to various other 'river women' figures: the Jamaican 'River Muma' or 'Mammy Water'; river goddesses of the Bahamas or of African-American communities.[20]

With her long, straight hair, she is reminiscent also of another figure, again popular throughout the Caribbean: that of the wicked 'White Lady'. This is a figure who, usually depicted as evil and dangerous, has typically been taken to be a symbol of, and a warning against, the evils of slavery and of colonialism, and of the dangers of the West in general.[21] Indeed Manman Dlo herself is also typically depicted as both dangerous and frightening. We are, for example, told how Ptit Georges, when he first sees Manman Dlo, 'remained as if paralysed' (Telchid, 'Mondésir', p. 98), while Simone Schwarz-Bart, in her epic tale *Ti-Jean l'horizon*, has her hero meet a Manman Dlo who asks him 'don't you know that the sight of me is fatal to mortals?',[22] and while Chamoiseau and Confiant similarly describe her as a 'diabolical' figure who bewitches all those who catch sight of her.[23] Indeed, in this, both Manman Dlo and the figure of the 'White Lady' are reminiscent also of mythical European river women, or mermaids, like Lorelei: Medusa-like, snake-haired women who are all specifically harmful and dangerous to men, as they lure and tempt them to their deaths at the bottom of rivers or of the sea.

What is clear through all of these associations is that, far from representing the figure of precolonial purity, Telchid's Manman Dlo is a creole figure *par excellence* – at once precolonial and colonial, oral and written, created out of, renewed and adapted, and now indistinguishable from all of these traditions and more. What is equally clear is that far from attempting to capture and to preserve, via transcription, a traditional, and somehow original, folktale, Telchid is, it would seem, instead actively deploying the 'Creoleness' – the contradictions and ambivalences – at the heart of the Antillean literary tradition. Indeed, as she herself recognizes, and as Glissant, as well as the writers of *In Praise of Creoleness* also suggest, it is this deployment, alone, which is capable, realistically, of leading towards the creation of 'new Antillean literatures'. Given that the Antilles are 'already written', in all senses, and that it is impossible now to 'progress' from the oral to the written, it is necessary instead to undertake a process of rewriting, transforming the oral and the written as they currently exist in order to create a literary tradition which is neither oral nor written, but which is both and more. That is, to work at the interstices between the oral and the written, between French and Creole, in order to 'create a literature which will obey all the demands of modern writing while taking roots in the traditional configurations of our orality'.[24]

Telchid's work, however, can be seen to be going further even than this, to be based more upon *re*configurations both of this 'traditional orality' and of the Antillean tradition also of written literature, notably, as I suggested earlier, in terms of the way in which both traditions typically represent and utilize the figure of woman. Within the Caribbean oral tradition, women have been represented in negative and stereotypical ways: at best as malleable, unthinking, or self-sacrificing and more usually, as with Manman Dlo, as evil and dangerous for men.[25] Within the Antillean written tradition – and here the discourses of négritude are exemplary – women have similarly been represented in negative, disempowering or purely functional ways: as the helpers or hinderers of masculine quests for identity or self-liberation, as the mothers and lovers of heroic male figures, as symbolic 'motherlands' to be returned to and exploited. Everywhere, they exist primarily in relation to men, almost never as subjects in their own right, and even less often – as is also true of the oral tradition – do they exist in relation to each other. Thus exiled from subjectivity, they are frequently represented as obviously marginal figures – as witches or as mad women.

It would at first seem that Titine herself occupies a similarly 'stereotypical' position in 'Mondésir', as central enigma or riddle – 'titim' – of the text. Hers is a position which is precisely between men: as symbolic mediatrix of an all-male battle between the oral and the written, as the property of Ptit George – 'his very own Titine, whom nobody else will ever marry' (Telchid, 'Mondésir', p. 99) – to be claimed as prize by Mondésir. However, as we have seen, she becomes neither Mondésir's prize, nor is she reclaimed by Ptit Georges. Equally, she is in no way a mediatrix of masculine liberation, for it is Mondésir and Ptit Georges who are left in a state of dispossession, of homelessness, of madness – in a position more often occupied, that is, by female figures of the Antillean tradition. Instead, Titine is in some manner 'rescued' by Manman Dlo, for the alternative that she gives Titine, to return to the bottom of the river, is entirely unexpected: it was not part of the original pact.

Manman Dlo rescues Titine both from an impossible choice between the oral and the written, and from a stereotypical position between men. Although it could certainly be argued that Titine's choice is somewhat limited, especially since she too is finally silenced, it is possible to see here at least an attempt to begin to imagine women who act as subjects, rather than who are entirely acted upon. What is more, it is once again around the already ambiguous figure of Manman Dlo that a less straightforward, or traditional, reading of the text can be seen to emerge, especially since she herself functions not only as the creole figure described earlier, but also as another deliberately non-stereotypical female figure, like Titine.

In Telchid's story, Manman Dlo is not, as is traditional, an evil or dangerous temptress of men. Very unusually, it is a woman whom she takes to the bottom of the river, and then it is not to drown her, but it is in order that she may live there with her. Indeed, she does so, as she tells Ptit Georges, because she is grieving about a daughter whom she has lost to the human world, a fact which reminds us once more of traditional tales of river-women, of young mermaids who assume a human form in order to go to live with human men on land, of daughters who are lost to their mothers forever and who usually suffer from this separation in the form of a curse – a curse, interestingly, which is often that of being doomed never to speak.

Telchid, it would seem, is attempting to imagine the other side of these stories, the side which has been silenced and covered over, whose marginalization has actually been central to the functioning of stories – both spoken and written – which are already marginalized themselves. That is, she is not only representing women in non-stereotypical ways but also, more than this, she is ensuring that it is the representation of that which is ordinarily very rarely portrayed – here specifically a relationship between women – which prevents the smooth functioning both of traditional narrative forms, and of the new, creole, narrative form that she is creating.

Telchid's own particular 'nouvelle littérature antillaise' may thus be seen to be new in more ways than one. Not only has she taken both a marginal, written form of literature, the *nouvelle*, and a form of marginalized oral literature which resembles it, the *conte*, and created out of them a 'creole' form which is a renewal of both. At the same time, she has begun to expand the idea of what 'Creoleness' itself may mean, she has begun to renew ideas about 'la nouvelle littérature antillaise' even as she participates in its creation. This is especially significant because much new Antillean writing, both literary and theoretical – and *In Praise of Creoleness* would itself be a good example – has typically continued to imagine Antillean cultural liberation in strictly gendered and androcentric terms. Indeed, remembering also that while women have always told tales to children in the Antilles, those professional storytellers, or *conteurs*, who address adult audiences, are almost always men, Telchid would seem to have become what may perhaps be called *une nouvelle conteuse* – in all of the many senses of the term.

15
Hybrid Texts: Family, State and Empire in a Poem by Black Cuban Poet Excilia Saldaña[1]

Catherine Davies

Cuba secured political independence from the Spanish metropolis in 1898 but was subsequently forced into a position of economic dependency, first by the United States and, later, the USSR. Not surprisingly, nationalism has been the main ideological imperative in Cuba throughout the twentieth century. After the Revolution of 1959 attempts were made to assimilate hitherto marginal sectors of society (primarily women and blacks) into the new socialist national project. A homogenous Cuban national identity was thus given priority over differences of class, race and gender in cultural and literary expression.

Despite this emphasis on national cultural homogenization, a constant feature of poetry written in post-revolutionary Cuba is the inscription of a diversity of discourses. This is particularly so in the case of black and mulatto women poets who are perhaps best placed to break with dominant identities and categories. The poetry of these women charts the crossing of the borders between Hispanic and African-Caribbean cultures, as did the *negrista* poets of the 1930s (Nicolás Guillén in particular), but it also queries long-established boundaries of racial and sexual difference. Such poems can be read as a form of sexual politics crossing racial, national and international borders.

In this essay I offer a close reading of a lengthy (15-page) poem by a mulatto woman, the poet Excilia Saldaña, entitled 'Monólogo de la esposa' ('The Bride's Monologue'). I consider it an example of a 'contact zone'[2] between local and global cultures which inscribes a plurality of discourses across cultural and gender boundaries primarily through intertextuality. Briefly, the poem relates a bride/wife's coming to consciousness and her rejection of the restrictive role of wife and daughter in an overwhelmingly patriarchal society. It voices the rebellion of black female subjectivity and reinvents a cultural space from a dissonant, feminist point of view. This poem is an example of what Maggie Humm refers to as 'script[s] of boundary crossing',[3] it captures the moment of transgression in the language of poetry and it disturbs the delimitations of the patriarchal body politic.

Excilia Saldaña was born in 1946 in Havana, the only child in a middle-class family of 'negros finos' (refined blacks). She was brought up in her grandparent's home with a passive mother and absent father. She left home in the early 1960s because her family disapproved of the 1959 Revolution. She has since published several books of stories and poems.[4] Saldaña is interested in African-Cuban culture but not in négritude; and she says she is not a feminist. The dramatic poem 'The Bride's Monologue', published in the Cuban cultural review *Casa de las Américas* in 1985[5] and staged in Sweden, had formed part of a book entitled *Mi nombre* (My Name) published in Mexico. This book consisted of five sections but was shredded because of numerous typographical errors. Another section of the book, *Mi nombre: Anti-elegia familiar* (My Name: a Family Anti-Elegy), was published separately in Havana in 1991.[6] The fact that Saldaña, like many Cuban authors, was unable to publish because of the political and economic crisis in Cuba in the early 1990s is symptomatic of her marginalization in the global cultural economy and print capitalism in general. According to Saldaña, the shredded book was a rendering in poetry of key moments of her (shredded) life-story. Like *Mi nombre: Anti-elegia familiar*, 'The Bride's Monologue' is a confessional psychobiography which clearly inscribes what some critics refer to as the double-consciousness (black/European) of the 'split' Caribbean writer.[7] The interplay of constantly deferred, metaphorical self-presentations makes the poem an example of a hybrid text which relates, in Homi Bhabha's words, 'the traumatic ambivalence of a personal psychic history to the wider disjunctions of a political existence'.[8]

In 'The Bride's Monologue' the Bride takes on the guise of a priestess: a Vestal Virgin/*santera*. Goddess and housewife, she keeps the sacred flame burning in the temple kitchen.[9] From inside the private place, the home, the Bride summons up and exercises her powers. By creating a spell, a vortex of disorder, the speaker-witch conjures up images of the men in her life (lovers, husbands, her father) and wonders why they have all failed her. She continually asks 'open questions' (Saldaña, 'Monólogo', p. 95), and she refuses to 'remain on the thresholds' (p. 87). Her hands are covered in blood. But what is the crime and who is guilty? The Bride solves the enigma with her 'old rusty key' (p. 96), a syncretic key inherited from her female ancestors, 'the fragile Kalabari/ of taut black skin/and the proud Castilian woman' (p. 98). The key, to racial and gendered identity, reveals the mulatta's own hybrid sexuality disavowed because of a past traumatic experience: she was raped by her father. Discovering the repressed trauma and responding to it enables the decentred subject to reconstruct a sexualized self.

This personal history will be considered from the perspective of current debates on multicultural engagement and intercultural expression that focus on processes of identity formation. The deferred possibilities of identity, when resolved into words and concepts, become static and lose the sense of ambivalence highlighted in current understandings of hybridity. Borderline moments, on the other hand, capture identity processes in the making. The term 'acculturation' and other assimilationist 'melting pot' theories have largely been rejected on account of the hierarchies of privilege and appropriation they imply. The 'third space' posits a way out of binarism. It is a space not of fusion or accumulation, but one in which often incommensurable, heterogeneous differences are held together.[10] Literary critics tend to focus on such spaces or moments in the text in which multiple possible readings co-exist simultaneously. Traditionally referred to as poetics or figurative language – association, connotation, pastiche, irony, inference and so on – this reading 'between the lines'[11] is the very stuff of literature.

Referring to the visual arts, Jean Fisher suggests the 'chimera' as the rhetorical figure which encapsulates the constant shifting of meaning outside the scope of communicable language. 'The chimera . . . is neither one thing nor another but both simultaneously, and not reducible to either'.[12] The notion of the 'chimera' suggests to a literary critic the metaphor, or the metaphoricity of language, which – if extended to imply intercultural exchange – implies translation (the movement of meaning).[13] For Bhabha translation is 'the performative nature of cultural communication. It is language *in actu* . . . rather than language *in situ*.[14] A 'borderline work of culture' creates 'a sense of the new as an insurgent act of cultural translation'.[15] Translation negotiates the often non-synchronous disjunctions between cultures, perhaps decanonizing the original,[16] and, in the process, creating 'new' possibilities of meaning.

I will follow through these ideas in relation to 'The Bride's Monologue', attempting to avoid what Fisher refers to as 'the Western desire for exotic separatism'.[17] On this occasion I am not interested so much in the problems associated with translating the text into English – my own translation has only 'a transmitting function' which, for Benjamin, was the 'hallmark of a bad translation'[18] – but I would like to comment on the ways the text 'translates' and incorporates previous texts. With reference to intertextual studies, Nikos Papastergiadis writes that in order to map 'the interruptive force of hybridity' and 'witness the innovative potential of the foreign text . . . we will have to measure *the degree to which the memory of the foreign code has been preserved* and examine the impact resulting from the insertion of the foreign text'.[19]

The foreign texts in 'The Bride's Monologue' belong predominantly to three literary canons pertaining to three powerful imperial cultures: the Ancient Greek, the Spanish and the British. There are numerous allusions to consecrated Hispanic authors such as Miguel de Cervantes, García Lorca, José Martí and Rubén Darío, to popular Spanish and Cuban songs and tango lyrics, to the Ancient Greek poet Sappho and to the Anglo-Irish author Oscar Wilde (both of whom queried established gendered identities). The most significant texts underlying Saldaña's palimpsest, however, are two tragedies: Shakespeare's *Macbeth* and Aeschylus' *Oresteia*. Particularly important are the two female protagonists of the tragedies: Lady Macbeth and Clytemnestra. 'The Bride's Monologue' is rich in embedded levels of meaning which may or may not be set in motion by the hypothetical reader, depending on the positionality of the reader and his or her familiarity with these other cultures and translations. Two questions arise: How do these foreign texts interrupt 'The Bride's Monologue' and how does the poem affect readings of the canonized texts? I intend to focus on the first question, ostensibly the easier of the two.

In 'The Bride's Monologue' the much repeated refrain 'These hands. These hands. These hands', 'There is not sufficient water to clean my hands' (p. 87), 'Will I never see these hands clean' (p. 89), the references to the viper, and the line 'which man not born of woman' (p. 98) point explicitly to *Macbeth*: 'for none of woman born/shall harm Macbeth' (*Macbeth*, IV.i.80), and 'What, will these hands ne'er be clean?' (V.i.35).[20] Similarly, various references in 'The Bride's Monologue' draw on Aeschylus: the line 'with no ox on my tongue' (p. 91), for instance, alludes to the words 'an ox stands huge upon my tongue' spoken by the watchman in *Oresteia*.[21] The references to the serpent, and the line 'I carpeted/the house to the bath chamber' (p. 91) point directly to Orestes' description of Clytemnestra as 'some water snake, some viper' who sets a trap with a 'bath curtain' (*Oresteia*, p. 129). What, then, do Lady Macbeth and Clytemnestra share and how do they relate to the Cuban Bride?

'The Bride's Monologue' tells of a violent crime which has stained the Bride's hands with blood and involves feelings of guilt and retribution. The crime on the surface level of the poem is, as previously mentioned, the father's rape of the daughter and this is heightened by allusions to the work of García Lorca where 'blood' (as in the play *Blood Wedding* and the *Gypsy Ballads*) connotes kinship and death. The line '!Que no quiero verla!' ('I don't want to see her/it!') ('The Bride's Monologue', p. 98) is borrowed from Lorca's *Lament for Ignacio Sánchez Mejías*.[22] In Saldaña's poem, due to the ambiguous meaning of the object pronoun 'la', the line refers simultaneously to the girl herself ('la niña'), the shame ('la vergüenza') and the blood ('la sangre'). It is for this reason that the Bride needs to 'exorcize' (p. 98) the demonized father from her memory through ritual. The poem, then, voices the subject's attempts to free herself of the trauma caused by the father's violation of her body (hence the virgin's blood) and of kinship taboos (the blood-line).[23] According to this reading, the poem's scope is the domestic sphere (the family, the kitchen) with an ostensibly feminist message: the woman/daughter/ housewife is a victim of male violence and parental abuse, her guilt is self-directed, and the father is the victimizer. Does the poem present, then, yet another example of the kind of 'universal...male dominance and female exploitation' theme which Chandra Mohanty believes obsesses First-World feminists in their readings of Third-World texts?[24]

Certain features of the poem suggest more challenging, complex subtexts. First, the Bride is not meek but a spirited, powerful, desiring subject invested with agency, a witch/priestess conjuring up supernatural forces to help rid her of the father-figure. Hence the significance of the scattered references to *santería* ritual: 'ebbó' (sacred stone).[25] Only by ridding herself of the father may the daughter construct a textual version of her fragmented, decentred self. The intertextual, intercultural references – to *Macbeth* and the *Oresteia* – confirm such a reading and take the drama one step further. They indicate a second crime which is not made explicit on the surface level of the poem.

What Lady Macbeth and Clytemnestra have in common is that they kill, or bring about the killing of, the King, the father-king of the family-state, the husband (Clytemnestra kills Agamemnon), or the father lookalike (Lady Macbeth instigates the murder of Duncan who reminds her of her father). These domestic tragedies, therefore, have a highly political subtext. The two women – queens in effect – are noble in status, cunning in statecraft and ambitious for power. They are not merely wives, or even regicides, but decisive power-brokers in the public sphere. In order to be this they must divest themselves of feminine sensitivity and assume what Clytemnestra refers to as 'male strength of heart' (*Oresteia*, p. 87). Their prime strategy is flattery and seduction: they lure their victims into their castle/homes and offer them feasts. They are assisted by supernatural, irrational female forces – the witches or 'weird sisters' in *Macbeth* and the Furies in *Oresteia*. In both cases the King is stabbed and his blood stains the women's hands, and both women are plagued by subsequent nightmares of guilt, or 'the torture of the mind' in the words of Lady Macbeth (*Macbeth*, III.ii.21). All these heterogeneous motifs are embedded in the shifting time frames of 'The Bride's Monologue', with the effect that the blood-stained 'Bride', the killer of the father-husband figure of authority, comes to represent an archetype as well as an individual voice.

Of significance, too, is Clytemnestra's motive for slaying her husband, the King: he killed their daughter, Iphigenia, as a sacrifice to the gods in order to hasten the progress of the Greek fleet about to invade Troy (so as to recover Helen). In Clytemnestra's words, 'he slaughtered like a victim his own child, my pain/grown into love' (*Oresteia*, p. 81). As the chorus of the *Oresteia* declares, 'Sisters, we have had wrong done to us' (p. 140). In 'The Bride's Monologue' the crime, then, is twofold: violation (or killing) of the daughter is followed by parricide (or regicide), and the effects of the crime extend well beyond the family. The poem is subversive in that it inscribes publicly two social taboos: incest and parricide.

The political connotations of killing the King in a domestic Cuban context are, of course, suggestive but perhaps simplistic. This is because the target of retribution in the poem is not just the father-figure but all social categories of men, and these, unlike the King, are explicitly associated with a Cuban (domestic) culture by means of a specifically localizing vocabulary. The Bride, who refers to herself as the 'goddess of Dolores Avenue' (the 'Avenue of Sorrow', which is Saldaña's home address; 'The Bride's Monologue', p. 88), invites these men to her house; they knock at her door, she dresses as a priestess and lets them in, carpeting 'the house to the bath chamber' (p. 91), just as Clytemnestra welcomed Agamemnon before she stabbed him in the bath. The suitors present her (in her kitchen-temple, the 'ile-ocha' in *santería* religion) with their distinctly Cuban offerings: pawpaw, 'caimitos' (two-star apple fruit), cowrie shells, 'jícaras' (cups). Then, it seems, the Bride sacrifices the men (or imagines she does) and lays them to rest on a clothes line where they hang out, significantly, 'in a democracy of wire and rope' (p. 90; an expression with obvious political overtones) until she takes them in to iron them: 'Starched and uncreased/ – hanging/in order of colour/on the clothes hangers –/they are in my cupboard' (p. 90). The figures, hierarchically arranged according to colour, represent the many facets of masculinity in a national, multi-ethnic context. The poem, then, is a feminist text, an indictment of patriarchy at the level of the home and the state, in which a female subject fights back, but then feels guilty.

The tension in this love-hate relationship is communicated through one crucial word, 'hypsipyle', which suggests a specifically Latin American postcolonial dimension. The Bride's suitors pin 'violent hypsipyles' on her dress. This is not a Spanish word; it is taken from a famous poem, 'Sonatina', written at the turn of the century by the poet Rubén Darío, founder of Spanish American *modernismo*. Darío writes: 'Oh quíen fuera hipsipila que dejó la crisálida' ('Oh, to be a hypsipyle that leaves the chrysalis'); here the neologism 'hipsipila' indicates an insect in a chrysalis half-formed between the larva and the imago, as well as the fairy-tale princess of the poem liberated, by a suitor, from the confines of her castle home. In 'Sonatina', then, the princess/insect frees herself/itself from the castle/chrysalis. Similarly, the Bride of the 'Bride's Monologue' wears a 'hypsipyle' as a token of her imminent release from the entrapment of the home, thus confirming a feminist reading of the poem. At the same time, however, 'The Bride's Monologue' refers to the original proper noun or name of the woman Hypsipyle who, in Greek mythology, saved her father (the king's son) from the women of Lemnos who had decided to kill all the men on the island.[26] A tension is thus set up between the Bride who might save the father (according to a Greek reading) and (in a Latin American reading) the Bride who must shed the father in order to develop; the latter option proves the most compelling.

'The Bride's Monologue', then, is about killing the father on both a local and inter-statal scale (echoing the rivalries in *Macbeth* between Scotland and England, and in the *Oresteia* between Argos and Troy) and, more importantly, at a postcolonial level in as much as a Latin American reading is set up in counterdistinction to classical European culture. Furthermore, the King of Scotland and the King of Argos represent not only the patriarch but also the Imperial King and the White King (British, Greek) who in 'The Bride's Monologue', reading between the lines, is killed off by the black, female, subaltern subject. Tentative intertextual connections can thus be made between a feminist and a postcolonial agenda.

An obvious subtext in this respect is the section of 'The Bride's Monologue' which reads.

> the poor little *cross-eyed mulatto girl*
> the object of mockery at school,
> who wanted to be the princess of an exotic kingdom

> guarded by a *hundred white men* with their hundred halberds
> an *owl* that never sleeps and a colossal *sacred stone.*

(p. 92)

In this section Saldaña borrows from two famous lines in Darío's 'Sonatina', where *the fair-haired, blue-eyed princess* is 'guarded by a *hundred black men* with their hundred halberds/a *hound* that never sleeps and a colossal *dragon*'.[27] In Saldaña's poem Darío's princess (which the bride wants to be before she kills her father) has been replaced by the cross-eyed mulatta who is guarded and served not by black men but by white men, and not by a European hound and dragon but an indigenous Cuban 'sijú' (owl) and an African-Cuban 'otá' (sacred stone). This clever reversal of Western aesthetic paradigms and the insertion of a black Cuban identity into a canonical poem which epitomizes Hispanic *modernismo* (the cultural movement which emulated the conquest culture of the European cosmopolitan élites) is effected by the female subject who refuses to be sub-altern (that is, subjected to another). In 'The Bride's Monologue', the Freudian 'dark continent', the barbarian who does not speak Greek, rids herself of the colonial master and inverts the mysogynistic, imperialist texts of the West with what Sara Suleri refers to as the 'female racial' voice.[28] The poem provides an example of how the feminist hybrid text (a mere poem, after all) disassembles, in speech and thought, the carefully structured edifices of the patriarchal family and its powerful ramifications at the level of state and empire. The poem unravels the threads of discourse that make up this immemorial pattern of social organization which has almost been set in stone, the cornerstone of Western culture as we know it, and dares to weave the threads together differently to offer alternative ways of thinking.

Appendix

The Bride's Monologue (excerpts)

The ringlets of the night hang from the sky.
Long tresses of silence spread across the shoulders of the house.
I comb them. Softly, I comb them:
I am the nameless one smoothing down the waves of dreams.
I am also a water-child
binding and unbinding memory's long mane of hair.
[...]
These hands. These hands. These hands.
There is never enough water to clean my hands,
to unstain the damned spot of blood

of my own blood–
for ever touching my hands. [. . .]
These hands. These hands. These hands.
What, will these hands ne'er be clean?

I am the one. The Bride.
All the sorrow in the world came to ask for my hand.
'I am not the Betrothed', I said, 'but the Bride.
Can you wash my hands?
Is there sorrow enough to wash my hands?'
[. . .]
These hands. These hands. These hands.
With what detergent can I rip off the bloody scab from my hands? [. . .]
No, the dead do not rest in cemeteries.
Their place of rest is on clothes-lines,
in the democracy of wire and rope
– where luxurious cloth hangs out with worn rags.
What an act of uncomparable love it is to iron them later!
Starched and uncreased
– hanging
            in order of colour
on the coat hangers –
they are in my cupboard, always ready to wear
[. . .]
I dressed
            in mallow and heliotrope,
I wore
            orchids and violets,
I put on my feet
            purple aubergines,
I carpeted
            the house to the bath chamber.
Each one arrived with his voice and his obsessions,
each one arrived with his obsessions and his ways:
[. . .]
my house full of spectres.
The impetuous ones took me by the waist
and pinned on my neck-line violent hypsipyles:
            'She shall dance, she shall sing!
            She shall liven up the fiesta! [. . .]
Less deluded than Ophelia
more changed than Aldonza
as war-like as Juliet
– biblical, classical, seductive –
light-footed,
without an ox on my tongue
I exclaimed:
Ah, my dead ones,
as we were saying yesterday: twenty years are nothing.

Where did I lose them last time round?
Who was it who needlessly killed our hopes?
Perhaps a god of envy [. . .]
      Or was it us
      – Sanchos and Quixotes of the Stain –
who changed a noble giant
to a common-place windmill?
Ah, my dead ones,
the ones who desired me in the oval portrait on my breast:
Yet each woman loves the thing she kills.
Ah, my dead ones,
the poor little cross-eyed mulatto girl,
      target of laughter at school,
who wanted to be the princess of an exotic kingdom
guarded by a hundred white men with their hundred halberds,
an owl that never sleeps and a colossal sacred stone,
is now a widow-queen with so much effort.
[. . .]
But I am the Bride
and I only have open questions
and a key made of lead
      which locks and does not open.
Ancient lustreless key
      in the glow of this key-keeper.
My grandmother used it and my mother
and the grandmothers of my grandmother
– the fragile Kalabari
      with taut black skin
and the stern woman from Castile,
      faithful rose, ivory flower – .
In the dressing-room with stone and Christ
in the hut with cattle and jungle,
      the same key
the same, that will not now close any gate.
My old rusted key
      in some lamenting corner
      in some crystal corner
      in some fetish corner with beads
      in some mud corner
      in some prayer and candle corner
      in some bloody corner where lie
      hundreds of decaying dead hands.

I return from the bloody corner.
There I found my father
      in an afternoon of games:
he is not a mulatto, he says, but a gypsy flamenco dancer.
And off we go in a caravan,
      reading palms and fingers.

And my hands are clean,
    and I put my arms around his neck. [...]
And father brings me out,
    and turns me round
and he twirls me in the smoke
      and he closes in at the siesta.
      In the vapours of rum,
      the girl was just a female.

(No, I don't want to see it!)
These hands. These hands. Who can
wash my hands, my eyes, my hair,
or my arms, my mouth, my lungs,
or my brain? What deep song,
what knave of diamonds, what king of clubs,
what ace of hearts, what jack
of spades, what bad luck, what heel-tapping,
what dove, what sacrifice, what retreat,
what man not born of woman,
Father, could exorcize you from my memory? [...]
I am the one. The Bride:
Apetedbi of the sacred water.
Nun of the feudal cloisters...
Penelope without Odysseus. [...]

Monologo de la esposa

Los crespos de la noche cuelgan del cielo.
Se esparcen por los hombros de la casa las guedejas del silencio.
Yo las peino. Suavemente yo las peino:
Soy la anónima alisadora de las ondas del sueño.
También soy una niña acuática
trenzando y destrenzándome
la cabellera del recuerdo.
[...]
Las manos. Las manos. Las manos.
No hay agua suficiente para limpiar mis manos,
para desteñir el estigma de sangre
    – de mi propia sangre –
tañendo para siempre mis manos. [...]
Las manos. Las manos. Las manos.
¿No he de ver limpias estas manos?

Soy yo. La Esposa.
Todo el dolor del mundo vino a pedir mi mano:
'No soy la Novia', le dije, 'sino la Esposa,
¿Puedes tú lavarme las manos?
¿Hay dolor suficiente para limpiar mis manos?
[...]

Las manos. Las manos. Las manos.
¿Con qué detergente arrancar la costra de sangre de mis manos? [. . .]
No, los muertos no descansan en los cementerios.
Sus lugar de reposo son las tendederas,
en la democracia de alambre y la soga
– donde conviven el paño lujoso y el jirón maltrecho. [. . .]
!Qué acto de amor incomparable es plancharlos luego!
Almidonados y lisos
– colgados
        por orden de colores
en los percheros –
listos están siempre en mi armario, para usarlos [. . .]

Vestí
        de malva y heliotropo,
me toqué
        con orquídeas y violetas,
calcé
        berenjenas moradas,
alfombré
        la casa hasta la bañadera.
Cada cual llegó con su voz y sus manías,
cada cual llegó con sus manías y sus maneras: [. . .]
mi casa llena de espectros.
Los vehementes me tomaban del talle
y prendían en mi escote hipsipilas violentas:
        !Que dance que cante!
        !Que alegre la fiesta!
[. . .]
Menos alucinada que Ofelia,
más transformada que Aldonza,
tan aguerrida como Julieta
– biblica, clásica, retrechera –
con los pies ligeros,
sin ningún buey sobre mi lengua
exclamé:
        Ay,   mis muertos,
como decíamos ayer: veinte años no es nada.
¿Dónde los perdí la vez postrera?
¿Quién fue que así mató nuestro destino sin razón?
¿Acaso un dios envidioso? [. . .]
        ¿O fuimos nosotros
        Sanchos y Quijotes de la mácula –
quienes convertimos un noble gigante
en tosco molino de viento?
Ay, mis muertos,
mis deseosos en el retrato ovalado de mi pecho:
Toda mujer ama lo que mata.
Ay, mis muertos,

la pobre mulatica bizca,
        centro de burla del colegio,
que quiso ser princesa de un exótico reino
que custodian cien blancos con sus cien alabardas,
un sijú que no duerme un otá colosal,
es ahora reina viuda de tantos empeños.
[...]
Pero yo soy la Esposa
y sólo tengo preguntas abiertas
y una llave de plomo
        que no abre, sino cierra.
Antigua llave sin brillo
        en el fulgor de esta llavera.
La usó mi abuela, y mi madre
y las abuelas de abuela
– la frágil carabalí
        de la tersa piel morena
y la adusta castellana,
        rosa fiel, flor marfileña – .
En la recámara de piedra y cristo
y en la choza de engorde y selva,
        la misma llave,
la misma que no puede ya cerrar ninguna reja.
Mi vieja llave herrumbrosa
        en algún rincón que se queja,
        en algún rincón de cristal
        en algún rincón de fetiche y cuentas,
        en algún rincón de barro,
        en algún rincón de oración y velas,
        en algún rincón de la sangre donde hay
        cientos de manos carcomidas y muertas.

Del rincón de la sangre vuelvo.
Allí encontré a mi padre
        en una tarde de juegos:
que no es mulato, dice, sino gitano de baile flamenco.
Y vamos en un carromato
        leyendo palmas y dedos.
Y las manos están limpias
        y se las cuelgo al cuello. [...]
Y me saca el Padre
        y me da la vuelta
y me gira en el humo
        y me cerca en la siesta.
        En los vapores del ron
        la niña fue sólo hembra.

(¡Que no, que no quiero verla!)
Las manos. Las manos, quién puede
lavar mis manos o mis ojos, o mi pelo,

o mis brazos, o mi boca, o mis pulmones,
o mi cerebro? ¿Qué cante jondo,
qué sota de oro, qué rey de bastos,
qué as de copas, qué caballo
de espadas, qué malaventura, qué taconeo,
qué paloma, qué ebbó, que recogimiento,
qué hombre no dado a lux por mujer,
Padre, podrá exorcizarte el recuerdo? [. . .]
Soy yo. La Esposa:
Apetedbí del omiero.
Monja feudal de clausura . . .
Penélope sin Odiseo.

16
Beyond Manicheism: Derek Walcott's *Henri Christophe* and *Dream on Monkey Mountain*

John Thieme

This essay considers the way in which two of Derek Walcott's earlier plays engage with the issue of finding an appropriate dramatic form for their Caribbean subjects, and relates this to their attempt to cross borders by moving outside the binary patterns in which colonial subjects find themselves inscribed. Much of Walcott's work has stressed the doubleness of Caribbean experience; he constructs oppositions between Europe and Africa, Crusoe and Friday, art and landscape, and, in his early work, presents himself as 'divided to the vein'[1] because of his split racial ancestry. However, from the outset, his writing attempts to dismantle the boundary fences of colonial discourse and dualistic modes of thinking, to arrive at a pluralist approach that could be seen as a literary staging of creolization. He has spoken of his early writing as an 'apprenticeship'[2] in which he sought to emulate the work of European masters. Arguably, this apprenticeship ended not only when he moved beyond imitativeness and found his own distinctive voice as a writer, but also – and this is complementary – when he evolved strategies for moving outside colonial definition. The two plays discussed here, *Henri Christophe* (1950), the first of his three dramatic treatments of the Haitian revolution and its aftermath, and what is arguably his finest play to date, *Dream on Monkey Mountain* (1967), both engage with the binarism central to colonial classifications, demonstrating the tragic consequences of such definition and, in the case of *Dream on Monkey Mountain*, suggesting ways in which the borderlines between Europe and the 'other' may be eroded.

Walcott has written of having been attracted to the subject of the Haitian Revolution because he saw parallels between the Haitian situation and the St. Lucian world in which he grew up, even though Haiti had become the first black republic in the Americas some 150 years before, while St. Lucia remained a colony when he was writing the play in mid-century. A dramatization of aspects of the history of post-revolutionary Haiti offered possibilities for an allegory exploring nation-building, leadership and the reconstruction of identity; and in the leading players in this history Walcott found tragic heroes racked by 'Manichean' crises about racial identity which again struck a chord in his own experience:

> I was drawn, like a child's mind to fire, to the Manichean conflicts of Haiti's history. The parallels were there in my own island, but not the heroes... [The black Jacobins'] self-disgust foreshadowed ours, that wrestling contradiction of being white in mind and black in body, as if the flesh were coal from which the spirit like tormented coal writhed to escape.[3]

Henri Christophe, the third of the triumvirate of ex-slave rulers who successively governed Haiti after the Revolution, a man torn between excessive violence and the commissioning of visionary architectural projects, particularly captured Walcott's imagination; in Christophe he located the raw material for a complex and flawed tragic hero,[4] whom he modelled on those of Elizabethan and Greek drama.

Walcott's decision to make Christophe his hero is particularly interesting. Earlier literary treatments of the events surrounding the Haitian Revolution and its aftermath had centred on the more obviously heroic figure of Toussaint L'Ouverture, the military and diplomatic genius of the first phase of the Revolution, and the individual most directly responsible for the ousting of the French. Wordsworth and Lamartine had focused on Toussaint, and in the twentieth-century Caribbean the Martiniquan poet, Aimé Césaire, an important precursor for Walcott, and the Trinidadian C. L. R. James had followed suit: in James's case not only in his classic study of the Haitian Revolution, *The Black Jacobins* (1938), but also in the play *Toussaint L'Ouverture* (1936).[5] However, as Judy Stone points out, 'Walcott chose for his Hamlet the enigma, the lesser man, but more complex mortal'.[6] Such a view is borne out in an early passage in the play, which refers to Christophe as 'a two-sided mirror' and suggests he constitutes a fusion of his two predecessors:

> under
> His easy surface, ripples of dark
> Strive with the light, or like a coin's two sides,
> Or like the world half-blind when moons are absent,

And brilliant in the glare of sun.
Under that certain majesty he hides
The teaching of Toussaint, the danger of Dessalines.[7]

Henri Christophe abounds in references to Elizabethan and Jacobean drama, and Walcott draws on the traditions of such theatre for the kind of 'complex' tragic hero he presents in the play. Bruce King has commented: 'The complexity of behaviour is Shakespearean, the disillusionment Websterian',[8] and Walcott himself has said that his black Jacobins were 'Jacobean...because they flared from a mind drenched in Elizabethan literature out of the same darkness as Webster's Flamineo, from a flickering world of mutilation and heresy'.[9] *Tamburlaine, Macbeth* and *Richard III* are other obvious intertexts, but arguably the most interesting parallels with Renaissance tragedy are with *Othello*, and these relate to Manichean binaries.

Walcott's use of the word 'Manichean' to describe similarities between the Haitian situation and late colonial St. Lucian society anticipates a trend in post-Fanonian analyses of colonial and related discourses to see Manichean allegory as lying at the heart of racial stereotyping. Such allegory, according to Abdul JanMohamed, insists on drawing demarcation lines between 'white and black, good and evil, salvation and damnation, civilization and savagery, superiority and inferiority, intelligence and emotion, self and other, subject and object'.[10] It is a practice which reached its peak in the pseudo-scientific racial binaries of the Victorian heyday of Empire, but its origins go back to the beginnings of Western culture,[11] and *Othello* affords a particularly powerful enactment of such allegory. While the play can be seen to contest such stereotyping, the hero is seduced into accepting a view of his social environment which is based on such dualism: arguably Othello's tragedy occurs because he succumbs to the Manichean binaries of Iago's rhetoric which promotes rational/sensual, civilization/savagery divisions; and although critics have debated the extent to which his racial identity informs his perceptions, it seems reasonable to conclude that his increasing absorption in animalistic imagery demonstrates the extent to which he comes to accept negative black stereotyping.

Whether or not one agrees with such a view of *Othello*, Walcott's Christophe certainly follows such a path in the penultimate scene of the play. He is persuaded by his secretary Vastey that the white archbishop Brelle is conspiring against him because of '[h]is obvious love for clear complexions', and seems to accept that Brelle still regards blacks as 'baboons' (*HC*, p. 45). Like Dessalines before him, Christophe feels he has achieved stature through his metamorphosis from slave to king, but he now falls victim to Vastey's Manichean rhetoric and it is not long before he is using it himelf:

> I am not a civilized man, father;
> I am at heart very primitive; there is that urge –
> A beast in the jungle among primitive angers
> Clawing down opposition; what is the expression – The instinct?
>
> (*HC*, p. 48)

The consequence is both a personal and a national tragedy, since both protagonist and country fail to achieve the 'federation of complexions' (*HC*, p. 31), which is one character's ideal for the country. The theme is clearly one which has relevance to all periods of Caribbean history; and it had a particular urgency in the late colonial period when the various territories were moving towards Independence: there was the possibility of political federation and debates about dismantling race and colour hierarchies were very much in the air.

Christophe's failure to achieve any sense of racial harmony is also narrativized through his relationship with Pétion, a mulatto general who rules the southern half of the country while he holds sway in the north, in the latter part of the play. Most significantly of all, however, his architectural visions are both entangled with an ideal of whiteness and characterized by a need for 'foreign' validation:

> I shall build chateaux
> That shall obstruct the strongest season
> So high the hawk shall giddy in its gyre
> Before it settles on the carved turrets.
> My floors shall reflect the faces that pass over them,
> And foreign trees spread out the shape of government;
> On emerald lawns I will hold councils.
> I'll pave a room with golden coins, so rich,
> The old archbishop will smile indulgently at heaven from
> The authenticity of my chateaux.
>
> (*HC*, p. 41)

It is perhaps the crowning tragic irony of the play that he seeks such 'authenticity' through what may be regarded as the perpetuation of colonial mimesis.

One *might* say the same of Walcott's play itself. *Henri Christophe* belongs to Walcott's 'apprenticeship' period and the intertextual weight of 'foreign' references is heavy enough to threaten the whole structure. According to such a view the ultimate Manichean tragic protagonist would be, not Christophe, but the author himself. There is evidence to support such a reading. Christophe and Dessalines are revolutionaries who perpetuate the Manichean divisions of the society rather than dismantle them as a consequence of being victims of 'that wrestling contradiction of being white in mind and black in body'; and the play engages in a not entirely dissimilar Manichean practice by cloaking its Caribbean subject in Elizabethan and Jacobean intertexts. However, in another sense *Henri Christophe* can be seen to move beyond Manicheism, to erode the borders drawn by colonial discourse, since it dramatizes the tragic consequences facing the protagonist who succumbs to a view that casts him as the inferior partner in the hierarchized Manichean equation.

Christophe's poetry clearly belies his self-estimate that he is a primitive sensualist. So where this particular binary is concerned, Walcott's poetry, like Shakespeare's in *Othello*, undermines the construction of black alterity in terms of the negative side of such Manichean binaries as civilization and savagery and rationality and sensuality. In short, Christophe emerges as a complex hybridized protagonist whose tragedy arises from his failure to see himself as such. The play stops short of staging his conflict in terms of formal hybridization and this, arguably, is *its* tragedy.

The dramatic mode of *Dream on Monkey Mountain* is altogether more complex. In the later play the top-heavy use of European intertexts is supplanted by an eclectic and hybridized repertory of formal elements, which draws extensively on the traditions of Caribbean masquerade, music and mime, among them a *burroquite* (or 'donkey dance'), singing and dancing by a religious sisterhood and an impromptu dance performance which includes the singing of a bongo. And performance, particularly mimesis, is in one sense the *subject* of *Dream on Monkey Mountain*, since it is about the powerful effects of colonial brainwashing, which encourages European mimesis in one kind of colonial subject and an adversarial opposition to such influence, in favour of an equally unsatisfactory attempt to return to 'pure' ancestral roots, in another. Both responses have injurious psychological consequences because they involve repression of the creolized nature of Caribbean societies.

Walcott's 'Note on Production' says that 'The play is a dream, one that exists as much in the given minds of its principal characters as in that of its writer' (*DMM*, p. 208). Initially this psychodrama seems to be located within the consciousness of the play's central character Makak, but, as the note indicates, it is intended to be a product of the collective consciousness of all the characters. Together, as the epigraphs to the two parts, taken from Sartre's introduction to Fanon's *The Wretched of the Earth*, indicate, they represent the dissociated Caribbean psyche, pulled two ways by the cultural schizophrenia induced by colonialism. Makak's dream, which involves a visionary return to Africa, is itself an exemplification of a syndrome identified by Sartre, in the passage quoted as the epigraph to the second part of the play: 'The status of "native" is a nervous condition introduced and maintained by the settler among colonised people with their consent' (*DMM*, p. 277). It is a vision of Africa induced by a European muse, a White Goddess figure, and so, as in *Henri Christophe*, the colonial subject seems to be the schizophrenic victim of Manichean binaries. However, in this case the play more obviously traverses such shadow lines, propounding an aesthetic and a view of Caribbean subjectivity which moves beyond this.

The dream reaches its climax in a scene of comic 'Apotheosis' (Part II, Scene 3), which is a riot of parody and pantomime. This functions as a kind of dream-within-a-dream, and since it is initiated by the figure of the colonial policeman Lestrade, it may seem to be primarily the product of his mind. It is, however, introduced by the play's Chorus and so, like the whole of the central section of the play, is best viewed as a collective fantasy. In this scene the Chorus is called 'the tribes' and seems to take on a communal African identity. It sings a 'chant of tribal triumph' (*DMM*, p. 308) and functions like the praise-singers of West African societies. Some of the detail is drawn from specific African traditions but much of it is generalized parody of African atavism. Earlier Walcott has mocked Caribbean mimicry of European standards; here he pokes fun at 'back to Africa' movements. And this is particularly apparent in the portrayal of Lestrade who moves from being a staunch defender of 'Roman law' and becomes an advocate of 'tribal law' (*DMM*, p. 311). At Lestrade's instigation, prisoners are brought before Makak in a fantasy of black revenge. They include such disparate figures as Sir Francis Drake, Mandrake the magician, Sir Cecil Rhodes and Al Jolson. Their common crime would seem to be their whiteness, but in some cases it is clearly more specific. Drake and Rhodes were archetypal imperialists; the comic-strip hero Mandrake has a black servant, Lothar; Al Jolson performed in blackface. In fact all the prisoners appear to be people who have exploited blacks, either economically or by appropriating their culture or by excluding them from 'official' versions of history. 'Tribal law' quickly condemns them to be hanged.

Next a comic catalogue of tributes is brought before Makak. These include 'An offer to revise the origins of slavery. A floral tribute of lilies from the Ku Klux Klan ... The Nobel Peace Prize ... An offer from Hollywood' (*DMM*, pp. 313–14), but all these tokens of restitution from the white world are summarily rejected by the tribes. At this point black intransigence will allow only an adversarial response which, like the négritudinist position, can be seen as the other side of the Manichean binaries constructed by colonialism and a stance which leaves the colonized subject still being determined by colonial discourses of alterity, albeit by turning them upside down. Makak's friend, Moustique, tells him he is in danger of replacing his former love for the white moon with a deep hatred which will require its destruction, and this proves prophetic. In a powerful poetic passage, Lestrade urges Makak to behead the apparition of the White Goddess who has inspired his dream of a return to Africa; the passage sums up the injurious effects of European cultural conditioning, while also suggesting that its power is dependent on the colonial subject's own complicity:

> She is lime, stone, marble, moonlight, lilies, cloud, foam and bleaching cream, the mother of civilization and the confounder of blackness. I too have longed for her. She is the colour of the law, religion, paper, art, and if you want peace, if you want to discuss the beautiful depth of your blackness, nigger, chop off her head! When you do this, you will kill Venus, the virgin, the Sleeping Beauty. She is the white light that paralysed your mind, that led you into confusion. It is you who created her, so kill her! kill her! The law has spoken.
>
> (*DMM*, p. 319)

Makak is finally persuaded and the scene ends with his beheading the apparition. In so doing he clearly exorcizes the stranglehold which the European side of his heritage has appeared to have on him. However, since the Goddess has been responsible for initiating his African dream, the beheading also involves a repudiation of African cultural essentialism. This is confirmed by the fact that immediately before he takes the action, Makak removes the African robe in which he has been dressed during the Apotheosis scene. So the 'two bewitchings'[12] of Africa and Europe, which the play seems to suggest are opposite sides of the same coin, are simultaneously rejected.

In the Epilogue Makak awakens from his dream and moves beyond the situation of being a colonial mimic. Hitherto he has been called only Makak ('Monkey'), but now he moves beyond aping European or supposed African modes of behaviour (which are themselves European inventions and correspond to the negative side of the binary oppositions identified by JanMohamed), and is given an individual name, Felix Hobain. The play ends with his eroding the borderlines drawn by colonial discourse as he seeks a return to an Edenic (pre-colonial?) past:

> Lord, I have been washed from shore to shore, as a tree in the ocean. The branches of my fingers, the roots of my feet, could grip nothing, but now, God, they have found ground... now this old hermit is going back home, back to the beginning, to the green beginning of this world.
>
> (*DMM*, p. 326)

The image of the uprooted tree washed across the ocean suggests the legacy of the Middle Passage.[13] However, the conclusion clearly argues against a return to Africa. 'Home' for Makak is the Caribbean landscape of his more immediate 'origins' and it is now viewed as a pre-Columbian environment which offers the promise of a fresh start. This notion is in keeping with the belief, central to all Walcott's later work and expressed most forcefully in his essay 'The Muse of History',[14] that historical determinism must be rejected in favour of an aesthetic in which the New World artist creates the Americas anew through an Adamic vision.

Though Makak is the central figure in *Dream on Monkey Mountain*, the Caribbean search for identity is also played out in the minds of other characters, most notably in that of Corporal Lestrade, who is an obvious foil to Makak. The racially mixed Lestrade begins as a vivid study in the negative effects of cultural schizophrenia. Named after the bumbling Scotland Yard detective of the Sherlock Holmes stories,[15] he initially appears as a staunch defender of the colonial order; he separates himself off from the island's blacks, viewing them as existing on a lower evolutionary plane than himself:

> In the beginning was the ape, and the ape had no name, so God call him man. Now there were various tribes of the ape, it had gorilla, baboon, orang-utan, chimpanzee, the blue-arsed monkey and the marmoset, and God look at his handiwork, and saw that it was good. For some of the apes had straighten their backbone, and start walking upright, but there was one tribe unfortunately that lingered

behind, and that was the nigger. Now if you apes will behave like gentlemen, who knows what could happen? The bottle could go round, but first it behoves me, Corporal Lestrade, to perform my duty according to the rules of Her Majesty's Government, so don't interrupt.

(*DMM*, pp. 216–17)

Such language can be related to the rhetoric of racial Manicheism, with its equation of blackness and animality, but as a mulatto Lestrade represents a challenge to such binaries, since he embodies both sides of the Manichean divide. Ultimately *his* inner struggle is as important in the play as Makak's – as in *Henri Christophe*, the central protagonist is black, but the mulatto dilemma looms equally large – and in repudiating blackness, he is rejecting half of himself. However, during the course of the dream he performs a complete about-face and, in a movement typical of shifts in Caribbean attitudes around the time of Independence, appears to replace his Eurocentric perspective with an Afrocentric one. Finally it is Lestrade who persuades Makak to behead the White Goddess and this act of symbolic emancipation frees *both* men from their roles as mimics, liberating them into an emergent *Caribbean* consciousness, in which local subjectivity frees itself from the strait-jacket of being constructed in terms of otherness, a predicament which is perpetuated by colonial subjects who internalize Manichean binaries and perpetuate them either by slavish (as opposed to carnivalesque) imitation or an adversarial response which fails to dismantle their conceptual divisions. In this sense the beheading of the Goddess can be seen to represent a movement forward into a postcolonial consciousness. The play challenges existing social and cultural divisions, presenting a hybrid view of subjectivity and employing a creole discursive continuum.

At the end of *Dream on Monkey Mountain* Lestrade re-emerges as the colonial administrator he was at the outset. This could support the view that the dream has been Makak's after all, but in the latter half of Part II Lestrade is centre-stage and the action seems to issue primarily from *his* mind. So he stands alongside Makak as another powerful study of a Manichean consciousness. The suggestion seems to be that coming to terms with hybrid origins is a crucial issue for all Caribbean people irrespective of their ethnic make-up; and again it is mirrored in the complex cultural provenance of the play and its 'dream' of a future in which the emphasis is on the Caribbean present, not on an unsustainable attempt to retrieve the fiction of a homogeneous ancestral past.

And insofar as *Dream on Monkey Mountain* depicts a collective dream, ultimately *all* the characters exorcize the stultifying legacy of such cultural essentialism, and the play promotes a positive view of creolization. In so doing it breaks down the abstract binaries that have dominated post-Cartesian Western thought in favour of an aesthetic which celebrates the ability to move across inherited epistemological borders. Whereas *Henri Christophe* shows the tragic consequences of succumbing to Manichean rhetoric, *Dream on Monkey Mountain* dramatizes the positive dimensions of Caribbean schizophrenia, as its characters traverse the ideological frontiers which have hitherto inhibited their independent development. Complementing this, the play itself employs a theatrical mode which, while drawing on a diverse and polyphonic range of intertexts, is rooted in folk forms and thus transcends both European and African atavism

17

'Canvas of Blood': Okigbo's African Modernism

David Richards

This essay draws material from a number of different times and places: London in 1995, Paris in 1907, Northern Spain in 1937, Arochukwu in the eighteenth and nineteenth centuries, Nigeria in the 1960s. It also transverses disciplines and genres: anthropology, literary criticism, history, poetry, sculpture, painting. Such intellectual, temporal and spatial vicissitudes require some preliminary coordinates to be announced if they are not to become, at best, nomadic, at worst, vagrant. So, *this essay is about collage.*

Collage is, of course, one part of a general modernist exploration of the technique of fragmentation, juxtaposition and defamiliarization which goes beyond simply the pasting of paper cut-outs. For Max Ernst, for example, it was 'the chance meeting of two distant realities on an unfamiliar plane, the culture of displacement and its effects – and the spark of poetry that leaps across the gap as the two realities converge'.[1] For Ernst, collage embodied 'the irrational tension between the elements of reality' which was 'the paradigm for his own visual world'.[2] But collage offers a possible paradigm, not only for a visual world, but also for postcolonial 'culture[s] of displacement' where meanings can associate, proliferate, collide, disintegrate and reform. Collage takes multiple elements from other sources and places them in new combinations. Elements bound to other contexts are made to occupy strange hybrid landscapes. Collage is therefore like language in that it offers the prospect of infinite recombinations of forms. But collage also contains an element which Rosalind Krauss has termed 'protolinguistic' since the elements recombined in collage 'open another field in which absence is the essence of meaning'.[3] The context from which the element is cut is absent from the collage, but the act of collage nonetheless draws attention to the fact of its absence: the new field which collage creates, its presence, is constructed out of absences, and absence makes collage possible. Collages also reach out beyond those older absent contexts to new and as yet unuttered statements to a world of infinite possibilities. Collage in Ernst's formulation offers, therefore, a *productive* notion of 'displacement' which seems to typify the work of contemporary postcolonial artists and writers.

But this essay is not only *about* collage, it *is*, also, a collage.

* * * * *

The exhibits at the Royal Academy of Arts exhibition 'Africa: the Art of a Continent' (4 October 1994–21 January 1995) were arranged as if to take the visitor on a metaphorical journey across Africa from Egypt in the entrance gallery through, successively, East, South, Central, West, Sahel and back to North Africa: many thousands of miles abbreviated into the Academy's exhibition spaces, an epic exploration undertaken at the pace of a meandering stroll. The 'monumental' and 'unpreced-ented'[4] nature of the exhibition was not only its glory but also its predicament: the geographical arrangement cut across historical time and there was little sense of how two adjacent artefacts from different cultures, perhaps from different millennia, could be made to corres-pond. 'Africa: the Art of a Continent' increased the quantity of our knowledge but hardly touched at all the depth of our understanding. Yet, although the exhibition's contents are not available to summary (what summary could be available from the conjunction of Ashanti gold weights, the minbar of the Sultan Qa'itbay and hundreds of other objects?), it also, strangely, conjured a sense of a familiar or anticipated vision of Africa from its spectacular arrangements. This is particularly the case with the exhibits from sub-Saharan Africa where it was not so much that the exhibition removed all the works from any meaningful African cultural contexts but that the works were made to inhabit and fulfil a thoroughly Western preconception: African art is, on the evidence of this exhibition, primitive, pagan and past. Africa became again what it had been, so that it may be recognized by the strolling spectator: parenthesized, a simulacrum of itself, historyless, ideally primitive and determined from without. The objects became opaque, *en abyme*, in suspense, obscured by and embedded in a series of grand theories of an evolutionary history or notions of the human psyche. African art serves to supply an archetypal reference, a locus, for a number of acute Western obsessions.

* * * * *

Primitive, pagan, past. So much is sustained by the perpetuation of an African art as totem, taboo, fetish. Without the anthropologically-sanctioned notion of the primitive, as Steven Tyler writes.

> [N]either modern poetry nor modern art would be what it is today... [it] has given modern artists the mood of distance and estrangement from their own familiar traditions, and, by enriching and relativizing the storehouse of knowledge, symbols, and odd and diverse facts out of which poets or artists fashion their work, has enabled their exploitation of the archaic, the exotic, the primitive, the primordial, the universality of myth and symbols, and the relativity of language and thought.[5]

Art historians offer a point of origin for the moment when the primitive entered the consciousness of the modern artist: in Paris in 1907, in the cellars of the Trocadero, where Picasso 'discovered' a collection of African masks which he included in his 'monumental' and 'unprecedented' canvas *Les Demoiselles d'Avignon*. Until *Les Demoiselles d'Avignon* the primitive had been used by Western figurative art as an allegorical or exotic subject; Picasso's innovation was to rework African forms of representation into the practice of painting. The masks he depicts are not simply primitive exemplars; their formal rendering of spatial planes becomes the stylistic medium for the painting itself. Picasso's discovery of the African masks held enormous significance for him in that he felt the masks expressed a primitive consciousness:

> For me the masks were not just sculptures. They were magical objects... intercessors... against everything – against unknown, threatening spirits... They were weapons – to keep people from being ruled by spirits, to help free themselves. If we give a form to these spirits, we become free.[6]

The formal and stylistic innovations the masks inspired in Picasso led directly to his collaborations with Braque and the creation of the 'moment' of Cubism and, in short, the revolutionary impact of African form on European art which, literally, reshaped its destiny during the years 1907–14. In a radical, even essential, way, African art *is* modernity. Yet that 'modernity' can only function if Africans themselves remain distinctly traditional and lacking modernity: 'primitive, pagan and past'.

Picasso's *Les Demoiselles d'Avignon* has become, oddly, the recognizable face of African art: a recognition bequeathed, not by Africans, but by modernism's treatment of African art. The subject of *Les Demoiselles d'Avignon*, female sexuality, is overlaid by, masked by, the primitive, which evokes an ambivalence characteristic not only of the treatment of female sexuality but also of African art in the West. The mask is of use to Picasso as a figurative and symbolic device in a 'collaged' vision where female sexuality converges with primitive fetish. Not being directly of 'interest' but merely a cipher for other concerns, the mask is, in this sense, drastically emptied of cultural significance other than its simple primitiveness. The mask's African significance would have been constituted by its function within the community of the carver who made it, but when that function is displaced the object becomes amenable to the designation of art. The mask's dislocation has transfigured a functional object into a modern artwork. The essential difference which separates the 'primitive' and the modern is function: while the object retains its function it cannot partake of modernity. Modernism's treatment of African art is predicated upon the action of rendering the primitive object an incalculable ellipsis.

In almost every respect, 'Africa: the Art of a Continent' conformed to this modernist view of African art where it is emptied of autonomous content and Africans themselves are reduced in significance to anonymous, 'primal', primary and unknowing contributors of source materials. In this scenario, the notion of a self-conscious African artist is excised: the African artist lacks that self-consciousness which the European modernist has in abundance. Without this kind of self-consciousness, Africans are denied the possibility to represent themselves to themselves, or to others. They exist only as the anonymous and unaware commodities of modernism but who themselves lack modernity.

Of course, European modernism is too large and various to be contained in these formulae, but it may be salutary to conceive of the celebrated moment of *Les Demoiselles d'Avignon* as, in truth, the celebrated moment of African tradition. But (if you see what I mean) without much that's traditional. Nor much that's African, either, for that matter. Picasso's and, more generally, modernism's 'collage' of African art draws as much attention to what is absent from its depiction as what is present, and invariably what is absent is the African-ness of African art. Whereas modernism sees African art as the paradigm of all that is primitive, pagan, past, African artists conceive their works as functional objects expressing and participating in the cultural discourse of myth, formal composition, history. This contradiction between the aims of modernism and the practice of African artists would seem to lead to an *impasse*: the radical incompatibility of modernism in an African context. Yet the newly independent states of postcolonial Africa gave birth to precisely that hybrid being – the African modernist.

* * * * *

The Nigerian poet, Christopher Okigbo, drew on an eclectic range of texts and cultural sources for his collection of poems *Labyrinths*. His work is a thoroughly modernist melange of writers and musicians, deities and ancestors, myths and legends, politicians and political events: Idoto, Orpheus, the Western Nigeria Crisis of 1962, Patrice Lumumba, Obafemi Awolowo, Hopkins, Debussy, Melville, Hawthorne, Cowley, Raja Ratnam, Mallarmé, Tagore, Lorca, Aeneas' helmsman Palinaurus, Ishthar, Tammuz, Gilgamesh, T. S. Eliot, Pound, Yeats, Ovid, Catullus, Horace, Virgil, Tacitus. There are also fragments of more personal memories and allusions: to his newly-born niece in 'Newcomer',[7] to his mother, Anna; to a school teacher and other individuals from his childhood. The references, quoted fragments and allusions to other contexts, the 'globules of anguish strung together on memory'[8] as he called them, belie a structure which Okigbo claimed was imminent in the poems and through which the poems are 'originally related'. The various sections constitute a 'fable' of 'man's quest for fulfilment' from a 'cleansing' 'ceremony of innocence' and initiation ('Heavensgate') to the 'projection' of 'outer and inner worlds', the sense of the loss of an 'inner' psychic awareness and the history of 'the collective rape of innocence' ('Limits'). The poems celebrate a 'spiritual and psychic' 'homecoming' and the interrupted 'quest' is resumed in the 'unconscious' until, finally, the poetic persona achieves a state of 'aesthetic grace' ('Distances').[9] This structure of an extraordinary psychological-religious quest is achieved in a modernist poetic of fragments.

Okigbo's heavily eclectic modernist style does not, however, deploy an extensive set of references to paintings. Indeed in the 72 pages which constitute his collected poems only one painting is directly acknowledged, compared to the dozens of allusions to music and poetry. Yet the single painting is central to the development of the sequence of poems; it is a key to Okigbo's strategy and meaning and is fundamental to an understanding of Okigbo's visual imagination. It occurs at the end of a series concerned with the destruction of traditional Igbo religious shrines by colonial force and missionary interventions and marks a turning point which will lead, eventually, to a reinvention of the poet as the locus both of a culture of displacement and of a recombination of converging realities. The lone image is of a painting by Picasso.

> But at the window, outside, a shadow:
>
> The sunbird sings again
> From the LIMITS of the dream;
> The Sunbird sings again
> Where the caress does not reach,
>
> *of Guernica*
> On whose canvas of blood,
> The slits of his tongue
> cling to glue...
>
> & *the cancelling out is complete*[10]

The reference links Picasso's *Guernica* to Nwanza, the sunbird who, in Igbo mythology and folktales, is a trickster-like symbol of energy and vitality – 'an embodiment of the creative conscience'.[11] This is a central crux in the complex argument of the 'organically related' poems: the moment where Okigbo's poetic voice changes from a detailing of the destruction of the traditional Igbo culture into a slow reconstruction of the fragments. *Guernica* is the song the Sunbird sings.

Picasso's painting seems to occupy a position of central importance in the poem, therefore, expressing symbolically a poetic process by which postcolonial Igbo culture may discover its voice. The painting seems also to have held a particular fascination for Okigbo personally, since Sunday Anozie, who knew Okigbo well, reported that the poet carried with him at Nsukka in 1961 a newsprint slide of *Guernica*. 'If any single painting influenced Okigbo at the early stage of his poetic career it was undoubtedly *Guernica*'.[12] Clearly, the image acts in the poem as a sort of short-hand expression of cultural spoliation, linking the Civil War atrocities against the Basques and the British colonization of the Igbo. Okigbo's evocation of Picasso's image of devastation has also been used by critics as an indication of Okigbo's eerily prophetic premonition of the Nigerian Civil War, and of his own death in August 1967 on the front at Nsukka. Robert Fraser writes:

> Here allusion and prognosis fuse, for the reference to Picasso's canvas of 1937 brings us up against the perennial violence of every age at the very moment at which it highlights the plight of the Igbo, poised, as

Okigbo wrote, a mere three years from the first bombing raids on Enugu.[13]

Yet this is to make too despondent a reading of Okigbo's engagement with modernism's prime exponent of African forms in European art. *Guernica* is clearly important to Okigbo, strategically as the sequence unfolds, and symbolically for its expressive content, but most significantly, perhaps, for its formal arrangement which he saw as offering a new *poetic*. Anozie remembers Okigbo's limited knowledge of, but intense enthusiasm for, Picasso's work:

> What Okigbo particularly admired in Picasso was his genius for isolating particular aesthetic qualities with an unequalled ruthlessness and brilliance, and for doing it to an unequalled range and diversity of qualities. One of Okigbo's brilliant ideas about poetry – and an ambition he used to vaunt to the present writer – was to do something analogous to Picasso in breaking down the human figure into fragments and building some of them up into a new construction within which the fragments retain their separate identities or, in other words, to break down art into its several elements and exhibit them separately.[14]

For Anozie, Okigbo's Sunbird sings not of 'the tragedy' of Guernica but of 'the art behind'.[15] Okigbo saw in *Guernica* what Picasso had seen in the African masks in the Trocadero: not (just) subject matter ('violence' and 'primitive' respectively) but also a formal innovation ('a new construction'). Yet ironically, the affinity Okigbo forges with Picasso, Picasso had appropriated from African art 30 years before, and reworked into his own highly individual style through an extended 'cubist' apprenticeship. It is an intriguing prospect that what Okigbo saw in Picasso's modernism and which he expresses as his ambition to emulate is nothing less than what Picasso had seen in African art: a new visual language of open planes and facets arranged in a complex relationship of related viewpoints connecting both an abstract and mimetic style. Whatever the potential ironies of Okigbo responding to the Africanness of Picasso's modernism, Okigbo entirely translates Picasso's visual language into his poetics. *Labyrinths* is *Guernica*. But with an important consequent difference. The visual language which Picasso read as African 'primitive', Okigbo read as 'modernity' and by this extraordinary *'cancelling out'* of the homologies recovered modernity for Africa. The 'ambition' which Okigbo announced to Anozie amounts to nothing less than the creating of a modern African poetry, accomplished by reclaiming African artistic traditions from European modernism.

In the context of the newly-independent African nation states, the forging of new African cultural identities was considered the vital task of a remarkable generation of writers. Achebe, Soyinka, Ngugi, Senghor and many others contributed lively – often vociferous – addresses to the debates around defining African cultural consciousness. Okigbo also made his stand: in a letter concerning an African arts festival, he wrote in 1966, 'About Dakar. I did not go... I found the whole idea of a negro arts festival based on colour quite absurd. I did not enter any work either for the competition, and was most surprised when I heard a prize had been awarded to *Limits*. I have written to reject it.'[16] Okigbo shared the disdain of many anglophone African writers for négritude, which was the target of his dismissive rejection. His letter indicates his unwillingness to allow a racial consciousness to be the defining characteristic of an African poetics. Négritude was an 'absurd' project to Okigbo: its desire to define and locate *Africanité* amounted to a restricted colour-blind vision. He was much more concerned with locating the African origins of the formal practices of modernism and reconstituting them for an African poetics. *Guernica* offered a limitless prospect, at once both African and modern, where the aesthetic of fragments offered an unfixed, de-centred field of allusions, conjuring, by turns, an idyllic pastoral interlude out of traces:

> For we are listening in cornfields
> among the windplayers,
> listening to the wind learning over
> its loveliest fragment... [17]

Or increasingly more complex geometrical/moral alternatives in his experiments with a version of analytical 'cubist' imagery:

> life without sin, without
>
> life: which accepted,
> way leads downward
> down orthocenter
> avoiding decisions
>
> Or forms fourth angle –
> duty, obligation:
>
> square yields the moron[18]

Or extraordinary conjunctions of fragments simultaneously engaged in a collage of several images. Here, the point of reference is to Hopkins' 'The Wreck of the Deutschland' 'collaged' into a poem about the assassination of Patrice Lumumba. The effect – like the events it describes – is discordant, with converging images breaking the lines into ellipses and discontinuities as the poem splinters into prismatic subdivisions.

> How does one say NO in thunder...
> For in breakers in sea fever compass or cross
>   makes a difference: certainly makes
>   not an escape ladder...
> Where is there for us an anchorage;
> A shank for a sheet, a double arch – [19]

*****

I have been arguing that Okigbo's poetry offers an important corrective to many prevailing assumptions about African cultures – assumptions which descend from a modernist appropriation of African materials. Okigbo's engagement with modernism, particularly Picasso's *Guernica*, enabled him to formulate a poetics of collaged fragments and to recover from modernist primitivism a version of African modernity. I wish now to argue that Okigbo's encounter with modernism enabled an extraordinary historical conception also. Just as Okigbo's poetics disavow the modernist version of African primitivism, they also counter notions of African historylessness.

In the Introduction to *Labyrinths*, Okigbo makes an unusual parenthetical historical conjunction:

> *Labyrinths* is thus a fable of man's perennial quest for fulfilment. (The title may suggest Minos' legendary palace at Cnossus, but the double headed axe is as much a symbol of sovereignty in traditional Ibo society as in Crete. Besides, the long and tortuous passage to the shrine of the 'long-juju' of the Aro Ibos may, perhaps, best be described as a labyrinth.)[20]

The particular model of Igbo history he adopts is the 'Aro Ibos', by which he meant Arochukwu, a powerful and centralized state which predominated in south-eastern Nigeria from c. 1690 until its destruction during the period of British colonization. Arochukwu is still shrouded in a 'labyrinthine' enigma because 'historiographical problems emanated from its history, namely, the Eurocentric neglect of African political institutions which did not conform to the European mind-set, and the modification of state formation theories to embody the trappings of racial bias'.[21] Apollos Nwauwa describes Arochukwu as a 'unique' confederation of three distinct ethnic groups – Igbo, Ibibio and Akpa – 'located astride two major trade routes which converged at the confluence of the Enyong and the Cross Rivers'.[22] Arochukwu controlled three essential resources: the main trade routes, the distribution of exotic goods and a justice system based on the 'long juju'. It is this last which Okigbo evokes as his exemplar for both poem and history. An oracle of local significance called *Ibini-Kupabi*, controlled by the Ibibio, had been in existence before the foundation of the confederacy but it was developed by Nachi, an itinerant Edda priest-doctor, into a place of pilgrimage and a powerful instrument of state control. The delta peoples consulted it, the Ibibio venerated it, the Igbo regarded it as *Chukwu*, the high god, and the people of the confederacy became *umuchukwu* (Children of the High God). The oracle combined religious and judicial functions to mitigate and arbitrate interethnic conflict, and the penalty for losing a case before the oracle was enslavement.[23]

There are a number of highly significant features in Okigbo's reference to the oracle of Arochukwu. The allusion to the 'double headed axe' as 'a symbol of sovereignty in traditional Ibo society' is unusual in the context of the notions of Igbo history which prevailed at the time in that it runs counter to the received view. One need look no further than the historical novels of Chinua Achebe to see 'traditional Ibo society' as being without monarchical authorities or centralized political élites: it is universally characterized by a particularly 'republican' timbre, essentially acephalous, even subject to social fragmentation.[24] Yet Okigbo writes in terms of 'sovereignty'.

Okigbo's revisionist version of Igbo history perhaps also indicates the contemporary political contexts of the poems. During the mid-1960s, when Okigbo was assembling the final versions of his poems into the *Labyrinths* collection (and writing his Introduction in October 1965) a strong separatist movement had developed in the Eastern Region of the Nigerian Federation in response to the massacre of some 10 000 to 30 000 Igbo by Hausa and Fulani peoples, who then dominated the Nigerian federal government. (These events would eventually lead to the formation of the Republic of Biafra in May 1967, and a civil war that raged until January 1970.) Arochukwu endured for more than two centuries as a successful synthesis of ethnicities welded into a sovereign entity: few readers could have missed the irony of Okigbo's historical allusion and it is hardly a coincidence that Okigbo awakens the historical memory of another lost 'sovereignty', the Arochukwu confederacy, just as the Nigerian confederacy was on the verge of falling into 'this iron dance of mortars'.[25]

Yet Okigbo also connects a number of significant elements in a typical collage-like manoeuvre: this cultural history and the poetic text are to be read in the same ways. Oracle and poem share the same contours: both are 'labyrinths', and the aesthetic and historical join. This extraordinary 'graphical' imagination enabled him to see ideas, art theories, historical events almost as shapes in a collage: a capacity for abstract visualization which emphasized dialogues and affinities between different cultures, historical periods, texts and artworks. He 'corrected' the primitivist misrepresentation of modernism by recovering modernism's African origins in a collaged 'Guernican' perception, just as he answered African 'historylessness' with a history lesson which also has a poetic 'shape'.

Throughout this essay I have tried to describe this feature of Okigbo's poetry as modernist collage ('the chance meeting of two distant realities on an unfamiliar plane, the culture of displacement and its effects – and the spark of poetry that leaps across the gap as the two realities converge'), but there is an oft-cited Igbo proverb which captures his collage poetics much better than this: 'where one thing stands, another stands by it'.[26] Which is to say that Okigbo was most 'modernist' when he was most African.

Closing Statement: Apprenticeship to the Furies

Wilson Harris

The Furies! What are the Furies? Are they nourished by our animosities, prejudices, biases? Are we intricately and complexly and dramatically part and parcel of the womb-body of the Furies? Are they in us yet far from us? Are they ghosts tapping at our window within abused elements, water, air, fire, earth? I have been intuitively involved in an imagination of the Furies – their protean shapes and configurations – for some considerable time. They are such a neglected medium in the humanities, yet deeply rooted simultaneously, that a late-twentieth-century interpretation is paradoxical and personal, and I have had to fall back on a gathering impetus within my own work, across the past four decades, to cope with and confront an insistent theme of the Furies.

In my latest fiction entitled *Jonestown* the question arises – 'How strange to entertain the regeneration of oneself through the furies one has long feared?'

Let me pause and stress 'regeneration of oneself', implicit in which is the regeneration of one's age, one's community. I shall return to this issue of regeneration (involving a crossing of borders of fear in the life of the imagination) as I lay out the premises of my discussion. But let me continue with the quotation I began to read, indeed let me re-read the opening question and continue to the end of the short passage that contains it:

> How strange to entertain the regeneration of oneself through the furies one has long feared? How steeped has one been – without quite knowing it – in uncanny dread of the masks one's dead mother wears, or has worn, across centuries and generations, the mystical wilds and wildernesses, the mystical brides?

Let me remind you at this stage of the dread Sirens (all presumed to be women), of dread Circe, of the three terrible winged goddesses with serpents in their hair, namely Alecto, Magaera and Tisophone which pursue and punish doers of unavenged crimes. Classical lore in Europe and the ancient Greek world tends to identify the revenge-syndrome with the female. Anton Ehrenzweig, in his book *The Hidden Order of Art*, appears to endorse an implicit preoccupation in Freud with the many disguises of the death-goddess or the 'killing goddess'. He emphasizes three women or a triple-goddess. It is a curious and interesting phenomenon that Canaima, the revenge figure in Guyana and South America, is male, indicating perhaps a shamanic force to Canaima. Shamans are susceptible to an inner body or womb, the womb of Dream. In Canaima's case his male imaginary womb, so to speak, is stoked with apparitions of revenge for crimes of which a people might not know, or have forgotten, they or their antecedents have committed.

The medium of the Furies – perhaps because of an identification with the female gender – has been (as far as I am aware) neglected in the humanities. Understandably so, for feminism and the rights of women are now celebrated causes. Yet, in my view, these causes may founder unless a profoundly creative and recreative and re-visionary grasp of the theatre of the womb-body of cultures and civilizations is visualized in depth. It is no exaggeration, I feel, to say that the life of the imagination may well be at stake without a vital approach to the Furies, their potency for terror, and simultaneously, paradoxically, for the regeneration of cosmic love.

We need, I think, to see women – when portrayed as embodiments of the Furies – *not* as individual characters in the psychology of the novel or the cinema but as human vessels inhabited by spectralities and concretions, by a cellular chemistry pertinent to the body of the womb in shamanic lore, the womb of nature and of civilization. Think of the human vessel in the genius of the Imagination symbolizing ingredients within itself and beyond itself which are richer and stranger than individual gender. When one looks deep into its cellular fabric – into the vessel of the womb in space and time in shamanic lore – one visualizes the seed of the land, one visualizes oceanic parables littered with stars and constellations, one visualizes the spring of rivers and the veined leaves of forests that have cradled cultures since time began. The womb, therefore, in shamanic lore, transgresses the boundaries of individual gender. The content of the vessel of the womb in nature and cosmos and Dream is both spectral and concrete. Ghosts are there in the blood of the living, ghosts of the living past and unborn future.

You see then, do you not, that though the Furies were portrayed as women, gender was a mask for far-flung – sometimes self-contradictory – natures, the natures of fire and water and the multitudinous fabric of the cosmos within the heart of human and animal passion, elemental passion as well, the passion of storm and lightning, the peace of halcyon days as well, the magical days of the halcyon bird.

The womb, let us say, is a seminal vessel. The active life of that spectral and concrete vessel implies, at one level, intercourse between man and woman, intercourse between the partiality of the male and the partiality of the female. Such partiality tells of a deeper hunger in the body of nature, it tells of an unfinished climax of body and spirit, it tells of the reach of spirit into far-flung responsibilities within essences of creation, the fluids of animal soul mirrored in, and interwoven with, the ecology of oceans and rivers and lakes upon which the individual floats at times like a bubble.

Wars and famines are not new to humanity across the centuries, landslides are not new, the earthquake is not new, the volcano is not new, but within the past three hundred years since the Industrial Revolution we have seen, through the historical lenses that we possess, the action of man-made instruments and machines in the miring of the globe on a scale that seems extraordinary, to say the least, when it invokes comparison with the loss of species and changes in environments within millennia prior to what is called the Enlightenment. Our man-made capacity to treat living landscapes and riverscapes and skyscapes as passive furniture, and the processes that have been set in train, are a potential and a real rifling of the body of the womb in nature which has borne us, in which our gestation as a species began.

It is not difficult, I would have thought, to appreciate how, in ancient times, abused nature or natures sought revenge and were dressed up in the theatre of cultures as 'killing goddesses'. Anton Ehrenzweig, in *The Hidden Order of Art*, and implicitly Freud – from whom he draws a measure of inspiration – place a remarkably high premium on the 'killing goddess' in the pessimistic, psychological vein that they bring to their books. The mind-set that Ehrenzweig and Freud elaborate implies a serious necessity to look deeply into the processes of revolutionary technique in the arts. I applaud this but on closest examination of their psychology I am left with the impression that we are lodged in a dead end in which to shore up the ruins of a loss of resurrectionary soul, a death of god, a death of cosmic love. And this, I would have thought, is substantive to the European novel-form through Thomas Hardy into Franz Kafka and into Thomas Mann's obsession with diseased, virtually incurable, character.

I do not have to tell you that the European novel-form – in the wake of European empires since the sixteenth century – has exercised an enormous influence upon all societies around the globe which tend, by and large, it seems to me, to bypass their own resources and to underestimate the bearing these might have on a re-visionary dynamic aligned to the Furies.

Having said all this I must confess that Ehrenzweig in *The Hidden Order of Art* does, it seems to me, leave a faint door ajar into the seminal mystery of the imagination beyond the Freudian dead end. A profound scanning of clues within the depth-body of the language of fiction (such as he analyses in Goethe) opens a vital communication with latent capacities to 'transcend the limits of individual existence'. The irony, it seems to me, is that such a 'transcending of the limits of individual existence' would shake the very foundations of modern theory, which is preoccupied in politics, as much as in fiction, with individual status, plot, and with an arsenal of technologies to cope with every threat to prosperity from envious regimes and from masses in foreign lands. Ehrenzweig, like a few other formidable European critics, seems fated, as far as I can see, to scan the technicalities of depth-resources in the arts yet to stop at the door he holds faintly ajar into other texts of the imagination than those enshrined in Freudian – and other related variants of – realism. Inevitably, the womb-body of civilization succumbs to latency or remains a prize to be rifled and disputed by all generations. That dispute registers, it seems to me, in the subconscious or the unconscious as a revenge-syndrome nursed by those who see themselves as despoiled or raped or injured.

This, curiously enough, fuels the character of the 'killing goddesses' in the modern cinema. Let me give the titles of four films that come to mind: *Play Misty for Me, Fatal Attraction, Black Widow, House of Cards*. The formidable 'killing' women who appear on the screen are capable of leading battalions. They carry many seductive and calculating faces and in that sense are triple or more agents of a revenge-syndrome in a world that has wounded them deeply. Needless to say, these films are manufactured for a mass market familiar with the rape of women in Bosnia, Rwanda, in the alleyways of many a metropolis (a woman was raped recently in a taxi cab by the taxi driver). It is incredible, but I read a report recently of rape in or close to a Buddhist temple in the Far East by a Buddhist priest.

Rape in theatres of war is nothing new but the horror it invokes never fades. It arouses us, in the depths of the unconscious and subconscious, to dread the womb-body of a civilization from which our age is sprung. How real is cosmic love in such dire affliction and distress?

I would argue that all this is pertinent to aroused Furies whom classical lore invested with the mask or persona of women intent on punishing the doers of unavenged crimes. I would also argue that the modern cinema – wittingly or unwittingly – invests in that revenge-syndrome with female protagonists who become deadly in the roles they play. Such roles may be archetypally consistent with the Furies but alas no 'transcending of the limits of individual existence' occurs. Rather it is just to say, I think, that a war of genders, male and female, becomes the individualistic plot and storyline of the films I have listed. If, however, we take seriously the cue from world events, the wrongs inflicted on women, then the womb of nature and civilization – in its acute association with theatres of abuse and conflict – inserts a witness to itself in the lament of consciousness embroiled in the rape of environments and settlements around the globe. It would take too long in this address to list the threat to species, rain-forests, oceans, rivers, but let me remind you of the horrendous glow of burning oil fields in the recent Middle East War.

Iraq is one of the cradles of civilization. The tyrannies of Saddam Hussein are visible triggers, in reports that appear in newspapers and journals, of the precipitation of conflict that has scarred the peoples of the region. Less visible is the archetypal person or vessel or mirror of a threatened landscape-cradle of civilization to which humanity is indebted. That debt may be stated crudely in modern currency, in the pounds or dollars or francs with which we buy barrels of oil still to be salvaged from a wounded earth. But the debt is numinously alive in the Furies were we to seek to re-trace our steps into the past and into what are now the ghost-armies of Alexander the Great. Bitter as such a re-tracery is, there are, I would think, pregnant cross-culturalities available to sensitive scholars that transcend the boundaries of revenge-politics.

Let me stress what I have been saying. In the modern cinema we perceive the portrayal of women in such films as *Play Misty for Me* or *Fatal Attraction* or *Black Widow* as archetypally consistent with the Furies whose vocation it was in classical myth to pursue the doers of un-avenged crimes. I have attempted to suggest that though these films do not relate directly to theatres of war in Iraq or Iran or former Yugo-slavia or Rwanda they are influenced by such horrendous conflicts in their portrayal of revenge-seeking women in the mass-media cinema. Such women are individualized as in the conventional novel. They are portrayed as being as strong and violent as men. They do not – in Anton Ehrenzweig's phrase – 'transcend the limits of individual existence'. As a consequence they lack something, in my view, which may open our imaginations to the regenerative potential in the Furies.

The supreme casualty that we suffer as things now stand in conventional realism is the death of cosmic love. Think about this honestly and carefully. Love may serve as an ornament of gratification for the individual who builds a fortress that makes him or her immune to the deep-seated malaise of humanity around the globe. Within that fortress we may manufacture entertainments and fictions – such as I have listed in the cinema – which run in parallel with diseased character in the modern novel. I alluded, you may remember, to Kafka and Hardy and Mann earlier in this talk. The difference, however, is that the complexity of disease in the European masters, who depict the fate of civilization in a pessimistic vein, is overshot in the cinema by a conflict of gender in which love becomes a feature of seduction and violence. The family becomes a fortress subject to invasion by marauding females. Such is surely the theme of *Fatal Attraction*.

It seems to me – when we take all this into account – that we are driven to see that a 'transcending of the limits of individual existence' is an enormous question that bears on the roots of love in the womb of space and time. Post-modern Freudian psychology breeds pessimism. Revenge-syndromes lifted into populist entertainment become a money-making industry, no doubt, but they polarize gender even as they endorse the 'killing goddess'.

I would like now to speak of the creation of texts that diverge from the narrative form which we associate with the European convention. This is a testing matter. I am, I must confess, not concerned with theory-for-the-sake-of-theory but with insights I have assembled in my writing career across close on four decades. I must emphasize strongly that it is not my intention to elevate such insights into a formula or into ruling criteria. Not at all. One is aware of a growing diversity in the areas of Caribbean and Latin American literatures, not to speak of Africa and Asia, all of which possess unique roots in the soil of tradition that may be aroused in peculiarly new ways to bear on the arts of the imagination.

Only recently I spoke at the October Gallery in London on the work of the painter Aubrey Williams, who died a few years ago, and was able in that context to say something of Leroy Clarke, Stanley Greaves, George Simon and Genevieve Cox. With regard to writers in the Caribbean and Central and South America, the long-neglected masterpiece *Pedro Paramo*, by the Mexical novelist Juan Rulfo, is gaining ground. In the Caribbean and Guyana one cannot but be aware of new developments in the work of writers such as Robert Antoni, Pauline Melville, Erna Brodber, Fred D'Aguiar, Lawrence Scott, the poet Mark McWatt, the poet David Dabydeen, and in the novel *Crossing the River* by Caryl

Phillips which is written in documentary prose even as it seems to question the ironies of hollow avocation or professional status within the conditioned mind of blended diasporan characters across two hundred years. It isn't easy to be confident of anything in the life of the humanities, and my specific purpose in mentioning a few names of largely new and talented poets and fiction-makers – and also, you may recall, painters – from the Caribbean and Guyana – is to suggest that there might well be a ground or turning point through and beyond the boundaries of the imagination long taken for granted by colonial peoples.

I trust I have cleared the air also – if this were at all necessary – in pursuing insights assembled from my own work across close on four decades. No dogma or formula is intended. The fiction I have written in and since *The Guyana Quartet* has been driven by a re-visionary dynamic that takes nothing for granted within its narrative body to bring into play a blend of pasts and presents and likely or unlikely futures. I say the fiction takes nothing for granted but I need to qualify this in a slightly unusual way. The truth is that across the long years of concentrated work I have not lost hope, within a severely nihilist climate and end-game philosophy of the Imagination, that through profoundly intuitive and changing texts and forms it is truly possible to visualize the action of cosmic love within the dire circumstances, the dire plight, that afflicts humanity. Cynics would argue that the action of cosmic love is lacking in theatres of crisis. Cosmic love – many would argue – is dead. This is nothing new. We live not only in a post-Freudian age steeped in pessimism and in escapism but also in a post-Nietzschean age. The death of cosmic love would seem to be a consequence of the death of God. Where is God when men's and women's bodies are seized by the affliction of war or famine or crisis?

I am saying – let me repeat – that conventional realism offers no reply. It may describe events but the frame it uses endorses the absence of cosmic love. It cannot breach the limits of individual existence. If anything it reinforces those limits. It consolidates the nation state and the vested interests of the nation state. It accepts love as the privileged premise or ornament of fortunate societies that may secure themselves from torment and seek in hedonism their philosophy. All this is understandable, I think, when we confess that we think and feel and judge and surrender to immediate experience within a frame of language and a psychology of the ego and super-ego that underestimates the womb of time and the vessel of the person. To revise and break the mould of such underestimation requires, I think, immeasurable persistence and dedication in and to resources beyond formulaic closure or institution-alised storyline or plot.

In *Jonestown* – my latest novel – Francisco Bone subsists in the womb of time and space and dream upon blended ages. The seas and landscapes upon which he moves form a multi-layered and all pervasive fabric in that they affect every detail, every object, in his life. Let me quote an instance from the actual text of the fiction. Look at him now in a class room in Albuoystown in the year 1939 – he is nine years old – to which he has returned from the future. He has travelled back across mountain-ous waves and seas from the dreadful carnage of Jonestown which occurred in November 1978 in Guyana. He has travelled back to his childhood in Albuoystown, a poor suburb in the city of Georgetown. Mr Mageye, his teacher, is at the blackboard. Here is the passage that I said I would read (the I-narrator is Francisco Bone):

> I was affected by the memory of a steep wave that had threatened to overwhelm the Virgin Ship on my crossing from 1978 disaster-ridden Jonestown back to 1939 Albuoystown.
>
> Black and steep as Night over Jonestown, blacker than the black-board at which Mr Mageye now stood.
>
> He (Mr Mageye) loved to play pranks. He would arouse laughter in his class and then resume his history lesson. He dodged behind blackboard and wave. As the Ship was about to fall through the roof of the world he occupied a crevice in the blackboard and peered through it as if it were a telescope. At that instant I heard the bells of the Sirens ringing. The ship righted itself.
>
> I heard the voice of the Sirens through the magical bells declaring that Mr Mageye was a rare phenomenon, a genuine and a sacred jester. He stood there in the telescopic wave with the look of a gentle Sphinx. The expression passed from his features, he moved back to the front of the blackboard, and he resumed the history lesson.

The womb of space which Francisco carries is now pregnant, as the passage I have read shows, with linkages between 'wave' and 'black-board', between a 'crack' in the blackboard and a 'telescope'. All this constitutes a kind of 'sacred jest' which is – if you read the entire work – a threshold into the action of cosmic love. The quantum physicist Nick Herbert, in his book *Quantum Reality*, emphasizes the one-track mind to which humanity is addicted, yet he suggests there might be microscopes to overcome such a biological flaw. The 'sacred jest' acknowledges the flaw but implies, simultaneously, layers in the womb of space and dream through which the collective or universal unconscious erupts into the subconscious and into the mystery of a creative and re-creative dynamic of consciousness.

I say 'mystery of consciousness' because science has not solved 'consciousness', how it comes about, what are its roots in the body, so to speak, of space and time. Let me emphasize, therefore, that the creation of texts which diverge from one-track realism must, I would think, of necessity seek to cross chasms in reality, to cross the familiar raw material of existence we would associate with a mere blackboard, for instance, to an element such as a storm or a wave upon which the elements write with the chalk of lightning. The schoolmaster Mr Mageye writes with mere chalk; the voice of the Sirens, secreted in the elements, may be converted into rhythms that write themselves upon a black towering wave and, in that instant, the dread voices of the Sirens which Odysseus feared in Homer's poem are edged with all the momentum of a salutary or saving lighthouse, salutary and regenerative omens. The new text brings together, therefore, motifs and imageries from the past and the present and the future in the womb of space and time into a re-visionary gestation or arousal of the light of consciousness. Cosmic love arises then within the dire precipice of storm. This, I am saying, is a different kind of fiction from conventional realism. It suggests that cosmic love may be visualized within the sweep of imageries sprung from different times and ages. All this is pertinent to the vessel of the person steeped in spectralities and concretions through which to transcend individual one-track destiny which may ally itself with freedom but, in fact, is intent on cementing a fortressed ego or super-ego for itself. Freedom should mean, I think, the action of memory to acquaint us deeply, profoundly, with the perilous voyages of humanity out of its cradles of dream in space and time so that the grain of cosmic love may come home to us in all its astonishing reality and fragility and originality.

Without that salvage of cosmic love within the convertible imageries of linked pasts and presents and futures what – may I ask – is art? Is art an ornament, a form of escapism, a sophisticated facade expressed enigmatically in Samuel Beckett's text *Imagination Dead Imagine*?

One may ponder upon that last word 'Imagine' in that short and complex text. It seems to me to endorse or indict or invoke the void of the fortressed individual whose roots in a whole humanity extending across the ages have been well-nigh severed. As a young man, I saw those roots imperilled with the forfeiture of the Caribbean federation in Guyana and the West Indies. Some Caribbean writers and thinkers, it seems to me, lock themselves at times in an insular cultural politics which eclipses genuine alternatives or parallel universes of sensibility in their own region and in the Americas.

The ancient Maya, ancient Mexico, are pertinent to this region. The ancient Maya possessed a concept of blended pasts and futures. Eric S. Thompson, an American scholar, points out in his book *Maya Civilization* that this concept baffled the European mind, though I would think that Chaos mathematics – a new phenomenon in European science – has edged a little closer into its potential significance for the modern mind. Long before I knew of it, the idea was intuitively alive in my own work as a sliding scale that re-visits the cradles of living landscapes and seeks bridges across chasms in reality. That quest for bridges is born, I think, of the activity of broken archetypes. Archetypes cannot be seized in their wholeness. The Blessed Fury (a term I now borrow from the text of *Jonestown*) which appears towards the end of *Palace of the Peacock*, dressed in nothing but her long flowing hair, is a measure of the broken Virgin-archetype. I could trace such measures and the links between broken Virgin-archetypes and broken Predator-archetypes in *The Guyana Quartet* and succeeding novels into *The Carnival Trilogy* and *Resurrection at Sorrow Hill*, but obviously that is impracticable. Instead, let me close my address with a few words on broken archetypes and their profound bearing on the Furies in *Palace of the Peacock*.

The Virgin-archetype, in its wholeness, would imply, in my understanding, intercourse, shorn of violence, with the womb-body of nature and reality. Let me repeat 'intercourse with nature and reality' that is shorn of violence. One may attempt to visualize, let us say, the birth of Christ from a Virgin as sprung from intercourse shorn of violence. I do not have to say how difficult this seems in real terms, in the so-called real world. It seems to reside in a realm beyond the human imagination. Yet the fact that we entertain it at all in religious myth means it is not entirely beyond the faculties of truth with which art and science wrestle. What we salvage from such an apparently impossible idea, I think, is a broken Virgin-archetype, broken, yes, but profoundly active. Think of a whole number which it is impossible to realize or seize. When it breaks it brings us numerous factors that take us deep into the past, to question fallacious absolutes, even as it enriches our creative conscience in addressing the all-too-human crises that afflict us in the present and for which we require new solutions to cope with the gravity and the tragedies that confront civilization. The broken archetype becomes, therefore, a re-visionary dynamic, in all its factors and strands, that we may address and immerse ourselves in within the womb of space and time.

The Blessed Fury which appears towards the end of *Palace of the Peacock* is a manifestation of the factorization of the Virgin-archetype. The mould of the absolute revenge-seeking Furies is broken and she moves on a line, let us say, between the revenge-politics of the Furies and the apparently impossible wholeness of the archetype to which she belongs. The long garment of hair which is her dress is close to nature and it diverges from absolute dogma or absolute historical costumery or investiture. There is a child at her side. She secretes elements of Arawak as well as European mythology within herself. She is actually one of three women who appear in the novel. They may be seen as a kind of triple goddess. But the emphasis on their killing force as set out in Freudian logic by Anton Ehrenzweig is deeply altered. I say 'triple goddess' with hindsight for I knew nothing of this when I wrote *Palace of the Peacock*. I learnt of it for the first time in the mid-nineteen seventies. It isn't easy to intellectualize my divergence from the 'killing goddess' that comes to occupy a nature we have abused. But let me remind you of what I was saying a moment or two ago. To find ourselves within a medium of broken wholenesses is to respond to infinite variables and factors in a quest for impossible fulfilment which we entertain, nevertheless, as a true goal, though we resist imposing it on ourselves as an accomplished feat. For to do so is to succumb to incorrigible bias in the name of truth.

As I already said, the woman dressed in her hair is one of three women. The others are Mariella and an ancient Arawak woman. They have been so abused that they carry all the potential to become revenge-seeking Furies. But in their alignment to the Blessed Fury they become susceptible to roots in living landscapes and in a voyaging humanity. Mariella is a woman and a kind of earth-goddess. The ancient Arawak woman invokes through rivers and waterfalls the long, epic journey that the aboriginal peoples of the Americas made from the Behring Straits into the North and Central and South Americas. They become regenerative vessels, though still sustaining terror-making faculties. They imbue the second death of the crew with a re-visionary crossing of chasms of reality in which many cultures in the Americas have foundered.

The mystery of the Furies, and the natures of revenge, and the possibilities for regeneration are, I would think, of profoundest proportion in crossing boundaries into a renewal of the archetypal life of the imagination as it seeks to engage with the roots of consciousness.

What is imagination? What is consciousness?

This is an age of crisis. Conflicts between genders, between races and cultures, between technology and nature, are looming more critically and terrifyingly perhaps than ever before within the frontiers of history and the traffic of refugees of body and spirit everywhere who are the children of the Furies. My innermost feeling is that humanity is at the crossroad in this, the last, decade of the twentieth century. This has been, let us remember, the century of the Holocaust. Capital punishment has not been abolished in the Caribbean and in many African states, such as Nigeria where the writer Ken Saro-Wiwa was recently hanged. In the Far East there is rising prosperity but the bondage of fear is strong, punitive logic is entrenched. And child prostitution, with the rising fear of Aids, is becoming a lucrative business.

A one-track mind-set or psychology of brute realism is undeniable in many areas of the globe. We cannot, in the deepest senses, alleviate the suffering of victims of crime, victims of social disability, unless we begin to take stock of the Furies, take stock of revenge-syndromes in ruthless competition and trade, in populist cultures, in entertainment, in politics. The abuse of the elements has set in train changing weather patterns, storm, famine, drought. But I am suggesting that the Furies also bring a most searching scrutiny into things we take for granted, into links between ages and realms we tend to bypass or eclipse; they also bring long-neglected keys which are pertinent to a literacy of the imagination, pertinent to the conversion of boundaries of fear into thresholds beyond the tyranny and the charisma of fear. Such paradox is native to the genius of creation, it is native to a buried core-response within communities in the womb of space and time and the tasks of the regeneration of our age.

'Apprenticeship to the Furies' was the keynote address delivered at the Border Crossings Conference, University of North London, January 1996.

Notes

Introduction

1 See, for instance, Edward Said, *Orientalism* (1978; Harmondsworth: Penguin, 1985); Wilson Harris, *Tradition, the Writer and Society* (London: New Beacon, 1967); Gauri Viswanathan, *Masks of Conquest: Literary Study and British Rule in India* (London: Faber and Faber, 1990); and Chris Baldick, *The Social Mission of English Criticism 1848–1932* (Oxford: Clarendon Press, 1983), pp. 70–2.

2 Vinay Dharwadker, 'The Internationalization of Literatures', in Bruce King (ed.), *New National and Post-Colonial Literatures: an Introduction* (Oxford: Clarendon Press, 1997), pp. 59–77.

3 Dharwadker, 'Internationalization of Literatures', pp. 71–7.

4 See, for instance, the essays in Lois Parkinson Zamora and Wendy B. Faris (eds), *Magical Realism: Theory, History, Community* (Durham, N.C.: Duke University Press, 1995).

5 Montserrat Ordóñez, 'One Hundred Years of Unread Writing', in Susan Bassnett (ed.), *Knives and Angels: Women Writers in Latin America* (London: Zed Books, 1990), pp. 132–44. Susan Forsyth's essay in Part III below looks critically at these publishing and translating constraints as they act on Native American literature.

6 Seamus Heaney, *An Open Letter* (Derry: Field Day, 1983), pp. 7, 13. Lyn Innes's and Willy Maley's essays in Part I below investigate some of the complexities involved in introducing Ireland and Scotland into debates on colonialism and postcolonialism. See also Susan Bassnett, *Comparative Literature: a Critical Introduction* (Oxford: Blackwell, 1993), pp. 48–70.

7 For a brief account of how these phenomena impinge on postcolonial writing, see Elleke Boehmer, *Colonial and Postcolonial Literature: Migrant Metaphors* (Oxford: Oxford University Press, 1995), pp. 232–43.

8 Homi K. Bhabha, *The Location of Culture* (London: Routledge, 1994).

9 For a succinct summary of some of the criticisms made of Bhabha's work, see Peter Childs and Patrick Williams, *An Introduction to Post-Colonial Theory* (Hemel Hempstead: Prentice Hall/Harvester Wheatsheaf, 1997), pp. 143–5.

10 Robert J. C. Young, *Colonial Desire: Hybridity in Theory, Culture and Race* (London: Routledge, 1995), p. 163.

11 Stuart Hall, 'Cultural Identity and Diaspora', in Jonathan Rutherford (ed.), *Identity: Community, Culture, Difference* (London: Lawrence and Wishart, 1990), pp. 223, 225, 226.

12 Dipesh Chakrabarty, 'Postcoloniality and the Artifice of History: Who Speaks for "Indian" Pasts?', *Representations*, 37 (Winter 1992), p. 4.

13 Partha Chatterjee, *Nationalist Thought and the Colonial World: a Derivative Discourse?* (London: Zed Books, 1986).

14 Chakrabarty, 'Postcoloniality and the Artifice of History', pp. 1, 20, 22, 21.

15 Gyanendra Pandey, 'In Defence of the Fragment: Writing about Hindu-Muslim Riots in India Today', *Representations*, 37 (Winter 1992), pp. 28–9.

16 James Ngugi [Ngugi Wa Thiong'o], Henry Owuor-Anyumba, Taban Lo Liyong, 'On the Abolition of the English Department', in Ngugi's *Homecoming: Essays on African and Caribbean Literature, Culture and Politics* (London: Heinemann, 1972), p. 146.

17 Salman Rushdie, *Imaginary Homelands: Essays and Criticism 1981–1991* (London: Granta Books, 1991), p. 62.

18 Nayantara Sahgal, 'The Schizophrenic Imagination', in Anna Rutherford (ed.), *From Commonwealth to Post-Colonial* (Sydney, Mundelstrup and Coventry: Dangaroo Press, 1992), p. 30.

19 Jawaharlal Nehru, *The Discovery of India*, quoted by Sunil Khilnani, *The Idea of India* (London: Hamish Hamilton, 1997), p. 169.

20 Chantal Zabus, *The African Palimpsest: Indigenization of Language in the West African Europhone Novel* (Amsterdam and Atlanta: Rodopi, 1991).

21 Childs and Williams, *Introduction to Post-Colonial Theory*, p. 2.

22 Arvind Krishna Mehrotra, 'Introduction' to *The Oxford India Anthology of Twelve Modern Indian Poets* (Delhi: Oxford University Press, 1992), p. 6.

23 Aijaz Ahmad, *In Theory: Classes, Nations, Literatures* (London: Verso, 1992), p. 98.

24 Bill Buford, 'Declarations of Independence', *The New Yorker* (23 and 30 June 1997), p. 6.

25 See, for instance, Vijay Mishra and Bob Hodge, 'What is post(-)colonialism?', *Textual Practice*, 5 (1991), pp. 399–414, and Aijaz Ahmad, 'Jameson's Rhetoric of Otherness and the "National Allegory"', *Social Text*, 17 (Fall 1987), pp. 3–25.

1 Postcolonial Studies and Ireland

1 See especially David Cairns and Shaun Richards, *Writing Ireland: Colonialism, Nationalism and Culture* (Manchester: Manchester University Press, 1988), David Lloyd, *Anomalous States: Irish Writing and the Postcolonial Moment* (Durham, N.C.: Duke University Press, 1993), and Declan Kiberd, *Inventing Ireland: the Literature of the Modern Nation* (London: Cape, 1995).

2 Here Edward Said is an important exception. His *Culture and Imperialism* (London: Chatto & Windus, 1993) includes a long section discussing Yeats as a nationalist poet who can be understood in the context of poets such as Aimé Césaire and Pablo Neruda.

3 Bill Ashcroft, Gareth Griffiths and Helen Tiffin, *The Empire Writes Back: Theory and Practice in Post-Colonial Literatures* (London: Routledge, 1989).

4 First published in *Social Text*, 15 (Fall 1986), pp. 65–88.

5 Edward Said, *Orientalism* (1978; Harmondsworth: Penguin, 1985).

6 These essays are reprinted in Chinua Achebe, *Hopes and Impediments* (Oxford: Heinemann International, 1988).

7 Said, *Orientalism*, p. 3.

8 Javed Majeed, *Ungoverned Imaginings: James Mill's* The History of British India *and Orientalism* (Oxford: Clarendon Press, 1992), pp. 87–122.

9 Thomas Moore, *Lalla Rookh* (London: Longman, Green, 1861), p. 354.

10 For further details on Gonne's comparisons between Ireland, India and other areas colonized by the British, see my book, *Woman and Nation in Irish Literature and Society, 1880–1935* (Hemel Hempstead: Harvester, 1993), chap. 8.

11   Jameson, 'Third-World Literature', p. 65. Jameson goes on to say: 'what is more damaging than that, perhaps, is its tendency to remind us of outmoded stages of our own first-world cultural development and to cause us to conclude that "they are still writing novels like Dreiser and Sherwood Anderson".'

12   Ibid., p. 69.

13   Aijaz Ahmad, 'Jameson's Rhetoric of Otherness and the "National Allegory"', *Social Text*, 17 (Fall 1987), pp. 3–25.

14   Vijay Mishra and Bob Hodge, 'What is Post(-)colonialism?', *Textual Practice*, 5 (1991), pp. 399–414.

15   Charles Kingsley, *His Letters and Memories of His Life, Edited by His Wife* (London: Kegan Paul and Co., 1877), quoted in C. L. Innes, *The Devil's Own Mirror: the Irishman and the African in Modern Literature* (Washington, D.C.: Three Continents Press, 1990), p. 12.

16   Robert Hughes, *The Fatal Shore* (London: Collins Harvill, 1987), p. 190.

17   Quoted, ibid., p. 188. Compare, over half a century later, a letter written in 1868 by Benjamin Disraeli to *The Times*: '[The Irish] hate our free and fertile isle. They hate our order, our civilization, our enterprising industry, our sustained courage, our decorous liberty, our pure religion. This wild, reckless, indolent, uncertain and superstitious race have no sympathy with the English character. Their fair ideal of human felicity is an alternation of clannish brawls and coarse idolatry. Their history describes an unbroken circle of bigotry and blood' (quoted by L. P. Curtis, *Apes and Angels* [Newton Abbot: Davidson & Charles, 1971], p. 81).

18   Quoted in Hughes, *Fatal Shore*, p. 444.

19   For an excellent discussion of Wilde in this light, see Declan Kiberd, *Inventing Ireland* (London: Jonathan Cape, 1995), pp. 33–50.

2   Crossing the Hyphen of History

1   *The Concise Oxford Dictionary of Current English*, 7th edn, s.v. 'border', 'borderer'.

2   For a recent exchange on Ireland's place within postcolonialism see: Colin Graham, 'Post-Nationalism/Post-Colonialism: Reading Irish Culture', *Irish Studies Review*, 8 (Autumn 1994), pp. 35–7; Gerry Smyth, 'The Past, the Post, and the Utterly Changed: Intellectual Responsibility and Irish Cultural Criticism', *Irish Studies Review*, 10 (Spring 1995), pp. 25–9; Colin Graham, 'Rejoinder: the Irish "Post-"? A Reply to Gerry Smyth', *Irish Studies Review*, 13 (Winter 1995/6), pp. 33–6; Willy Maley, 'Varieties of Nationalism: Post-Revisionist Irish Studies', *Irish Studies Review*, 15 (Summer 1996), pp. 34–7; Eugene O' Brien, 'The Epistemology of Nationalism', *Irish Studies Review*, 17 (Winter 1996/7), pp. 15–20.

3   Homi K. Bhabha, '"Race", Time, and the Revision of Modernity', *Oxford Literary Review*, 13 (1991), pp. 193–219.

4   Edmund Spenser, *A View of the State of Ireland*, in James Ware (ed.), *Two Histories of Ireland* (Dublin, 1633), p. 21.

5   See my 'Rebels and Redshanks: Milton and the British Problem', *Irish Studies Review*, 6 (1994), pp. 7–11; and '"This Sceptred Isle": Shakespeare and the

British Problem', in John Joughin (ed.), *Shakespeare and National Culture* (Manchester: Manchester University Press, 1997), pp. 83–108.

6 Marilyn Reizbaum, 'Canonical Double Cross: Scottish and Irish Women's Writing', in Karen R. Lawrence (ed.), *Decolonizing Tradition: New Views of Twentieth-Century 'British' Literary Canons* (Chicago: University of Illinois Press, 1992), pp. 165–90.

7 See James Spedding, Robert Leslie Ellis and Douglas Denon Heath (eds), *The Works of Francis Bacon* (London: Longmans and Co., 1857–75), vol. 4, p. 16.

8 Bacon, *Works*, vol. 10, p. 313.

9 Bacon, *Works*, vol. 11, p. 114.

10 *Concise Oxford Dictionary of Current English*, s.v. 'trefoil'.

11 Bob Purdie, 'The Lessons of Ireland for the SNP', in Tom Gallagher (ed.), *Nationalism in the Nineties* (Edinburgh: Polygon, 1991), pp. 66, 72–3.

12 See Sean Duffy, '*Braveheart*... brave attempt', *History Ireland*, 3, no. 4 (1995), pp. 5–6.

13 David Lloyd, *Anomalous States: Irish Writing and the Postcolonial Moment* (Dublin: Lilliput Press, 1993), p. 89.

14 Ibid., p. 112.

15 Bill Ashcroft, Gareth Griffiths and Helen Tiffin, *The Empire Writes Back: Theory and Practice in Post-Colonial Literatures* (London: Routledge, 1989), p. 33. Two of the most significant works on Ireland in recent years have largely ignored the impact and influence of Scotland. See Luke Gibbons, *Transformations in Irish Culture* (Cork: Cork University Press, 1996), and Richard Kearney, *Postnationalist Ireland: Politics, Culture, Philosophy* (London: Routledge, 1996). Both Gibbons and Kearney, despite their differences, are locked into an Anglo-Irish framework that fails to grasp the Scottish dimension of the British Problem/Irish Question.

16 See Maurice Roche, *Rethinking Citizenship: Welfare, Ideology and Change in Modern Society* (Cambridge: Polity Press, 1992).

17 'The Deconstruction of Actuality: an Interview with Jacques Derrida', conducted by Brigitte Sohm, Cristina de Peretti, Stéphane Douailler, Patrice Vermeren and Emile Malet, trans. Jonathan Rée, *Radical Philosophy*, 68 (1994), p. 34.

18 D. W. Brogan, *Citizenship Today: England – France – the United States* (Chapel Hill: University of North Carolina Press, 1960), pp. 8–9.

19 See Etienne Balibar, 'Citizen Subject', trans. James B. Swenson Jr., in Eduardo Cadava, Peter Connor and Jean-Luc Nancy (eds), *Who Comes after the Subject?* (London: Routledge, 1991), pp. 33–57.

20 Owen Dudley Edwards (ed.), *A Claim of Right for Scotland* (Edinburgh: Polygon, 1989), p. 13.

21 Spenser, *View of the State of Ireland*, p. 39.

22 See 'Valedictory', an interview with Tom Vernon, in Alan Bold (ed.), *The Thistle Rises: an Anthology of Poetry and Prose by Hugh MacDiarmid* (London: Hamilton, 1984), p. 287. MacDiarmid was an advocate of 'a sort of union of the Celtic countries in the British Isles' (p. 289).

23 Jacques Derrida, 'Limited Inc a b c ...', trans. Samuel Weber, *Glyph*, 2 (1977), p. 209.

3 The Politics of Hybridity

1   The main sources for the vogue of hybridity as a critical – and increasingly cultural/creative – concept are the essays collected by Homi K. Bhabha in *The Location of Culture* (London: Routledge, 1994). Further references to this book will be given in parentheses in the text. For an analysis of the historical provenance and contemporary function of the term, see Robert J. C. Young, *Colonial Desire: Hybridity in Theory, Culture and Race* (London: Routledge, 1995), and also the selections included under the rubric 'Hybridity' in Bill Ashcroft, Gareth Griffiths and Helen Tiffin (eds), *The Post-Colonial Studies Reader* (London: Routledge, 1995), pp. 183–209.

2   The term is Benita Parry's, as employed in her essay 'Resistance Theory/ Theorising Resistance, or Two Cheers for Nativism', in Francis Barker, Peter Hulme and Margaret Iversen (eds), *Colonial Discourse/Postcolonial Theory* (Manchester: Manchester University Press, 1994). Further references to this essay will be given in parentheses in the text.

3   On the relationship between postcolonial criticism and Western capitalism see Arif Dirlik, 'The Postcolonial Aura: Third World Criticism in the Age of Global Capitalism', *Critical Inquiry*, 20 (Winter 1994), pp. 328–56; and Anne McClintock, 'The Angel of Progress: Pitfalls of the Term "Postcolonialism"' (1992), in Barker, Hulme and Iversen (eds), *Colonial Discourse/Postcolonial Theory*, pp. 253–66.

4   On Fanon's critique of nationalism see chapters 3 ('The Pitfalls of National Consciousness', pp. 119–65) and 4 ('On National Culture', pp. 166–89) in *The Wretched of the Earth*, trans. Constance Farrington (1961; Harmondsworth: Penguin, 1967).

5   Judith Butler, *Gender Trouble: Feminism and the Subversion of Identity* (London: Routledge, 1990), p. 31.

6   Bhabha discusses the concept of 'image analysis' in an important essay not included in *The Location of Culture*. See his 'Representation and the Colonial Text: a Critical Exploration of Some Forms of Mimeticism', in Frank Glover-smith (ed.), *The Theory of Reading* (Sussex: Harvester Press, 1984), pp. 93–122. On Lloyd's engagement with Bhabha and his critique of the 'narrative of representation', see the essays 'Adulteration and the Nation' in *Anomalous States: Irish Writing and the Postcolonial Moment* (Dublin: Lilliput Press, 1993), pp. 88–124, and 'Ethnic Cultures, Minority Discourse and the State', in Barker, Hulme and Iversen (eds), *Colonial Discourse/Postcolonial Theory*, pp. 221–38. Further references to these essays will be given in parentheses in the text.

7   Neil Lazarus, 'National Consciousness and the Specificity of (Post) Colonial Intellectualism', in Barker, Hulme and Iversen (eds), *Colonial Discourse/Postcolonial Theory*, p. 214.

8   Mark Storey (ed.), *Poetry and Ireland since 1800: a Source Book* (London: Routledge, 1988), 'Introduction', p. 8.

9   Thomas MacDonagh, *Literature in Ireland: Studies Irish and Anglo-Irish* (Dublin: The Talbot Press Limited, 1916), pp. 169–70. For Gibbons's analysis see 'Challenging the Canon: Revisionism and Cultural Criticism', in Seamus Deane (gen. ed.), *The Field Day Anthology of Irish Writing* (Derry: Field Day, 1991), vol. 3, pp. 561–8.

10 Kumkum Sangari, 'The Politics of the Possible' (1987), partially reprinted in Ashcroft, Griffiths and Tiffin (eds), *Post-Colonial Studies Reader*, pp. 143–7, see p. 144.

11 In 'Ethnic Cultures, Minority Discourse and the State' (1994) Lloyd writes: 'Only within the context of representative government and the ethical state formation can the concept of the minority emerge as the differential anti-thesis of the majority... precisely that which constitutes minorities as "interest groups" susceptible of representation deprives them of the capacity to enter fully into the larger narrative of representation. For whereas the general logic of representation assumes its ground to be the formal individual whose contingent interests are none the less sublated in ethical development, the minority is constituted as an impossibility of sublation, as a generic individual whose particularity represents a difference inassimilable to the universal ends of the representative state' (p. 233).

12 David Harvey, *The Condition of Postmodernity: an Enquiry into the Origins of Cultural Change* (Oxford: Basil Blackwell, 1989), p. vii.

13 Richard Kearney, 'Introduction: an Irish Intellectual Tradition?: Philosophical and Cultural Contexts', in Kearney (ed.), *The Irish Mind: Exploring Intellectual Traditions* (Dublin: Wolfhound Press, 1985), pp. 7–38.

14 Seamus Deane, 'Heroic Ideals: the Tradition of an Idea', in Field Day Theatre Company, *Ireland's Field Day* (London: Hutchinson, 1985), p. 57.

15 On the troubled relations between postcolonial theory, history, historicism and historiography, see Bill Schwarz, 'Introduction: Conquerors of Truth: Reflections on Postcolonial Theory', in Schwarz (ed.), *The Expansion of England: Race, Ethnicity and Cultural History* (London: Routledge, 1996), pp. 9–31.

16 See the essay 'Can the Subaltern Speak?' (1988), reprinted in Patrick Williams and Laura Chrisman (eds), *Colonial Discourse and Postcolonial Theory: a Reader* (Hemel Hempstead: Harvester Wheatsheaf, 1993), pp. 66–111.

17 See David Cairns and Shaun Richards, 'Discourses of Opposition and Resistance in Late Nineteenth- and Early Twentieth-Century Ireland', *Text and Context*, 2, no. 1 (Spring 1988), pp. 76–84.

18 See Derrida's essay 'Declarations of Independence', *New Political Science*, 15 (1986), pp. 7–15.

19 David Lloyd explores the paradoxes attending the practice of state-foundation in his essay 'The Poetics of Politics: Yeats and the Founding of the State' (1993). See *Anomalous States*, pp. 59–87.

20 Jenny Sharpe, 'Figures of Colonial Resistance' (1989), partially reprinted in Ashcroft, Griffiths and Tiffin (eds), *Post-Colonial Studies Reader*, pp. 99–103, see p. 100.

21 See the interview 'The Postcolonial Critic', in S. Harasym (ed.), *The Postcolonial Critic: Interviews, Strategies, Dialogues – Gayatri Chakravorty Spivak* (London: Routledge, 1990), pp. 67–73.

4 Inside-Out

1 Stuart Hall, 'Cultural Identity and Diaspora', in L. Chrisman and P. Williams (eds), *Colonial Discourse & Post-colonial Theory: a Reader* (Hemel Hempstead: Harvester Wheatsheaf, 1993), pp. 394–5.

2 Iain Chambers, *Migrancy, Culture, Identity* (London: Routledge, 1994), p. 6.
3 On the colonial 'othering' of the Irish, see, in particular, D. Cairns and S. Richards, *Writing Ireland: Colonialism, Nationalism and Culture* (Manchester: Manchester University Press, 1988). For discussion of the notion of the Irish as 'marginal Britons', see D. G. Boyce, 'The Marginal Britons: the Irish', in R. Colls and P. Dodd (eds), *Englishness: Politics and Culture 1880–1920* (London: Croom Helm, 1986).
4 R. F. Foster, 'Knowing Your Place: Words and Boundaries in Anglo-Irish Relations', in his *Paddy and Mr Punch: Connections in Irish and English History* (Harmondsworth: Penguin, 1995), p. 86.
5 R. F. Foster, 'Marginal Men and Micks on the Make: the Uses of Irish Exile, c. 1840–1922', *Paddy and Mr Punch*, p. 301.
6 Michael Kearney, 'Borders and Boundaries of State and Self at the End of Empire', *Journal of Historical Sociology*, 4, no. 1 (1991), p. 52.
7 See H. K. Bhabha, *The Location of Culture* (London: Routledge, 1994). L. P. Curtis argues that: 'The psychological importance of Paddy [as the stereotyped Irishman] can be best explained in terms of a defense mechanism known as projection...[T]he gentlemen who relied upon this stereotype were merely projecting onto an assumedly inferior group all those emotions which lay buried within themselves and which the English social system encouraged – and at times compelled – them to repress.' L. P. Curtis, *Anglo-Saxons and Celts: a Study of Anti-Irish Prejudice in Victorian England* (Bridgeport, Connecticut: University of Bridgeport, 1968), p. 65.
8 T. Eagleton, *Heathcliff and the Great Hunger* (London: Verso, 1994), pp. 127–8.
9 R. Kearney, *Postnationalist Ireland: Politics, Culture, Philosophy* (London: Routledge, 1997), p. 201. Original emphases.
10 J. Rutherford, 'A Place Called Home', in Rutherford (ed.), *Identity: Community, Culture, Difference* (London: Lawrence and Wishart, 1990), p. 24. On issues surrounding economics, class and Irish emigration, see Jim MacLaughlin, *Ireland: the Emigrant Nursery and the World Economy* (Cork: Cork University Press, 1994).
11 I. Ang, 'On Not Speaking Chinese: Postmodern Ethnicity and the Politics of Diaspora', *New Formations*, 24 (Winter 1994), p. 10.
12 For a critique of such assumptions, see M. Hickman and B. Walter, 'Deconstructing Whiteness: Irish Women in Britain', *Feminist Review*, 50 (Summer 1995), pp. 5–19.
13 See F. Anthias and N. Yuval-Davis in association with H. Cain, *Racialized Boundaries: Race, Nation, Colour and Class and the Anti-Racist Struggle* (London: Routledge, 1992), p. 44. Prior to 1995, as they note, despite the Irish being the largest ethnic group in Britain, the Commission for Racial Equality refused to recognize them as such. On gender and 'double invisibility', see B. Walter, *Gender and Irish Migration to Britain*, Geography Working Paper no. 4 (Cambridge: Anglia Polytechnic University, 1989). Mary Lennon, similarly, comments: 'we weren't immigrants...we had been made invisible... [the benefits of which are] offered to me if I keep my mouth shut...which I'm not prepared to do'. M. Lennon, in S. James (ed.), *Strangers and Sisters: Women, Race and Immigration* (Bristol: Falling Wall Press, 1985), pp. 72–4.

14 S. Rushdie, *Imaginary Homelands: Essays and Criticism 1981–1991* (London: Granta, 1992), p. 10.

15 W. B. Yeats, *John Sherman* (1891) in *John Sherman and Dhoya* (Dublin: Lilliput Press, 1990), p. 19. Subsequent page references will appear in parentheses in the text.

16 P. Ó Conaire, *Exile* (1910), trans. G. Mac Eoin (Indreabhán, Conamara: Cló Iar-Chonnachta, 1994), p. 9. Subsequent page references will appear in parentheses in the text.

17 On such racializations, see H. A. MacDougall, *Racial Myths in English History: Trojans, Teutons, and Anglo-Saxons* (Montreal: Harvest House, 1982). On *Punch* in particular, see L. P. Curtis, *Apes and Angels: the Irishman in Victorian Caricature* (Bridgeport, Connecticut: University of Bridgeport, 1968). Roy Foster offers a critique in *Paddy and Mr Punch*.

18 Ang, 'On Not Speaking Chinese', p. 10. Gilroy's essay is entitled 'It Ain't Where You're from, It's Where You're at: the Dialectics of Diaspora Identification', in *Small Acts* (London: Serpent's Tail, 1993), pp. 120–45.

19 R. F. Foster, *Modern Ireland 1600–1972* (Harmondsworth: Penguin, 1989), p. 370.

20 R. F. Foster, 'Marginal Men and Micks on the Make', *Paddy and Mr Punch*, p. 289.

21 See particularly Jacques Lacan, 'The Mirror Stage as Formative of the Function of the I as Revealed in Psychoanalytic Experience', in Lacan, *Ecrits: a Selection*, trans. Alan Sheridan (London: Tavistock, 1977), pp. 1–7.

22 P. Pearse, quoted in R. D. Edwards, *Patrick Pearse: the Triumph of Failure* (London: Faber, 1979), pp. 78–9 (my emphasis).

23 S. Hall, 'Minimal Selves', in L. Appignanesi (ed.), *Identity: the Real Me*, ICA Document 6 (London: Institute of Contemporary Arts, 1987), p. 44.

24 Samuel Beckett, *All That Fall* (London: Faber & Faber, 1957), p. 10.

25 In addition to Kavanagh's many poems documenting the poverty of Irish rural life, see his novel *Tarry Flynn* (New York: Devin-Adair, 1949). For Ó Faoláin's critique, see, for example, *Come Back to Erin* (London: Jonathan Cape, 1940).

26 K. O'Brien, *Mary Lavelle* (1936; London Virago, 1984), p. 94. On issues surrounding imperialism, nationalism and the position of Irish women, see, for example, Sabina Sharkey, 'Gendering Inequalities: the Case of Irish Women', *Paragraph*, 16, no. 1 (1993), pp. 5–22.

27 S. Beckett, 'First Love' (1970), *The Expelled and Other Novellas* (Harmondsworth: Penguin, 1980), p. 18.

28 S. Beckett, *Murphy* (1938; London: Picador, 1973), p. 75. Subsequent page references will appear in parentheses in the text.

29 D. Kiberd, *Inventing Ireland: the Literature of the Modern Nation* (London: Jonathan Cape, 1995), p. 531.

30 M. Heidegger, 'Letter on Humanism', *Basic Writings* (New York: Harper and Row, 1977), p. 219.

31 Bertold Brecht, epigraph to Edna O'Brien's *A Pagan Place*, cited by Fintan O'Toole, 'The Ex-Isle of Erin: Emigration and Irish Culture', in Jim Mac Laughlin (ed.), *Location and Dislocation in Contemporary Irish Society: Emigration and Irish Identities* (Cork: Cork University Press, 1997), p. 168.

32   See B. Gray, 'Irishness – a Global and Gendered Identity?', *Irish Studies Review*, 16 (Autumn 1996), pp. 24–8. See also M. Hickman, 'The Irish in Britain: Racism, Incorporation and Identity', *Irish Studies Review*, 10 (Spring 1995), pp. 16–19; and M. Lennon et al. (eds), *Across the Water: Irish Women's Lives in Britain* (London: Virago, 1988).

33   The charge against Field Day is primarily that their concentration upon questions of nation and nationalism results in the exclusion of other issues, particularly surrounding sexual politics – this being evidenced by the all-male Field Day collective, and particularly by the relative lack of women writers included in the anthology. On the controversy, see Francis Mulhern, 'A Nation, Yet Again', *Radical Philosophy*, 65 (Autumn 1993), pp. 23–9, and Luke Gibbons's response, 'Dialogue without the Other?', *Radical Philosophy*, 67 (Summer 1994), pp. 28–31.

34   E. Donoghue, 'Going Back', in D. Bolger (ed.), *Ireland in Exile: Irish Writers Abroad* (Dublin: New Island Books, 1993), pp. 158–60. Subsequent page references will appear in parentheses in the text.

35   A. Devlin, *After Easter* (London: Faber & Faber, 1994), p. 58. Subsequent page references will appear in parentheses in the text.

36   F. Fanon, 'On National Culture', *The Wretched of the Earth*, trans. Constance Farrington (Harmondsworth: Penguin, 1967), p. 176.

37   For interesting research linking the high rates of mental illness amongst Irish emigrants in Britain with the identity instabilities resulting from (post)colonial discourses, see L. Greenslade, 'White Skin, White Masks: Psychological Distress and the Irish in Britain', in P. O'Sullivan (ed.), *The Irish in the New Communities* (Leicester: Leicester University Press, 1992), pp. 210–25.

38   Ang, 'On Not Speaking Chinese', p. 18.

39   R. Kearney, 'Migrant Minds', in *Across the Frontiers: Ireland in the 1990s* (Dublin: Wolfhound Press, 1988), p. 186.

40   R. Kearney, 'Myth and Motherland', in Field Day Theatre Company, *Ireland's Field Day* (London: Hutchinson, 1985), p. 80.

41   See G. C. Spivak, 'Subaltern Studies: Deconstructing Historiography', in D. Landry and G. MacLean (eds), *The Spivak Reader* (London: Routledge, 1996), pp. 203–35, and P. Gilroy, *The Black Atlantic: Modernity and Double Consciousness* (London: Verso, 1993).

5   States of Dislocation

1   M. Sarup, 'Home and Identity', in G. Robertson et al. (eds), *Travellers' Tales* (London: Routledge, 1994), p. 98.

2   F. O'Toole, *Black Hole, Green Card* (Dublin: New Island Books, 1994), pp. 8–19.

3   F. O'Toole, *The Ex-Isle of Erin* (Dublin: New Island Books, 1997), p. 157.

4   Ibid., p. 158.

5   S. R. Bald, 'Negotiating Identity in the Metropolis: Generational Differences in South Asian British Fiction', in R. King, J. Connell and P. White (eds), *Writing across Worlds: Literature and Migration* (London: Routledge, 1995), p. 70.

6   B. Ashcroft, G. Griffiths and H. Tiffin, *The Empire Writes Back: Theory and Practice in Post-Colonial Literatures* (London: Routledge, 1989), p. 196.

7   S. Rushdie, *Imaginary Homelands: Essays and Criticism 1981–1991* (London: Granta Books, 1991), p. 19.
8   R. F. Foster, *Paddy and Mr Punch: Connections in Irish and English History* (Harmondsworth: Penguin, 1995), p. 305.
9   W. Trevor, *Excursions in the Real World* (Harmondsworth: Penguin, 1994), p. xiii.
10 Ibid.
11 I. Chambers, *Migrancy, Culture, Identity* (London: Routledge, 1994), p. 6.
12 Ibid., pp. 23–4.
13 Ibid., p. 27.
14 Rushdie, *Imaginary Homelands*, p. 210.
15 E. Boehmer, *Colonial and Postcolonial Literature: Migrant Metaphors* (Oxford: Oxford University Press, 1995), p. 237.
16 H. K. Bhabha, 'How Newness Enters the World: Postmodern Space, Postcolonial Times and the Trials of Cultural Translation', in *The Location of Culture* (London: Routledge, 1994), pp. 223–9.
17 Ibid., p. 227.
18 Ibid., p. 230.
19 W. Trevor, *Felicia's Journey* (1994; Harmondsworth: Penguin, 1995), p. 25. All subsequent quotations from this book are indicated in parentheses in the text.
20 A. Memmi, *The Colonizer and the Colonized* (London: Earthscan, 1990), p. 15.
21 P. Carter quoted in Chambers, *Migrancy, Culture, Identity*, p. 5.
22 Memmi, *Colonizer and Colonized*, p. 113.
23 Ibid., pp. 109–10, 113–14.
24 Ibid., p. 109.
25 M. Leitch, *Gilchrist* (London: Secker & Warburg, 1994), pp. 55–6. All subsequent quotations from this book are indicated in parentheses in the text.
26 D. G. Boyce, 'The Marginal Britons', in Robert Colls and Philip Dodd (eds), *Englishness: Politics and Culture 1880–1920* (London: Croom Helm, 1986), pp. 230–53.
27 A. Nandy, *The Intimate Enemy: Loss and Recovery of Self under Colonialism* (Oxford: Oxford University Press, 1982), p. xvi.
28 Rushdie, *Imaginary Homelands*, p. 10.
29 Bhabha, *Location of Culture*, p. 227.
30 Rushdie, *Imaginary Homelands*, p. 16.
31 Bhabha, *Location of Culture*, p. 227.
32 Ibid., p. 252.
33 F. Fanon, *Black Skin, White Masks* (London: Pluto, 1986), p. 229.

6 'It's a Free Country'

1   This paper is a revised version of my article '"It's a Free Country": Bharati Mukherjee's Vision of Hybridity in the Metropolis', first published in *Wasafiri*, 24 (Autumn 1996), pp. 18–21.
2   Homi K. Bhabha, 'DissemiNation: Time, Narrative, and the Margins of the Modern Nation', in Bhabha (ed.), *Nation and Narration* (London: Routledge, 1990), p. 299.

3   T. Coraghessan Boyle, *The Tortilla Curtain* (London: Bloomsbury, 1995), p. 311.

4   Benedict Anderson, *Imagined Communities: Reflections on the Origin and Spread of Nationalism* (London: Verso, 1983).

5   Bhabha, 'DissemiNation', p. 299.

6   Ibid., p. 297.

7   Robert J. C. Young, *Colonial Desire: Hybridity in Theory, Culture and Race* (London: Routledge, 1995), p. 4.

8   Ibid., p. 24.

9   'In the production of the nation as narration there is a split between the continuist, accumulative temporality of the pedagogical, and the repetitious, recursive strategy of the performative. It is through this process of splitting that the conceptual ambivalence of modern society becomes the site of *writing the nation*.' Bhabha, 'DissemiNation', p. 297.

10 Ibid.

11 These lectures were broadcast on BBC Radio 4 in July 1995.

12 Bharati Mukherjee, 'Immigrant Writing: Give Us Your Maximalists', *New York Times Book Review* (28 August 1988), p. 28.

13 Ibid., p. 29.

14 Bharati Mukherjee, 'A Four-Hundred-Year-Old-Woman', in Philomena Mariani (ed.), *Critical Fictions: the Politics of Imaginative Writing* (Seattle: Bay Press, 1991), p. 26.

15 Homi K. Bhabha, 'Signs Taken for Wonders: Questions of Ambivalence and Authority under a Tree Outside Delhi, May 1817', in Henry Louis Gates, Jr. (ed.), *'Race', Writing and Difference* (Chicago: University of Chicago Press, 1986), p. 173.

16 Bharati Mukherjee, 'Loose Ends', in *The Middleman and Other Stories* (London: Virago, 1988) p. 48.

17 Ibid., p. 52.

18 Mukherjee, 'Orbiting', in *Middleman*, p. 75.

19 Bharati Mukherjee, *Jasmine* (London: Virago, 1989), p. 198.

20 Ibid., p. 181.

21 Ibid., p. 186.

22 Ibid., p. 20.

23 Ibid., p. 156.

24 Kristin Carter-Sanborn, '"We Murder Who We Were": Jasmine and the Violence of Identity', *American Literature*, 66, no. 3 (1994), pp. 573–93; Gurleen Grewal, 'Born Again American: the Immigrant Consciousness in *Jasmine*', in Emmanuel S. Nelson (ed.), *Bharati Mukherjee: Critical Perspectives* (New York: Garland, 1993).

25 Grewal, *Born Again American*, p. 194.

26 Bhabha, *Letters from Chicago*, Broadcast no. 3.

27 Homi K. Bhabha, 'The Commitment to Theory', *New Formations*, 5 (Summer 1988), p. 6.

28 Ibid.

29 Boyle, *Tortilla Curtain*, p. 101.

30 Ibid., p. 198.

31 Bhabha, 'DissemiNation', p. 301.

7 I Came All the Way from Cuba So I could I Speak Like This?

1 See Miren Uriarte, 'Los cubanos en su contexto: teoríos y debates sobre la inmigración cubana en los EE.UU.', *Temas*, 2 (1995), pp. 64–78.

2 See Eliana Rivero, 'Cubanos y Cubanoamericanos: perfil y presencia en los Estados Unidos', *Discurso Literario*, 7, no. 1 (1989), pp. 81–101. (The translation of this and following quotations are mine.)

3 See Silvia Burunat y Ofelia García (eds), 'Veinte años de literatura cubanoamericana', *Antología 1962–1982* (Tempe: Bilingual Press/Editorial Bilingüe, 1988).

4 I am aware that using 'US' when referring to what is usually called 'America' and 'american' when referring to the US context may seem strange. This choice has two reasons: the need of precision and the reluctance to the use of a term which implies an expropriation of a name that was initially used to define the whole of the Americas, not only the northern part. Besides, it is not pertinent to use 'North America' when not referring to Canada. Finally the acceptance of the term 'american' is because it has been codified in the hyphenated terms.

5 See Julio Rodríguez-Luis, 'Sobre la literatura hispánica en los Estados Unidos', *Casa de las Américas*, 193 (1993), pp. 37–48.

6 Eliana Rivero, 'Cubanos y Cubanoamericanos', p. 84.

7 See Eliana Rivero, '(Re)Writing Sugarcane Memories: Cuban Americans and Literature', in Fernando Alegría (ed.), *Paradise Lost or Gained? The Literature of Hispanic Exile* (Houston: Arte Público Press, 1986), pp. 164–82.

8 See Eliana Rivero, 'Tanta agua bajo estos puentes...', *Fuentelibre, revista de cultura*, 2, nos 5/6 (Summer 1995), p. 38.

9 See Gloria Anzaldúa, *Borderlands/La Frontera* (San Francisco: Aunt Lute Books, 1987), pp. 195, 194.

10 See Antonio Cornejo Polar, 'Una Heterogeneidad no dialéctica: sujeto y discurso migrantes en el Perú moderno', *Revista Iberoamericana*, 176–7 (1996), p. 841.

11 See Antonio Vera-León, 'Escrituras bilingües y sujetos biculturales: Samuel Beckett en La Habana', *La Isla Posible* (Barcelona: Destino, 1995), p. 77.

12 See Gustavo Pérez-Firmat, 'Trascender el exilio: la literatura cubano-americana, hoy', *La Gaceta de Cuba* (September–October 1993), p. 21 (This text was first published in 1987).

13 See Homi K. Bhabha, 'How Newness Enters the World: Postmodern Space, Postcolonial Times and the Trials of Cultural Translation', in *The Location of Culture* (London: Routledge, 1994), p. 219.

14 See Stuart Hall, 'Cultural Identity and Diaspora', in Jonathan Rutherford (ed.), *Identity: Community, Culture, Difference* (London: Lawrence and Wishart, 1990), pp. 222–37, see p. 226.

15 All quotations come from Cristina García's *Dreaming in Cuban* (New York: Ballantine, Books, 1992) and Achy Obejas, *We Came All the Way from Cuba So You Could Dress like This?* (Pittsburgh: Cleis Press Inc., 1994). Subsequent page references will be given in the text.

16 See Homi K. Bhabha, 'Introduction', *The Location of Culture*, p. 5.

17 Ibid.

18 See Nara Araújo, 'Literatura femenina, feminismo y crítica feminista en Cuba', *Letras Femeninas*, 11, nos 1–2 (1995), pp. 165–71.

8 Border Anxieties

1 All references to Fanon's *Peau noire, masques blancs* (Paris: Editions de Seuil, 1952) and the 1967 Markmann translation, *Black Skin, White Masks* (New York: Grove Press) will be given in the text, using the abbreviations *Pn* and *BS*, followed by page numbers. The responsibility for amendments to Markmann's translation is my own, although I would like to thank Michael Temple and Vicky Lebeau for their helpful comments on Markmann's translation.

2 'On the Grounds for Detaching a Particular Syndrome from Neurasthenia under the Description of "Anxiety Neurosis"', in James Strachey et al. (trans. and ed.), *The Standard Edition of the Complete Psychological Works of Sigmund Freud* (London: Hogarth Press and the Institute of Psycho-Analysis, 1953–1974), vol. 3, pp. 85–117. Further references to this work will use the abbreviation *SE*, followed by the volume and page numbers.

3 I'm thinking only of *Peau noire* here. In the final chapter of *Les Damnés de la terre*, on colonial war and mental disorders, for example, the phobias and anxiety states produced by war present a different dialectic or problematic to the one studied here.

4 What fascinates me about this trope of adestination in *Peau noire* is the way that it has come to be passed on as a disturbing remainder or surplus in readings of Fanon's sexual politics, as if this figure of the evacuated black subject could be posed as the enigmatic sign of what Fanon himself desires and demands. Hence, Fanon's brief and enigmatic remark on the woman of colour – 'Nous n'en savons rien' ('I know nothing about her') (*Pn*, p. 145, *BS*, p. 180) – continues to influence and guide the anxious reading of his work by feminist-oriented critics. It is impossible, for example, not to see something exemplary or overdetermined in Diana Fuss's attempts to locate a place other than *Peau noire* for the *che vuoi*? Fanon asks of rape in the context of interracial desire. See 'Interior Colonies: Frantz Fanon and the Politics of Identification', *Diacritics*, 24 (Summer–Fall, 1994), pp. 20–42. In a related context, Kobena Mercer, has, in his comments on the representations of Martiniquan homosexuality in *Peau noire*, argued that Fanon's 'contradictory logic – which initially suggests that Fanon knows little about homosexuality... reveals that he knows all too much'. See Kobena Mercer, 'Decolonisation and Disappointment: Reading Fanon's Sexual Politics', in Alan Read (ed.), *The Fact of Blackness: Frantz Fanon and Visual Representation* (London and Seattle: Institute of Contemporary Arts and Bay Press, 1996), p. 125. Here there is a fracture of a demand which Fanon knowingly fails to know and one which returns to haunt the response it solicits. The question is whose demand is this and how does one place the *che vuoi* of this encounter?

5 This may go some way to explaining, or at least accounting for, one of the most enigmatic sentences in *Peau noire*: 'Since the racial drama is played out in the open ["plein air"], the black man has no time ["n'a pas le temps"] to make it unconscious ["l'inconscienciser"]' (*Pn*, p. 122, *BS*, p. 150). Given the

belated adestination of the black psyche – *vis-à-vis* the succession of racist phantasms – the claim that white phobic projection gives rise to a posthumous, cryptomnesic existence for the black, strikes me as an affirmation of what Fanon says elsewhere on the belatedness of black identity.

6 'The Negro's behaviour makes him akin to an obsessive neurotic type, or, if one prefers, he puts himself into a complete situational neurosis' (*Pn*, p. 48, *BS*, p. 60). The wide-ranging terrain of 'Le Nègre et la psychopathologie' – from psychoanalysis to anti-semitism to the politics and aesthetics of négritude – has often obscured the extent to which Fanon's analysis of racist fantasy and the historical affects of cultural difference remains closely bound up with a concern with the psychoneuroses, especially that of phobia. In this respect, most commentators on Fanon have tended to follow the justly renowned readings by Homi Bhabha, in *The Location of Culture* (London and New York: Routledge, 1994), with his emphases on fetishism, paranoia and ambivalence. There is, however, a distinction to be made between Bhabha's highly influential theory of colonial discourse, with its emphasis on the stereotype as fetish, and Fanon's thinking on phobia. Bhabha, in 'The Other Question', recognizes the ways in which phobia and fetishism intersect in Fanon: 'It is precisely this function of the stereotype as phobia *and* fetish that, according to Fanon, threatens the closure of the racial/epidermal schema for the colonial subject and opens the royal road to colonial fantasy' (*Location of Culture*, pp. 72–3, italics added). But in his elaboration of this *via regia*, or royal road, the entire question of phobia goes missing, never to be mentioned again. It is not simply because phobia is the absent sign of *The Location of Culture* that I refer to it. This avoidance of phobia and of neurosis, already replaced by speculations on fetishism and ambivalence in Bhabha's works, seems to affix itself to a certain guardedness about the specificities of Fanon's own indebtedness to psychoanalysis, as if the Fanonian legacy must be diverted, or anxiously turned away from, its own good or bad investiture in a psychoanalysis of the neuroses in order to preserve the theoretical purity of its truth. This avoidance of Fanon's own theoretical genesis recalls the border scene presented above of the Martiniquan philosopher suddenly grasped by an anxiety which is already his, an anxiety or anxious expectation that will, in turn, reintroduce him to his 'true face', his simulacrum, and imaginary double, as he lands in France.

7 In other words, the specific relation between the phobia and the drive is variable. Otto Fenichel, in *The Psychoanalytic Theory of the Neuroses* (New York: W. W. Norton and Co., 1945), writes: 'In part the paths of displacement depend on the nature of the drives that are warded off. Anxiety over being eaten, for example, may correspond to oral-sadistic longings' (p. 199).

8 Sigmund Freud, *Inhibitions, Symptoms, and Anxiety, SE*, vol. 20, p. 109.

9 Sigmund Freud, 'Anxiety', in *A General Introduction to Psychoanalysis* (New York: Washington Square Press, 1924), p. 417.

10 Charles Odier, *L'angoisse et la pensée magique: Essai d'analyse psychogénétique appliquée à la phobie et la névrose d'abandon* (Neuchâtel and Paris: Delachaux, 1947); translated as *Anxiety and Magic Thinking* (New York: International Universities Press, 1950), p. 135.

11 Freud, 'Anxiety', p. 418.

12 According to Freud in 'The Unconscious', the substitute, 'on the one hand, is connected by association with the rejected idea; and, on the other, has escaped repression by reason of its remoteness from that idea'. *SE*, vol. 14, p. 182.

13 Homi Bhabha, 'Foreword: Remembering Fanon', in Frantz Fanon, *Black Skin White Masks* (London: Pluto, 1986), p. xix.

14 It is precisely here where the cast of racists in *Peau noire* begin, more or less, to present themselves as a group of determined phobics who, having repressed their perverse longings for the enigmatic black 'thing', secretly envy the prostitute who rushes headlong into her desire for this 'thing', a fetishistic desire which she expresses openly and repeatedly (*Pn*, pp. 137–8, *BS*, p. 171).

15 This is why I cannot agree with Françoise Vergès's claim that Fanon 'constructs a superego for the black man which has a persecutory dimension', for the sadistic superego in question, experienced as anxiety in the body in the black man and as racist violence outside it, is not instituted by him in order to remove himself from access to either the symbolic or the veridical dimensions of culture. This dispossession is imposed. See Read, *Fact of Blackness*, p. 136.

16 This phrase is taken from Helene Deutsch, *Psychoanalysis of the Neuroses*, trans. W. D. Robson-Scott (London: Hogarth Press, 1951), p. 196. It refers to the role of aggression in anxiety neurosis. The influence of Deutsch's theories of female masochism is noticeable through out 'Le Nègre et la psychopathologie'.

17 Fanon's commentary on sado-masochistic fantasies in childhood appears to be in dialogue with another study of paternal punishment and beating fantasy, Freud's 'A Child Is Being Beaten', in *SE*, vol. 17, pp. 175–204. I'm not able to confirm that he had this text in mind when writing about a girl's aggressive and ambivalent identification with the sibling being beaten. However, the parallels Fanon introduces into this imagined scene of beating – the sense of guilt turned against the self and the pleasure at being beaten oneself – suggest a familiarity with Freud's paper.

18 Fenichel, *Psychoanalytic Theory of the Neuroses*, p. 196.

19 In an unpublished paper given at the French Research Seminar at the University of Sussex (1997), titled 'Psychopolitics: Frantz Fanon's *Black Skin, White Masks*', Vicky Lebeau asked whether Fanon's interpretation could, in fact, be distinguished from the mechanism of projection – reversal and transference of affect – that it is supposed to explain.

20 Writing on interracial homosexual and heterosexual desire, for example, Fanon introduces a classic trope of inversion: 'the Negrophobic woman is in fact nothing but a putative sexual partner – just as the Negrophobic man is a repressed homosexual' (*Pn*, p. 127, *BS*, p. 156). For an interesting commentary on Fanon's homophobia, see Kobena Mercer, 'Busy in the Ruins of Wretched Phantasia', in *Mirage: Enigmas of Race, Difference and Desire* (London: Institute of Contemporary Arts, 1995).

21 Bhabha, 'Remembering Fanon', p. xxvi.

22 'Fanon uses the *imago* – the stereotype – to put us on the track of an unconscious and a dreaming possessed not, or not only, by the subject's own wishful-shameful fantasies but by the real; or, more precisely, by the fantasies which make up the real, including those racial and sexual phan-

toms which Bhabha locates on the cultural scene.' Lebeau, 'Psychopolitics', p. 11.

23 The importance of this concept of 'real fantasies' in Fanon's analysis of culture was first brought to my attention by Lebeau in the paper mentioned above. For my own commentary see 'Bonding over Phobia' in Chris Lane (ed.), *Psychoanalysis and Race* (New York: Columbia University Press, 1998).

24 This sacrificial dedication is avowed through neurotic conflict, an immediate source of which concerns the child's attitude to his Antillean family which he must learn to reject if he is to be accepted on the French (white) mainland. Fanon says, 'the family structure [of the black child] is cast back into the *id*' (*BS*, p. 149), i.e., becomes connected to drive-anxiety and a potential source of neurotic conflict. Moreover the internal fantasy-object of himself (as white) introjected from exposure to French culture will be shown to have scarcely anything to do with the experiences of living in France. The loss of this fantasy-object and of his parental superego will, in fact, trigger supreme conflict in an attempt to ward off the anxiety of this loss of two primary objects of attachment – his parents and his white self.

25 Bhabha, *Location of Culture*, p. 40.

9 Nationalism's Brandings

1 Urvashi Butalia, 'Community, State and Gender: Some Reflections on the Partition of India', *Oxford Literary Review*, 16 (1994), pp. 31–67.

2 Ibid., p. 55.

3 *Pinjar* [The Skeleton] was originally written in Punjabi in 1950 and translated into English by Khushwant Singh in 1987. See Amrita Pritam, *The Skeleton and That Man* (New Delhi: Stirling, 1987). Pritam is a well-known feminist poet and prose writer who writes both in Punjabi and Hindi.

4 Veena Das, *Critical Events: an Anthropological Perspective on Contemporary India* (Delhi: Oxford University Press, 1995), p. 68.

5 Gyanendra Pandey, 'The Prose of Otherness', in David Arnold and David Hardiman (eds), *Subaltern Studies VIII* (Delhi: Oxford University Press, 1994), p. 190.

6 Ibid., p. 190.

7 Ritu Menon and Kamla Bhasin, 'Recovery, Rupture, Resistance: Indian State and Abduction of Women during Partition', *Economic and Political Weekly* (24 April 1993), p. WS-2.

8 Butalia, 'Community, State and Gender', p. 56.

9 Das, *Critical Events*, p. 64.

10 Urvashi Butalia, 'Introduction', *Seminar*, 420 (1994), pp. 12–14.

11 Pandey, 'Prose of Otherness', p. 205.

12 Menon and Bhasin, 'Recovery, Rupture Resistance', p. WS-2. The historian Mushirul Hasan too lauds literature's transcendental qualities, its ability to 'repudiate "communal" categories and transcend religious, regional and territorial barriers'. See Mushirul Hasan, *India Partitioned: the Other Face of Freedom*, 2 vols (New Delhi: Roli Books, 1995), vol. 1, p. 10.

13 Veena Das, review of the three volume *Stories about the Partition of India*, ed. Alok Bhalla (New Delhi: Indus, 1994), *Seminar*, 420 (1994), p. 58.

14 I am referring here to her piece (co-authored by Ashis Nandy) titled 'Violence, Victimhood and the Language of Silence', in *The Word and the World: Fantasy, Symbol and Record* (London: Sage, 1986).

15 Pandey, 'Prose of Otherness', p. 219.

16 Butalia, 'Community, State and Gender', p. 63.

17 Saadat Hasan Manto, *Kingdom's End and Other Stories*, trans. Khalid Hasan (London: Verso, 1987). Both 'Toba Tek Singh' and 'Open Up' ('Khol Do') are also the Manto stories most often referred to by these critics as powerful manifestos of post-Partition violence. The first works with the powerful ironies of a slip of legislation which determines the exchange of lunatics by the governments of India and Pakistan two years after the declaration of the official partition. The second deals with the return of an unconscious daughter to an old father who has been awaiting her arrival. The horror of the story lies in its ending, where upon hearing the command of an observing doctor to '*open* the window', the much battered and abused daughter in a robot like fashion begins to untie the cord of her shalwar (baggy trousers). The father seeing the movement shouts with joy, 'my daughter is alive' (p. 38).

18 Gayatri Chakravorty Spivak, *The Post-colonial Critic*, ed. Sarah Harasym (London: Routledge, 1990), p. 19.

19 Pritam, *Pinjar*, p. 1.

20 Ibid., p. 33.

21 Ibid., p. 37.

22 Ibid., p. 34.

23 Pierre Bourdieu, *The Logic of Practice* (Cambridge: Polity Press, 1990), p. 73.

24 Ibid., p. 68.

25 Pritam, *Pinjar*, p. 2.

26 Louis Althusser, 'Ideology and Ideological State Apparatuses', *Lenin and Philosophy and Other Essays* (New York: Monthly Review of Books, 1971), pp. 127–86.

27 Slavoj Zizek, *Tarrying with the Negative: Kant, Hegel and the Critique of Ideology* (Durham: Duke University Press, 1993), p. 76.

28 Pritam, *Pinjar*, p. 23.

29 Ibid., p. 18.

30 Judith Butler, *Bodies That Matter* (London: Routledge, 1993), p. 34.

31 Pritam, *Pinjar*, p. 39.

32 Ibid., p. 7.

33 Butler, *Bodies That Matter*, p. 35.

10 Internalized Exiles

1 Jorge Klor de Alva, 'The Postcolonization of the (Latin) American Experience: a Reconsideration of "Colonialism"', in Gyan Prakash (ed.), *After Colonialism: Imperial Histories and Postcolonial Displacements* (Princeton, N.J.: Princeton University Press, 1995), pp. 241–75..

2 Irene Silverblatt, 'Becoming Indian in the Central Andes of Seventeenth-Century Peru', in Prakash (ed.), *After Colonialism*, pp. 275–98.

3 See Martín Lienhard: 'Of Mestizajes, Heterogeneities, Hybridisms and Other Chimeras: On the Macroprocesses of Cultural Interaction in Latin America',

Journal of Latin American Cultural Studies, 6, no. 2 (1997), pp. 183–200. Lienhard's paper explains and contextualizes the work of the major Latin American theorists in this area. For a similarly informative overview on Latin American literary criticism, see Patricia D'Allemand, 'Urban Literary Production and Latin American Criticism', *Bulletin of Latin American Research*, 3 (1983), pp. 359–69.

4 Fernando Ortiz, 'Del fenómeno social de la transculturación y de su importancia en Cuba' (On the Social Phenomenon of Transculturation and Its Importance in Cuba), *Revista Bimestre Cubana*, 46 (1940).

5 Angel Rama, *Transculturación narrativa en América Latina* (Narrative Transculturation in Latin America) (Mexico: Siglo XXI, 1983).

6 Diana Palaversich, 'Postmodernismo, postcolonialismo y la recuperación de la historia subalterna' (Postmodernism, Postcolonialism and the Recuperation of Subaltern History), *Revista de Literatura Latinoamericana*, 24, no. 1 (March 1995), pp. 3–15.

7 See Roberto Querejazu Calvo, 'La "borradura" de Bolivia del mapa' (The 'Erasure' of Bolivia from the Map), *Presencia Literaria* (La Paz) (4 September 1994), p. 7. The author points out that Britain had no diplomatic presence in Bolivia at this time.

8 Jesús Urzagasti, *Tirinea* (Buenos Aires: Editorial Sudamericana, 1969). Further references to this work will be given in the text.

9 Néstor Taboada Terán, *Manchay Puytu, el amor que quiso ocultar Dios* (Manchay Puytu, the Love God Sought to Hide) (Cochabamba: Los Amigos del Libro, 1977). *Manchay*, in the Quechua language, means 'fear'. *Puytu* refers to the large storage jar featured in the story.

10 René Poppe, *El Paraje del Tío y otros cuentos mineros* (The Tío's Niche and Other Mining Stories) (La Paz: Editorial Juventud, 1978). The term *Tío* translates literally from Spanish as 'uncle'. However, the referent here is a deity belonging to, and ruling, the mine environment. It has been condemned by the Roman Catholic Church as a manifestation of Satan, but is nevertheless tolerated due to the strength of the miners' belief, to offend which would be to endanger production as well as lives. The *Tío* is also notable for jealous protection of his territory and intolerance of any female presence in the mine.

11 Luis H. Antezana, 'Rasgos discursivos en la narrativa minera boliviana' (Discursive traits in Bolivian mining fiction), *Revista Iberoamericana*, 52, no. 134 (enero/marzo 1986), pp. 111–26.

11 Writing Other Lives

1 D. Brown, *Bury My Heart at Wounded Knee: an Indian History of the American West* (New York: Holt, Rinehart and Winston, 1970).

2 M. Crow Dog with R. Erdoes, *Lakota Woman* (New York: HarperPerennial, 1991).

3 An oversight addressed in Peter Hulme's 'Including America', in *Ariel*, 26, no. 1 (January 1995), pp. 117–23.

4 For discussion of American Indian policy, see V. Deloria (ed.), *American Indian Policy in the Twentieth Century* (Norman and London: University of Oklahoma Press, 1985), particularly Tom Holm's essay 'The Crisis in Tribal Government';

and M. Annette Jaimes (ed.), *The State of Native America* (Boston, Mass.: South End Press, 1992).

5   E. Burgos-Debray (ed.) and Ann Wright (trans.), *I, Rigoberta Menchú: an Indian Woman In Guatemala* (London: Verso, 1984).

6   W. Churchill, *Struggle for the Land: Indigenous Resistance to Genocide, Ecocide and Expropriation in Contemporary North America* (Monroe, Maine: Common Courage Press, 1993), pp. 24–6.

7   J. Clifford, *Routes: Travel and Translation in the Late Twentieth Century* (Cambridge, Massachusetts, and London: Harvard University Press, 1997).

8   A. McClintock, A. Mufti and E. Shohat (eds), *Dangerous Liaisons: Gender, Nation, and Postcolonial Perspectives* (London: University of Minnesota Press, 1997).

9   Ibid., p. 1.

10   M. Brave Bird with R. Erdoes, *Ohitika Woman* (New York: HarperPerennial, 1993).

11   J. Fire/Lame Deer and R. Erdoes, *Lame Deer: Sioux Medicine Man* (1973; London: Quartet Books, 1980).

12   See D. Murray, *Forked Tongues: Speech, Writing and Representation in North American Indian Texts* (London: Pinter Publishers, 1991), A. Krupat, *For Those Who Come after: a Study of Native American Autobiography* (Berkeley, Los Angeles, and London: University of California Press, 1985), and H. D. Brumble III, *American Indian Autobiography* (Los Angeles: University of California Press, 1988) for discussions on 'Translation', 'An Approach to Native American Texts' and 'Editors, Ghosts, and Amanuenses' respectively.

13   A. Krupat (ed.), *Native American Autobiography: an Anthology* (Madison and London: The University of Wisconsin Press, 1994), p. 3.

14   V. Crapanzano, *Tuhami: Portrait of a Moroccan* (Chicago: University of Chicago Press, 1980).

15   M. Shostak, *Nisa: The Life and Words of a !Kung Woman* (London: Earthscan Publications, 1981).

16   J. G. Neihardt, *Black Elk Speaks* (1932; Lincoln and London: University of Nebraska Press, 1995).

17   The complexities of this are highlighted in R. DeMallie, *The Sixth Grandfather: Black Elk's Teachings Given to John G. Neihardt* (Lincoln and London: University of Nebraska Press, 1985), and J. Rice, *Black Elk's Story: Distinguishing Its Lakota Purpose* (Albuquerque: University of New Mexico Press, 1991).

18   Brumble, *American Indian Autobiography*, p. 22.

19   Ibid., p. 81.

20   R. D. Theisz, 'The Critical Collaboration: Introductions as a Gateway to the Study of Native American Bi-autobiography', in *American Indian Culture and Research Journal*, 5, no. 1 (1981), pp. 65–80.

21   J. Beverley, 'The Margin at the Center: On Testimonio (Testimonial Narrative)', *Modern Fiction Studies*, 35, no. 1 (Spring 1989), pp. 11–28.

22   Ibid., p. 13.

23   Ibid.

24   J. Beverley and M. Zimmerman, *Literature and Politics in the Central American Revolutions* (Austin: University of Texas Press, 1990), p. 173.

25 Beverley, 'Margin at the Center', pp. 14–16.
26 Burgos-Debray, *I, Rigoberta Menchú*, p. 1.
27 Beverley and Zimmerman, *Literature and Politics*, p. 187.
28 Ibid., p. 189.
29 Lame Deer and Erdoes, *Lame Deer*, pp. 271–2.
30 Brave Bird with Erdoes, *Ohitika Woman*, p. ix.
31 Ibid., p. x.
32 Beverley and Zimmerman, *Literature and Politics*, p. 173.
33 Brave Bird with Erdoes, *Ohitika Woman*, p. xi.
34 J. Clifford, *The Predicament of Culture: Twentieth-Century Ethnography, Literature, and Art* (Cambridge, Massachusetts, and London: Harvard University Press, 1988), p. 34.
35 Brave Bird with Erdoes, *Ohitika Woman*, p. xiii.
36 See Leonard Crow Dog and Richard Erdoes, *Crow Dog: Four Generations of Sioux Medicine Men* (New York: HarperCollins, 1995), which tells Leonard's story, as do *Lakota Woman*, *Ohitika Woman* and W. Churchill and J. Vander Wall's *Agents of Repression: the FBI's Secret Wars against the Black Panther Party and the American Indian Movement* (Boston: South End Press, 1988).
37 Brave Bird with Erdoes, *Ohitika Woman*, p. xiii.
38 Ibid., p. xiii.
39 Ibid., p. 150.
40 Ibid., p. xiii.
41 Ibid.
42 Ibid.
43 Ibid.
44 Crow Dog with Erdoes, *Lakota Woman*, p. 214.
45 Ibid., p. 118.
46 See Churchill and Vander Wall, *Agents of Repression*.
47 Crow Dog with Erdoes, *Lakota Woman*, p. 74.
48 Ibid.
49 Brave Bird with Erdoes, *Ohitika Woman*, p. xiv.
50 Crow Dog with Erdoes, *Lakota Woman*, p. 3.
51 Ibid., p. 5.
52 Ibid.

12 'The Limits of Goodwill'

1 Mudrooroo Narogin, *Writing from the Fringe: a Study of Modern Aboriginal Literature* (Queensland: University of Queensland Press, 1989), p. 165. Peter Quartermaine in his book *Thomas Keneally* (London: Edward Arnold, 1991) has also drawn attention to this critique of Keneally's Aboriginal writing.
2 S. Slemon, 'Unsettling the Empire: Resistance Theory for the Second World', in B. Ashcroft, G. Griffiths and H. Tiffin (eds), *The Post-Colonial Studies Reader* (London and New York: Routledge, 1995), p. 110. Slemon acknowledges Alan Lawson as his source for the term 'Second World' (that is, 'the territory of white settler colonial writing').
3 Bain Attwood, *The Making of the Aborigines* (Sydney: Allen & Unwin, 1989), chap. 6.

4   T. Keneally, *Outback* (London: Hodder and Stoughton, 1983), p. 14.
5   'A "fatal impact" has, however, been detected in European historiography far
    more frequently than it actually occurred, and this no doubt is linked with
    the appeal of a romantic narrative that nostalgically regrets the destruction of
    idealized, precolonial communities. Though generally sympathetic to the
    plight of the colonized, such perceptions frequently exaggerate colonial
    power, diminishing the extent to which colonial histories were shaped
    by indigenous resistance and accommodation.' N. Thomas, *Colonialism's
    Culture: Anthropology, Travel and Government* (Cambridge: Polity Press,
    1994), p. 15.
6   T. Keneally, *Bullie's House* (Sydney: Currency Press, 1981), p. xviii.
7   A. Shoemaker, *Black Words, White Page: Aboriginal Literature 1929–1988*
    (Queensland: University of Queensland Press, 1989), p. 201.
8   Ibid., p. 249.
9   Maureen Watson, cited in Shoemaker, *Black Words, White Page*, p. 278.
10 Interview on BBC Radio 3 programme *The Third Ear*, 2nd April 1991.
11 Trinh T. Minh-Ha, 'Writing Postcoloniality and Feminism', in Ashcroft, Grif-
    fiths and Tiffin (eds), *Post-Colonial Studies Reader*, p. 264.
12 Attwood, *Making of the Aborigines*, p. 135.
13 Narogin, *Writing from the Fringe*, p. 13.
14 Ibid., p. 2.
15 Keneally, *Bullie's House*, p. xviii.
16 David Theo Goldberg sums up the destructive aspect of scientific discourse in
    a colonial situation: 'These practices of naming and knowledge construction
    deny all autonomy to those so named and imagined, extending power,
    control, authority and domination over them'. D. T. Goldberg, *Racist Culture:
    Philosophy and Politics of Meaning* (Oxford: Blackwell, 1993), p. 150.
17 Trinh T. Minh-Ha, 'Writing Postcoloniality and Feminism', p. 267.
18 Ibid., p. 267.
19 Keneally, *Bullie's House*, p. xvii.
20 Ibid., p. xi.
21 Ibid., p. xiii.
22 Shoemaker, *Black Words, White Page*, p. 276.
23 Keneally, *Bullie's House*, p. xv.
24 Shoemaker, *Black Words, White Page*, p. 250.
25 Ibid., p. 248.
26 Trinh T. Minh-Ha, 'Writing Postcoloniality and Feminism', p. 265.
27 Keneally, *Outback*, p. 8.
28 Trinh T. Minh-Ha, 'Writing Postcoloniality and Feminism', p. 268.
29 B. Ashcroft, G. Griffiths and H. Tiffin, *The Empire Writes Back: Theory and
    Practice in Post-colonial Literatures* (London and New York: Routledge, 1989),
    pp. 172–3.
30 George Melly, 'Aussie Odyssey', *New Society* (24 November 1983), p. 325.
31 Thomas, *Colonialism's Culture*, pp. 173–8.
32 T. Keneally, *Towards Asmara* (London: Hodder and Stoughton, 1989), p. 240.
33 Thomas, *Colonialism's Culture*, p. 191.
34 G. Griffiths, 'The Myth of Authenticity', in Ashcroft, Griffiths and Tiffin
    (eds), *Post-Colonial Studies Reader*, p. 238.
35 T. Keneally, *Flying Hero Class* (London: Hodder and Stoughton, 1991), p. 145.

13 The Trickster at the Border

1 Antonio Benítez-Rojo, *The Repeating Island: the Caribbean and the Postmodern Perspective*, 2nd edition, trans. James E. Maraniss (Durham: Duke University Press, 1996), p. 4 (Spanish language edition 1989).

2 Stuart Hall, 'Cultural Identity and Diaspora', in Jonathan Rutherford (ed.), *Identity: Community, Culture, Difference* (London: Lawrence and Wishart, 1990), pp. 222–7.

3 Mary Louise Pratt, *Imperial Eyes: Travel Writing and Transculturation* (London: Routledge, 1992), p. 7.

4 Fanon's analysis in 'Algeria Unveiled' of the way in which Algerian women combined both the veil and the wearing of Western dress as a precise revolutionary tactic corresponds, for instance, to Pratt's definition of autoethnography as 'instances in which colonized subjects undertake to represent themselves in ways that *engage with* the colonizer's own terms. If ethnographic texts are a means by which Europeans represent to themselves their (usually subjugated) others, autoethnographic texts are those the others construct in response to or in dialogue with those metropolitan representations' (*Imperial Eyes*, p. 7).

5 'The effect of mimicry on the authority of colonial discourse is profound and disturbing. For in "normalizing" the colonial state or subject, the dream of post-Enlightenment civility alienates its own language of liberty and produces another knowledge of its norms... the reforming, civilizing mission is threatened by the displacing gaze of its disciplinary double...' Homi K. Bhabha, 'Of Mimicry and Man: the Ambivalence of Colonial Discourse', in *The Location of Culture* (London: Routledge, 1994), p. 86.

6 For a useful discussion of this argument see Peter Hulme, 'Including America', *Ariel*, 26, no. 1 (January 1995), pp. 117–23.

7 Terms used by Wilson Harris in his early influential essay, 'History, Fable and Myth in the Caribbean and Guianas', first published in Georgetown in 1970 and reprinted in *Caribbean Quarterly*, 16, no. 2 (1970), p. 17. All further references are to this text; a revised and shortened version was also published in *Explorations: a Selection of Talks and Articles 1966–1981*, ed. Hena Maes-Jelinek (Aarhus: Dangaroo Press, 1981), pp. 20–42.

8 Gordon Brotherston, *Book of the Fourth World: Reading the Native Americas through Their Literature* (Cambridge: Cambridge University Press, 1992), pp. 2–3.

9 Gordon Brotherston, 'Towards a Grammatology of America: Lévi-Strauss, Derrida, and the Native New World Text', in Francis Barker et al. (eds), *Europe and Its Others*, vol. 2 (Essex: University of Essex, 1984), p. 73.

10 Bhabha, 'The Commitment to Theory', in *Location of Culture*, p. 31.

11 Harris, 'History, Fable and Myth', p. 9.

12 'Region-wide distribution of Population by Ethnic Group of Head of Household', in *Household Income and Expenditure Survey* (Statistical Bureau, 1993); I am indebted to Janette Forte of the Amerindian Research Unit at the University of Guyana for making various ethnographical information available to me.

13 See essay by Lee Drummond, 'On Being Carib', in *Carib-Speaking Indians: Culture, Society and Language*, ed. E. B. Basso (Tucson: University of Arizona Press 1977), pp. 76–88; and the discussion by Peter Hulme, 'Caribs and

Arawaks', in *Colonial Encounters: Europe and the Native Caribbean 1492–1797* (London: Routledge, 1986), pp. 45–87.

14 Walter E. Roth, 'An Inquiry into the Animism and Folklore of the Guiana Indians', in *Thirtieth Annual Report of the Bureau of American Ethnology, 1908–1909* (Washington: The Smithsonian Institution, 1915), pp. 103–386, see especially pp. 320–6.

15 Wilson Harris, 'Couvade', in *The Sleepers of Roraima: a Carib Trilogy* (London: Faber and Faber, 1970), p. 13. Page references to this story will be given in the text.

16 Roth, 'Inquiry', p. 321.

17 The father still cannot eat certain foods that may damage the child, or go out hunting for fear of hitting the infant spirit. When he goes out walking he must leave a trail, being careful to make a small ladder if he climbs a fence, and to construct a small boat out of the tairu leaf if he wades into the water, to ensure that the infant spirit does not get lost, which would cause the child to die. See Roth, 'Inquiry', pp. 324–5.

18 In Lacan's reading, the child's entry into subjectivity is always a damaged one, for the newborn baby so entirely identifies with the mother's body that its first confrontation with itself as a separate being ('the mirror phase') is a traumatic one, and produces a subjectivity that is always split.

19 Harris, in an interview with Alan Riach in Alan Riach and Mark Williams (eds), *The Radical Imagination: Lectures and Talks* (Liège: Université de Liège, 1992), p. 40; in this instance the French term 'Couvade' also signals the 'lying-in' period, once practised in Europe, in which a man would take to his bed while his wife was in childbirth.

20 See Harris, 'The Phenomenal Legacy', *The Literary Half-Yearly*, 11, no. 2 (July 1970), p. 3.

21 Timehri, meaning 'hand of God', are believed to have been inscribed long ago and are often referred to as Arawak as well as Carib; though, as mentioned above, these two terms should not be seen as mutually exclusive.

22 Brotherston, *Book of the Fourth World*, p. 44.

23 Mark McWatt, 'Form and Originality: the Amerindian Fables of Wilson Harris', *Journal of West Indian Literature*, 1, no. 2 (1987), p. 38.

24 Lauri Honko, 'The Problem of Defining Myth', in Alan Dundes (ed.), *Sacred Narrative: Readings in the Theory of Myth* (Berkeley: University of California Press, 1984), p. 49.

25 McWatt, 'Form and Originality', p. 39.

26 Harris, 'History, Fable and Myth', p. 22.

27 Hall, 'Cultural Identity and Diaspora', pp. 226–7.

14 Between Speech and Writing

1 Ralph Ludwig, (ed.), *Écrire 'la parole de nuit': la nouvelle littérature antillaise* (Paris: Gallimard, 1994).

2 Other recent collections include *La parole de terre en larmes* (1988), which is a collection of stories mainly by relatively unknown Guadeloupean writers who took part in a competition organized by Guadeloupe's 'centre for cultural activity', and *Nouvelles d'outre-mer* (1989), a collection of stories by

writers from the four French overseas departments of Guadeloupe, Martinique, Guyane and La Réunion, and again the product of a competition organized to encourage and promote new writers.

3 For a useful discussion of the possible reasons behind the short story's comparative lack of prestige, see Johnnie Gratton and Brigitte Le Juez, *Modern French Short Fiction* (Manchester: Manchester University Press, 1994), pp. 4–5.

4 Clare Hanson, *Rereading the Short Story* (London: Macmillan, 1989), p. 2.

5 Quoted, ibid., p. 3.

6 Patrick Chamoiseau and Raphaël Confiant, *Lettres créoles: Tracées antillaises et continentales de la littérature 1635–1975* (Paris: Hatier, 1991), p. 35.

7 Telchid, 'Mondésir', in Ludwig, *Écrire*, p. 101. All translations of quotations from French texts are mine unless otherwise indicated.

8 Ina Césaire and Joëlle Laurent (eds), *Contes de vie et de mort aux Antilles* (Paris: Nubia, 1976), p. 11.

9 Hector Poullet and Sylviane Telchid, '"Mi bèl pawol mi!" ou éléments d'une poétique de la langue créole', in Ludwig, *Écrire*, p. 187.

10 Ibid., p. 190.

11 Edouard Glissant, 'Le chaos-monde, l'oral et l'écrit', in Ludwig, *Écrire*, p. 112.

12 Glissant, ibid., p. 117.

13 Poullet and Telchid, '"Mi bèl pawol mi!"', p. 185.

14 See, for example, Glissant, 'Le chaos-monde', p. 113, and Jean Bernabé, Patrick Chamoiseau and Raphaël Confiant, *Éloge de la créolité/In Praise of Creoleness*, Bilingual Edition, trans. M. B. Taleb-Khyar (Paris: Gallimard, 1991), p. 96.

15 Ludwig, *Écrire*, p. 18.

16 See, for example, Glissant, *Le discours antillais* (Paris: Seuil, 1981), p. 251.

17 Raphaël Confiant, 'Questions politiques d'écriture créole', in Ludwig, *Écrire*, p. 172.

18 Bernabé, Chamoiseau and Confiant, *In Praise of Creoleness*, pp. 87–8.

19 Chamoiseau and Confiant, *Lettres créoles*, p. 51.

20 Carole Boyce Davies, '"Woman is a Nation..." Women in Caribbean Oral Literature', in Carole Boyce Davies and Elaine Savory Fido (eds), *Out of the Kumbla: Caribbean Women and Literature* (Trenton, New Jersey: Africa World Press, 1990), p. 171. See also, for example, Laura Tanna, *Jamaican Folktales and Oral Histories* (Kingston: Institute of Jamaica, 1984) and *A Treasury of Afro-American Folklore* (New York: Crown Publishers, 1976).

21 Boyce Davies, '"Woman is a Nation"', p. 171.

22 Simone Schwarz-Bart, *Ti Jean l'horizon* (Paris: Seuil, 1979), p. 68.

23 Chamoiseau and Confiant, *Lettres créoles*, p. 22.

24 Bernabé, Chamoiseau and Confiant, *In Praise of Creoleness*, pp. 97–8.

25 Boyce Davies, '"Woman is a Nation"', p. 165.

15 Hybrid Texts

1 A shorter version of this essay has appeared in my book *A Place in the Sun? Women Writers in Twentieth-Century Cuba* (London: Zed Books, 1997).

2   Paul Gilroy, *The Black Atlantic: Modernity and Double Consciousness* (London: Verso, 1993), p. 6.

3   Maggie Humm, *Border Traffic: Strategies of Contemporary Women Writers* (Manchester: Manchester University Press, 1991), p. 2.

4   Excilia Saldaña, *Kele Kele* (Havana: Letras cubanas, 1987), *El refranero de la víbora* (Havana: Letras cubanas, 1989), and *La noche* (Havana and Berlin: Gente nueva, 1989).

5   Excilia Saldaña, 'Monólogo de la esposa', *Casa de las Américas*, 152 (1985), pp. 86–100. I would like to thank *Casa de las Américas* for permission to reproduce parts of the poem. All translations in this essay are my own.

6   For a detailed study of *Mi nombre: Anti-elegia familiar* see Catherine Davies, 'Cross-Cultural Homebodies in Cuba: the Poetry of Excilia Saldaña', in A. Brooksbank Jones and C. Davies (eds), *Latin American Women's Writing: Feminist Readings in Theory and Crisis* (Oxford: Clarendon Press, 1996), pp. 179–200.

7   Michael Gilkes, *Creative Schizophrenia: the Caribbean Cultural Challenge*, The Third Walter Rodney Memorial Lecture (Warwick: University of Warwick, 1986), p. 1.

8   Homi K. Bhabha, *The Location of Culture* (London: Routledge, 1994), p. 10.

9   In Yoruba religion the *orishas* or gods may be worshipped in any *ile ocha* (shrine) at home, which is referred to as the *casa-templo* (the house-temple) in Cuba.

10   Bhabha, *Location of Culture*, pp. 218–19.

11   Walter Benjamin, *Illuminations* (1955; Glasgow: Fontana-Collins, 1979), p. 82.

12   Jean Fisher, 'Some Thoughts on "Contaminations"', *Third Text*, 32 (Autumn 1995), p. 7.

13   The etymological meaning of 'translate' is 'to bear/across'(Latin), that is, to 'trans/fer'. Similarly, 'metaphor' means 'to transfer a word from its literal signification' and derives from the Greek for 'trans/fer', that is, *meta* (change)/*phor* (*fer*: to bear).

14   Bhabha, *Location of Culture*, p. 228.

15   Ibid., p. 7.

16   Paul de Man, *The Resistance to Theory*, cited in Bhabha, *Location of Culture*, p. 228.

17   Fisher, 'Some Thoughts', p. 5.

18   Benjamin, *Illuminations*, p. 69.

19   Nikos Papastergiadis, 'Restless Hybrids', *Third Text*, 32 (Autumn 1995), p. 16. My emphasis.

20   All references are to William Shakespeare, *Macbeth*, ed. Bernard Lott (London: Longmans, 1966). Further references will be given in the text.

21   Aeschylus, *Oresteia*, trans. Richard Lattimore (Chicago: University of Chicago Press, 1953), p. 129. All further references are to this edition, and will be given in the text.

22   Federico García Lorca, *Llanto por Ignacio Sánchez Mejías* (Madrid: Instituto Cultural de Cantabria, 1982), p. 77.

23   Interestingly, incest is as much a taboo in Yoruba culture (*santería* belief in Cuba) as it is in Christianity.

24   Chandra Talpade Mohanty, 'Under Western Eyes: Feminist Scholarship and Colonial Discourses', *Feminist Review*, 30 (1988), p. 208.

25 The 'rey' (king) featured in the poem refers not only to the head of the patriarchal family but also to the most important figure in each *cabildo* (group) of the *lucumi* (Cuban yoruba) religion. See George Brandon, *Santería from Africa to the New World* (Bloomington and Indianapolis: Indiana University Press, 1993).

26 Sir Paul Harvey, *The Oxford Companion to Classical Literature* (Oxford: Oxford University Press, 1984), p. 219.

27 The corresponding stanza runs:
Pobrecita princesa de los ojos azules
Está presa en sus oros, está presa en sus tules,
en la jaula de mármol del palacio real,
el palacio soberbio que vigilan los guardas,
que custodian cien negros con sus cien alabardas,
un lebrel que no duerme y un dragón colosal.

(Poor little princess with eyes so blue
imprisoned in her gold, imprisoned in her tulle
in the Royal Palace's marble cage
the splendid Palace protected by guards
who watch over a hundred black men with their hundred halberds
a hound that never sleeps and a colossal dragon.)
Rubén Darío, *Prosas Profanas y otros poemas* (1896), ed. Ignacio M. Zulueta (Madrid: Castalia, 1987), p. 98. The emphases in Darío's and Saldaña's texts are my own.

28 Sara Suleri, 'Woman Skin Deep: Feminism and the Postcolonial Condition', *Critical Inquiry*, 18 (1992); reprinted in Patrick Williams and Laura Chrisman (eds), *Colonial Discourse and Post-Colonial Theory: a Reader* (Hemel Hempstead: Harvester Wheatsheaf, 1993), p. 246.

16 Beyond Manicheism

1 D. Walcott, 'A Far Cry from Africa', in *In a Green Night* (London: Jonathan Cape, 1962), p. 18.

2 E. Hirsch, 'An Interview with Derek Walcott', *Contemporary Literature*, 20, no. 3 (1980), p. 282.

3 D. Walcott, 'What the Twilight Says: an Overture', in *Dream on Monkey Mountain and Other Plays* (New York: Farrar, Straus and Giroux, 1970), pp. 11–12. Subsequent references will be given in the text, using the abbreviation *DMM*.

4 In a remark which demonstrates little alertness to the ways in which historiography and narrativization mediate the representation of character, but nevertheless indicates how Toussaint and Christophe have habitually been constructed, R. D. Hamner sees Christophe as more suitable than Toussaint for Walcott's purposes because he 'possessed *hamartia* – an essential element for classical tragedy'. See Hamner's *Derek Walcott* (Boston: Twayne, 1981), pp. 52–3.

5 C. L. R. James, *The Black Jacobins: and the San Domingo Revolution* (1938; 2nd edn, New York: Vintage, 1963). *Toussaint L'Ouverture* was revised as *The Black*

Jacobins, in E. Hill (ed.), *A Time... and a Season: 8 Caribbean Plays* (St. August-ine: University of the West Indies, Extramural Studies Unit, 1976). Subse-quent Caribbean plays on the Haitian Revolution include Aimé Césaire's *La Tragédie du Roi Christophe* (1963) and Denis Martin Benn's *Toussaint L'Ouver-ture* (1968).

6 J. S. J. Stone, *Studies in West Indian Literature: Theatre* (London: Macmillan, 1994), p. 95.

7 *Henri Christophe: a Chronicle in Seven Scenes* (Bridgetown: Advocate Co., 1950), p. iii. Subsequent references will be given in the text, using the abbreviation *HC*.

8 B. King, *Derek Walcott and West Indian Drama: 'Not Only a Playwright but a Company', The Trinidad Theatre Workshop 1959–1993* (Oxford: Clarendon Press, 1995), p. 95

9 'What the Twilight Says', *DMM*, p. 11.

10 A. R. JanMohamed, *Manichean Aesthetics: the Politics of Literature in Colonial Africa* (Amherst: University of Massachusets Press, 1983), p. 4.

11 In Plato's *Phaedrus*, for example, the soul is likened to a chariot drawn by two horses – one white, the other black. The charioteer, who stands for the rational element in the soul, has the problem of getting the two horses to pull together, since, while the white horse is compliant, the black horse tends to follow its sensual instincts and can only be made to cooperate through the use of the whip.

12 Sartre uses this phrase in the passage from his Introduction to *The Wretched of the Earth* which Walcott quotes as the epigraph to Part II of the play (*DMM*, p. 277).

13 Cf. V. S. Naipaul's very similar use of the image of trees from other continents washed ashore on Caribbean beaches in *The Mimic Men* (London: André Deutsch, 1967), *passim*, where the only significant difference is that the trees more obviously have an Indian provenance for the novel's narrator, the Indo-Caribbean Ralph Singh.

14 D. Walcott, 'The Muse of History', in Orde Coombs (ed.), *Is Massa Day Dead?* (Garden City, New York: Anchor/Doubleday, 1976), pp. 1–26.

15 Cf. 'What the Twilight Says', where in a list of '[t]he derelicts who mimed their tragedies' in the Castries of his youth, Walcott refers to a figure called 'Lestrade, sallow and humped like a provincial Sherlock Holmes' (*DMM*, p. 23).

17 'Canvas of Blood'

1 Max Ernst, *Beyond Painting*, quoted in Werner Spies (ed.), *Max Ernst: a Retro-spective* (London: Tate Gallery, in association with Prestel, 1991), p. 21.

2 Spies (ed.), *Max Ernst*, p. 33.

3 Rosalind Krauss, 'The Motivation of the Sign', in William Rubin (ed.), *Picasso and Braque: a Symposium* (New York: MOMA, c. 1992), pp. 262–3.

4 Cornel West, 'Preface' to Tom Phillips (ed.), *Africa: the Art of a Continent* (London: Royal Academy of Arts; Munich: Prestel, 1995), p. 9.

5 S. A. Tyler, 'The Poetic Turn in Post-modern Anthropology: the Poetry of Paul Friedrich', *American Anthropologist*, 86, no. 2 (1984), p. 329.

6   Picasso to Malraux, quoted by William Rubin in his essay 'Picasso', in Rubin (ed.), *'Primitivism' in Twentieth-Century Art* (New York: MOMA, 1984), vol. 1, p. 255.

7   Sunday O. Anozie, *Christopher Okigbo: Creative Rhetoric* (London: Evans Brothers, 1972), p. 7.

8   Christopher Okigbo, 'Introduction', *Labyrinths with Path of Thunder* (London: Heinemann, 1971), p. xiv.

9   Ibid., pp. xi–xii.

10 'Fragments out of the Deluge', *Limits XII, Labyrinths*, p. 35.

11 Anozie, *Christopher Okigbo*, pp. 96–7.

12 Ibid.

13 Robert Fraser, *West African Poetry: a Critical History* (Cambridge: Cambridge University Press, 1986), p. 119.

14 Anozie, *Christopher Okigbo*, pp. 96–7.

15 Ibid.

16 Letter to Sunday Anozie, 5 May 1966, quoted in Anozie, *Christopher Okigbo*, p. 22.

17 Okigbo, 'The Passage', *Heavensgate I, Labyrinths*, p. 5.

18 Okigbo, 'Initiations', *Heavensgate I, Labyrinths*, pp. 6–7.

19 Okigbo, 'Lament of the Silent Sisters', *Labyrinths*, p. 39.

20 Okigbo, 'Introduction', *Labyrinths*, p. xiv.

21 Apollos O. Nwauwa, 'The Evolution of the Aro Confederacy in Southeastern Nigeria, 1690–1720: a Theoretical Synthesis of State Formation Process in Africa', *Anthropos*, 90, nos 4–6 (1995), p. 353.

22 Ibid., p. 358.

23 Ibid., p. 359; and Patrick Manning, *Slavery and African Life: Occidental, Oriental and African Slave Trades* (Cambridge: Cambridge University Press, 1990), p. 89.

24 Onuora Ossie Enekwe, *Igbo Masks: the Oneness of Ritual and Theatre* (Lagos: Nigeria Magazine, 1987), p. 42.

25 Okigbo, 'Elegy for Alto', *Path of Thunder, Labyrinths*, p. 71.

26 Chinua Achebe, *Morning Yet on Creation Day* (New York: Anchor Press, 1975), p. 160.

Index

Note: The part and chapter titles of this book often provide a good indication of the themes and concepts discussed; these are not generally repeated in the index.